JACK THE RIPPER'S NEW TESTAMENT

Occultism and Bible Mania in 1888

By
Nigel Graddon

Adventures Unlimited Press

Other Books by Nigel Graddon:

THE LANDING LIGHTS OF MAGONIA
U-33: HITLER'S SECRET ENVOY
OTTO RAHN AND THE QUEST FOR THE HOLY GRAIL

Other Books of Interest:

VIMANA
ARK OF GOD
ANCIENT TECHNOLOGY IN PERU & BOLIVIA
THE MYSTERY OF THE OLMECS
PIRATES AND THE LOST TEMPLAR FLEET
TECHNOLOGY OF THE GODS
A HITCHHIKER'S GUIDE TO ARMAGEDDON
LOST CONTINENTS & THE HOLLOW EARTH
ATLANTIS & THE POWER SYSTEM OF THE GODS
THE FANTASTIC INVENTIONS OF NIKOLA TESLA
LOST CITIES OF NORTH & CENTRAL AMERICA
LOST CITIES OF CHINA, CENTRAL ASIA & INDIA
LOST CITIES & ANCIENT MYSTERIES OF AFRICA & ARABIA
LOST CITIES & ANCIENT MYSTERIES OF SOUTH AMERICA
LOST CITIES OF ANCIENT LEMURIA & THE PACIFIC
LOST CITIES OF ATLANTIS, ANCIENT EUROPE & THE MEDITERRANEAN
LOST CITIES & ANCIENT MYSTERIES OF THE SOUTHWEST
YETIS, SASQUATCH AND HAIRY GIANTS
THE ENIGMA OF CRANIAL DEFORMATION
THE CRYSTAL SKULLS

JACK THE RIPPER'S NEW TESTAMENT

Occultism and Bible Mania in 1888

By
Nigel Graddon

Adventures Unlimited Press

Jack the Ripper's New Testament
By Nigel Graddon

ISBN 978-1-948803-13-7

Published by:
Adventures Unlimited Press
One Adventure Place
Kempton, Illinois 60946 USA
auphq@frontiernet.net

AdventuresUnlimitedPress.com

10 9 8 7 6 5 4 3 2 1

Jack the Ripper's New Testament

Occultism and Bible Mania in 1888

Other books by Nigel Graddon

Otto Rahn and the Quest for the Grail: The Amazing Life of the Real Indiana Jones

(Adventures Unlimited Press)

The Mystery of U-33: Hitler's Secret Envoy

(Adventures Unlimited Press)

The Landing Lights of Magonia: UFOs, Aliens and the Fairy Kingdom

(Adventures Unlimited Press)

The Looking Glass Ripper

(writing as Gordon Finlay, CreateSpace Independent Publishing Platform)

CONTENTS

How oft when thou, my music, music play'st,
Upon that blessed wood whose motion sounds
With thy sweet fingers when thou gently sway'st
The wiry concord that mine ear confounds,
Do I envy those jacks that nimble leap,
To kiss the tender inward of thy hand,
Whilst my poor lips which should that harvest reap,
At the wood's boldness by thee blushing stand!
To be so tickled, they would change their state
And situation with those dancing chips,
O'er whom thy fingers walk with gentle gait,
Making dead wood more bless'd than living lips.
  Since saucy jacks so happy are in this,
   Give them thy fingers, me thy lips to kiss.

—William Shakespeare, *Sonnet 128*

Acknowledgements

This book would be incomplete without a big thank you to Jonothon for his penetrating insights and unrivalled knowledge, Kathleen for reprising her sharp-eyed proofing labours, Julien for his wonderful artwork, and Eric Stedman for permission to reproduce his facial reconstructions of Catherine Eddowes and Mary Kelly.

Original artwork by courtesy of Julien Decaudin

Introduction

There is a period...when old opinions have been shaken or destroyed, and new opinions have not yet been formed, a period of doubt, of terror, and of darkness, when the voice of the dogmatist has not lost its power, and the phantoms of the past still hover over the mind, a period when every landmark is lost to sight, and every star is veiled, and the soul seems drifting helpless and rudderless before the destroying blast. It is in this season of transition that the temptations to stifle reason possess a fearful power. [1]

This book is not presented as yet another exhaustive study into the fine detail of the Whitechapel murders, nor is it another dramatic attempt at disclosing the Ripper's identity. Eminent researchers with far more knowledge of the topic have contributed admirably to these laudable efforts.

Besides, if I were I intent on going down this well travelled road, where on earth would I begin if my end goal was to produce with flourish and fanfare my new pet candidate from the seemingly limitless population of psychopaths that was roaming London's streets in 1888?

Precisely what is it that can be said to encapsulate the unvarnished and absolute truth of the events perpetrated by Jack the Ripper? As far as I can ascertain, the following sentence sums up all the *known* facts. In 1888 a number of women in London were slain in varying degrees of brutality by a person or persons unknown, the perpetrator(s) thereafter becoming known in popular vernacular as "Jack the Ripper."

I see nothing else that may be definitively stated as an undeniable fact concerning the Whitechapel murders. There is no unequivocal consensus as to the precise number of victims. Furthermore, despite

---

[1] Lecky, W., *History of the Rise and Influence of the Spirit of Rationalism in Europe*, London, 1870, vol. II

one hundred and thirty years of investigation by countless researchers there is certainly no consensus as to the identification of the assailant (which in the absence of incontrovertible proof may be one person or more than one working in collaboration or independently).

Personally, I do not believe that the identity of the Ripper will ever be known such that the answer satisfies all parties which, when faced one remarkable day in the future with information deriving from an absolutely authoritative unimpeachable source, have no choice but to come together in common agreement.

That is not to say that such an unimpeachable source does not exist. I believe that it does but like the Brotherhood of the Cruciform Sword sworn to protect the Holy Grail in *Indiana Jones and the Last Crusade*, I suspect that the Ripper secret has its own resolute guardians. For them the passage of time is not a solvent that gradually weakens the necessity to keep a lid on a matter of extreme sensitivity, shame and embarrassment for those at the top of the State.

Why, then, am I sitting at my Apple Mac in the winter months of 2017-2018 typing these words if I am not especially interested in the minutiae of the Ripper murders or in proffering the name of a new suspect? I could not have been more than six or seven years of age when, browsing one day in the late 1950s through my paternal grandparents' bookcase in suburban Birmingham, I came across a heavy volume with a dark blue, hardback cover: *The 50 Most Amazing Crimes in the Last 100 Years*, published by Odhams Press in 1936. My mother never tired of telling people that her first son learned to read at a precociously young age. I don't know about that but I recall having no difficulty delving into its contents, one of which was the gruesome but compelling story of Jack the Ripper. It was a description of events that always stayed with me. Based on neither logic nor reason, I gradually developed an *idée fixe* that Jack the Ripper was not a single person. Once the notion took root, I was unable to shake off a conviction that there was more to the Whitechapel murders

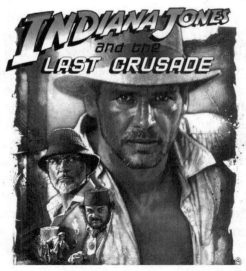

Indiana Jones and the Last Crusade 1989

than met the eye. As I grew into adulthood, decades giving way swiftly one after another, my instincts on the matter never wavered.

Beset with these reservations, I briefly toyed with the idea of writing "a book about Jack the Ripper" but quickly realised that all I would be doing was rehashing the familiar, certainly not offering anything to clothe my skeletal theories with a wholly unfamiliar interpretation of events. Instead, synchronous circumstances propelled me along a ten-year journey researching and writing about German philologist and Himmler's Grailhunter, Otto Wilhelm Rahn (1904-1939), any thoughts about exploring the grisly matters perpetrated during the Autumn of Terror put aside.

In 1995, at the beginning of that journey, it did not occur to me to link the two seemingly disparate topics. Why would anyone think to do so? The two subjects were galaxies apart. But as my investigations mounted, firstly into Rahn and later into mysterious U-Boat activities in Scotland during the first weeks of the war, I began to sense the presence of a connective force, a force that linked the killing of five prostitutes in London in 1888 with the evolution of National Socialism and Hitler's rise to power. It was an absurd notion but one I found myself increasingly unable to discard.

A research colleague with a track record of keen insight and astute authorship once suggested that Jack the Ripper was a heavily politicised, sleight of hand invention for public consumption, a remark that merits reflection. It suggests that we must ask not *who* was the Ripper but *what* was he and *why* was he created. The average Englishman loves blood and guts and the story of the Ripper murders satisfies that passion. One might also pause to consider if the killings served as a populist shroud to conceal other, high stake activities.

Considered in the context of these observations the error, if one may be permitted to describe it as such, is to regard the Ripper murders as simply a crime story. Instead, one may venture to meditate upon a feature of the Ripper story that appears to have elicited little attention, namely its role as a keyhole phenomenon through which may be observed a train of absorbing events and esoteric happenings seemingly unconnected with Whitechapel's raw and bloody narrative.

In the latter years of the Enlightenment, a period beginning with the scientific revolution in the 1620s and culminating in the momentous events of 1789, there took place a profound reaction against the prevailing mood in Europe. For one hundred and fifty years society's emphasis had focused upon liberalism, tolerance and the advocacy of individual reason over blind faith in monarchical rule and unbending Church dogma. The reaction took the form of an unfettered return to archaic beliefs and an intellectual investment in the power of superstitions.

The Whitechapel researcher ignores the nineteenth–century occult revival at the expense of attaining a complete picture of the social and political environment in which the murders took place. It is my belief that a thorough familiarity with the arteries and tributaries which nourished the phenomenon can help to explain facets of the Ripper period that continue to puzzle those drawn to the topic, including the fundamental issue as to why we are no further forward in naming its *dramatis personae*.

In his matchless work, *From Hell*, published in serial form between 1989 and 1998, storyteller Alan Moore has his Ripper—Sir William Withey Gull, Physician-in-Ordinary to Queen Victoria—telling his accomplice, coach driver John Netley: "One day men will look back and say I gave birth to the twentieth century." Fanciful or prescient?

Moore's passage echoes the words of late historian James Webb who described the significance of the principle nineteenth–century thinkers and their contribution to societal evolution. Each of these pioneer personalities was capable of capturing, interpreting and disseminating the contemporary Zeitgeist whereas some went further. These more adroit influencers had the capacity to think on their feet to address the immediate problems of the day. While still others in their midst were able to exert a powerful influence over an extended period of time, thereby inspiring others to come up with ideas of their own.

Moore was not the first to say that the Ripper's activities were driven by occult considerations but his introduction of a magical time element was an innovative contribution to the topic.

Consider the paradox in quantum science that the observed and the observer are wholly interdependent, the actions of the one predicated upon the presence of the other and vice versa. Sub-atomic particles whizz and spin along pathways mysteriously created by the physicist's own presence. The same law applies to historical events. Scientist and alchemist Isaac Newton probably did more to bridge the primitive understanding of one's era with the potentials of future scientific endeavour more than any other great thinker before or since. John Maynard Keynes wrote of Newton:

> He was the last of the magicians…he regarded the universe as a cryptogram set by the Almighty…By pure thought, by concentration of mind, the riddle, he believed, would be revealed to the initiate.

---

[2] Webb, J., *Flight from Reason*, MacDonald & Co., 1971
[3] "Newton the Man" in *The Royal Society*, Newton Tercentenary Celebrations, 1947

In what way may Jack the Ripper by his very presence in Whitechapel in the fall of 1888 have similarly shaped the nature of European affairs to come?

In 1997 pseudonymous essayist Simon Whitechapel developed the notion, setting out his theory in *Headpress* magazine. Pointing out that 1888 was a trisarithmic year, he claimed that the killings were ritualistic in nature and that their outcome was always intended to bear fruit in the next such year, 1999. I believe that "Whitechapel's" ideas are worthy of consideration, not in the literal sense of an unlikely 111-year action plan but, like Moore and Webb, in the context of the metaphysical aspects of time and its illusory nature behind the outer workings of "Jack the Ripper."

There is a further aspect associated with a time element that should be explored in any holistic treatment of the Whitechapel murders: the motivations and machinations of a 2000-year old Church. Religious faith in England in 1888 was practised in a jumble of different groups, none of which could legitimately claim more popularity than another. The main church was the Anglican Church, even though it reached no more than one in five of the population and despite the fact that it was promoted as a religion intended to fit modern lifestyles. Even more diluted was the appeal of other competing groups: the Catholics and Protestant dissenters such as the Methodists, Presbyterians, Baptists, Quakers and the Puritans. There was precious little to distinguish between them to command the loyalty of common folk, hence the rapid success of movements like spiritualism and Theosophy that offered the promise of a more personal engagement with the unseen world of spirit.

In the early 1990s I was developing an emerging niggle of thought that Church, religion and faith may have been connected to events in Whitechapel. I was also still harbouring the idea to write a book and introduce new elements of thought. With this in mind I opened a number of lines of enquiry, including the "Claston" question.

The idea that the British authorities secretly gave Mary Kelly safe passage to Canada where she and a son, Michael, lived under the name Claston originates from researcher Melvyn Fairclough.[4] In his book Fairclough speaks about a diary purportedly kept by Chief Inspector Frederick George Abberline that includes remarks about an escape by Kelly. The diary story was roundly criticised and Fairclough's research conclusions discredited. Nevertheless, I had (and still possess) considerable sympathy for the theory that Kelly flew the coop, a

---

[4] Fairclough, M. *The Ripper and the Royals*, Duckworth, 1991

scepticism fuelled by a number of well known evidential inconsistencies including seemingly irreconcilable conflicts in witness statements, particularly those relating to the morning after the event.

Being a stickler for covering all bases, I decided to cast a line and see what would bite. I made efforts to contact anyone named Claston who was living in the North American continent. In later pages I will go into the detail of what the fishing expedition revealed but suffice to say my inner hound was roused to chase the hare. As fully expected, I neither found Kelly's descendants nor an indication, let alone proof of an escape but I did find a Claston—and a very interesting one at that.

In our communication "my" Claston made a number of thought-provoking comments, one of which was that if I wanted to get to the bottom of the Ripper murders I should consider "contemporary biblical translation." This remark made me sit up and take notice because I had been thinking along similar lines, not for any reason backed up by specific evidential possibilities but because of a growing hunch fuelled by bits and pieces of seemingly unconnected strands of thought.

By the nineteenth century there were many influential figures in the worldwide Christian community, principally in England and America, who were calling for a fresh translation of the Bible, which had been largely unchanged since the publication in 1611 of the *King James Bible*, commonly known as the *Authorized Version* and usually abbreviated as the KJV.

A remarkable characteristic shared by many of the religious figures at the forefront of the revision program was a keen fascination for occult and esoteric matters. For example, Brooke Foss Westcott (1825-1901) who later became Bishop of Durham co-founded with his superior at Westminster Cathedral, future Archbishop of Canterbury Edward White Benson, the Cambridge University Ghost Club. The Ghost Club was the parent of today's Society for Psychical Research and its companion Fabian Society. As Cambridge undergraduates, Westcott and close friend Fenton John Anthony Hort (1828-1892) also founded the Hermes Club, which became a model for subsequent Hermetic societies that emerged in the years that both preceded and coincided with the Ripper murders.

By the time of the publication of the revised New Testament in 1881, the revised Old Testament in 1885 and the Bible Apocrypha in 1894 the nineteenth–century revision movement had been active for eighty years, a blink of an eye in Christian history. To an ecumenical movement that has survived for two millennia, passing centuries are but ticks of a clock that never winds down. Its mechanism is maintained by the Church's absolute belief in its role as God's chosen interlocutor, a sacred duty that prevails until the Day of Judgement.

Pending the trumpet blasts there is no force on earth that can be allowed to divert the Church from discharging its obligations.

As history has shown again and again, woe betide anyone who seeks to thwart the Church's holy work. It has been calculated that between thirteen million and nineteen million have been killed in the name of Christianity (during the Crusades, the Inquisition, the Thirty Years War and the French Wars of Religion), the figure rising to twenty-five million if the Holocaust is attributed to "Christian" violence rather than to ethnic genocide.

In the case of the Ripper murders I do not believe that they were necessarily perpetrated by men of the cloth but I do detect a whiff of ancient incense wafting through the nighttime streets of late Victorian Whitechapel. In my mind's eye I see an emissary of a dark god stalking its thoroughfares, swinging before it a smoking thurible whose sweet perfume mesmerises all those in its path, blinding them to the true nature of the ageless horror in their midst.

But does the figure of the dark god conceal even deeper shadows cast by a wholly different order of truth? Dawn succeeds the darkest hour and, by this same principle, 1888 was not just Jack's year but also a truly special time in the evolution of philosophy and mankind's pursuit of spiritual unfoldment. The momentous stresses that brought the Age of Reason to a close and initiated the Age of the Irrational provided the perfect conditions for the birth of Europe's esoteric movements and, for the intelligentsia, the emergence of a profound concentration on archaic beliefs and superstitions.

In an esoteric sense the nineteenth century resembled a giant alembic of otherworldly ideas, the most profound being the birth of spiritualism in 1848 and the founding of the Theosophical Society in 1875. The occult and metaphysical heat generated by these revolutionary movements as men and women sought in them new spiritual meaning had by 1888 brought the alchemist's pot to the boil. Such was the wild, unfettered, chaotic, mystico-political environment in which the Whitechapel murders took place. The scene is set. Let us now step into a boat and like traversing the hidden River Fleet beneath London's ancient streets begin to explore Whitechapel's religious and occult tributaries.

Jack the Ripper strikes

The swinging thurible in the Cathedral of Santiago de Compostela

Chapter 1

"Mr. Splitfoot"

In an existential sense the world went mad on 31 March 1848, the date that spiritualism was "invented."

What is spiritualism? It is the belief in the continued existence of the human personality after death in a spirit form with which, through mediumistic channels, the living may communicate. Adherents of the movement believe that the next world is one in which spirits evolve into higher forms, hence bestowing upon them the power to inform, guide and educate humans on moral and ethical issues.

The medium helps the spirit to communicate with its human audience through various physical, mental and luminous phenomena, rappings, table-turnings, spirit voices, aports (the paranormal transfer of an item from one place to another), telepathy, clairvoyance, automatic writing and, rarely, the materialisation of ectoplasmic forms.

Occultism, on the other hand, is based on the belief that phenomena are a consequence of working with unknown natural forces (the elementals).

The principle reference sources for this chapter's material are James Webb's first volume on the *Age of the Irrational*,[5] and Joscelyn Godwin's excellent history of occultism and esoteric development in the English-speaking world.[6]

Even before that momentous early spring day in New York State's Wayne County the carriage of reason, once a fine coach with shiny brass and all the trappings, had become increasingly rickety. The mysterious events in the tiny hamlet of Hydesville finally delivered its deathblow, bowling all four wheels into the brush. The Hydesville phenomena occurred in the period when Europe and America were experiencing an overwhelming reaction against the excess of logic

---

[5] Ibid.

[6] Godwin, J., *The Theosophical Enlightenment*, State University of New York Press, 1994

generated by the eighteenth-century Age of Reason. As man began to achieve greater mastery of his physical environment consequent to the Industrial Revolution and parallel increases in scientific development, his hold upon his relationship with the intangibles in the universe became more precarious. Rapid change of this nature has the tendency both to confuse and to frighten. After 1789 the threat of social revolution terrified large swathes of Europe. In the short but significant European "Revolutions of 1848," which began five weeks before Hydesville more than fifty violent but largely uncoordinated attempts were made to bring down governments, remove old monarchical structures and create independent national states.

One cannot, of course, attribute the demise of cool reason and the birth of spooky spiritualism solely to the Fox sisters and the rappings of "Mr Splitfoot" in their country cottage. To observers, the beginnings of spiritualism would have appeared inevitable when considered alongside the increasing episodes of esoteric phenomena that occurred during the preceding seventy-five years.

Spiritualism became a fashionable form of entertainment for those, especially in the middle classes, who loved the frisson of encountering the unknown and, of course, the prospect of holding hands in a darkened séance room without fear of censure. Others were not so glib about the burgeoning phenomenon and welcomed it as the cutting edge of the natural sciences and a new expression of religious belief in a world where many had pronounced the death of God.

The extraordinary mystical experiences of Swedish engineer turned prophet Emanuel Swedenborg (1688-1772) gradually attracted widespread attention, which culminated in the establishment in 1782 of the Church of the New Jerusalem in Eastcheap in the City of London. Swedenborg was just as much at home holding conversations with angels and spirits as he was with his fellow man. He taught that there had already been two great judgements that had befallen mankind: the Flood that brought an end to the hypothetical "Most Ancient Church" and the Crucifixion that signalled the demise of the "Ancient Representative Church." Swedenborg prophesised that this current "Third Age," that of the Christian Church, will shortly be overthrown.

The Church of the New Age was primarily established to inaugurate the coming era. The teachings of the New Church quickly spread. By 1828 the tenth General Convention of the American New Church proudly reported that the Swedenborgian doctrine was taught in eighty congregations statewide, compared with just forty-nine that would be reported in Britain a year later.

Emanuel Swedenborg, by Edwin Roffe, from *Compendium of Swedenborg's Theological Writings*, 1896

Certain that the Holy Alliance (a loose organization of most of the European sovereigns, formed in Paris in 1815 by Alexander I of Russia, Francis I of Austria and Frederick William III of Prussia) would be instrumental in fulfilling Swedenborg's Millennium prophecies, Robert Marsh, a leading light of the British New Church, wrote to each member enclosing books from the New Jerusalem Temple in Manchester. To the New Church's astonishment, Frederick William actually wrote back on official stationery as if in endorsement of the movement's New Age mission.

The next personality that stands out among the pre-eminent figures of a movement that had yet to be termed spiritualism was German physician and astronomy devotee, Franze Anton Mesmer (1734-1815). Mesmer postulated that between animate and inanimate objects there exists a universal connective force that he dubbed animal magnetism, later termed Mesmerism.

A follower of the highly influential sixteenth-century Swiss metaphysician Paracelsus, Mesmer was proposing as early as 1765 that the influence of the stars on the human body might be facilitated by the workings of a "subtle fluid," an invisible physical medium that had the power to transfer cosmic forces to material form.

In his experiments Mesmer attempted to draw forth this power through the use of magnets, an agonising process for some patients who experienced convulsions, hysteria, vomiting, spewing of blood and, finally, unconsciousness. Being a Mesmer guinea pig was evidently not for the faint-hearted. Nevertheless, Mesmer's ideas were highly influential, not least because his experiments popularised the idea of trance and, hence, laid the groundwork for the advent of the mediumistic aspects of spiritualism.

Moreover, the use of Mesmerism gradually began to grow in the world of practical medicine but not without difficulties for the early pioneers in the field. In 1838 physician Professor John Ellitson's adoption of "mesmeric sleep" resulted in peer pressure forcing him to resign his post at University College Hospital, London. Such negative views did not hold ground for long and by the time Scottish physician James Braid coined in 1843 the term hypnosis surgical operations conducted under mesmeric influence were becoming increasingly popular.

Other noted exponents of Mesmerism were Mary Baker Eddy (1821-1910), the founder of Christian Science, the "rediscovery" of Scriptural healing methods, and Phineas Parkhurst Quimby (1802-1866), who could diagnose illness while in trance. Eddy once came to

Quimby for healing for spinal pain. She believed that her beloved husband, Gilbert, had been poisoned by arsenic that had been mentally administered by enemies in Boston. In later pages we shall read of a parallel case in which leading late nineteenth-century French occultist Joséphin Péladan suspected that his brother, Adrien, had been similarly murdered occultly from a distance.

At the opposite end of the sensationalist spectrum a number of quacks masquerading under Doctor this or Professor that were capitalising on the new trance fad to elevate many popular superstitions into the realm of respectable sciences. Disturbingly, some were claiming to use trance to see and communicate with dead people, a relatively new phenomenon for the time.

The Shaker community in New York had since 1837 been telling of communications with the spirit world through the mediumship of young women. In January 1848 furniture-restorer Alphone Cahagnet published an account of the trance activities of Adèle Maginot who saw visions of the departed much in the same way as mediums claim to obtain today. Through these means Cahagnet was convinced that he had invented a "celestial telegraph" for communication with the departed.

It was obvious that the time was ripe for more such high strangeness, which was duly provided two months later by the three Fox sisters: Leah, Margaret (Maggie) and Catherine (Kate). Leah and Maggie, the two oldest, convinced Kate that the rappings in their cottage were the means by which they were communicating with spirits. Maggie described one evening's rappings incident:

We went to bed early because we had broken so much of our rest that I was almost sick.

My husband had just gone to bed when we first heard the noises this evening. I had just laid down when it commenced as usual. I knew it from all the other noises I had ever heard in the house. The girls, who slept in the other bed in the room, heard the noise and tried to make a similar noise by snapping their fingers. The youngest girl is about twelve years old.

She is the one who made her hand go. As fast as she made the noises with her hands and fingers, the sounds followed up in the room. It did not sound different at that time, but it made the same number of raps the girls did. When she stopped, the sounds would stop for a short time. The other girl, who is in her fifteenth year, then spoke in sport, and said, "Now do just as I do. Count one, two, three, four, etc.," at the same time striking one hand in the other.

The blows which she made were repeated as before. It appeared to answer her by repeating every blow she made. She only did it once. She then began to be startled, and I said to the noise, "Count ten," and it made ten strokes or noises.

Then I asked the ages of my different children successively, and it gave the number of raps corresponding to the ages of each of my children.

I then asked it if it was a human being making the noises, and if so, to manifest it by the same noise. There was no noise. I then asked it if it was a spirit—if it was, to manifest it by two sounds. I heard two sounds as soon as the words were spoken.

Kate bought into the story and it was not long before the three commenced new careers as mediums, a step that instigated the birth of modern spiritualism. Leah, the oldest, took charge of their newfound careers, which soon garnered extensive publicity and success.

One particularly gullible individual was helpful to the sisters in kickstarting their careers as professional mediums. Rochester Quaker Isaac Post began out of curiosity to engage in conversations with the Hydesville rapper.

In time, Post became convinced that what was at work were "the forces of human and spiritual magnetism, in chemical affinity," for which some people, such as the Foxes, possessed more "medium power" than others. Post brushed aside the suspicion that rappings were associated with the souls of murder victims and the like, believing that they were of a telegraphic nature that originated from philosophic and scientific minds, many of which had been pioneers in early studies of electricity.

Nevertheless, many were convinced that the rappings were the work of the Devil but the invisible knocker said that he was not "Mr. Splitfoot," the nickname that the girls gave the rapper but the spirit of peddler Charles B. Rosna, who indicated that he had been murdered five years earlier and buried in the cellar. Arthur Conan Doyle reported in his writings that the Foxes' neighbours did some digging and found bones identified as human but it was not until 1904 that a complete skeleton was excavated from the cellar wall.

For some years Kate and Maggie gave séances at New York and other places. One eminent believer, Horace Greeley, later a candidate for the U.S. presidency, was convinced of their honesty and went so far as to provide the funds for the completion of Kate's education.

Meanwhile, independent investigators, sceptics to a man, concluded that the raps were produced by the sisters cracking their bone joints such as toes, knees, ankles and hips. Investigators from the

University of Buffalo conducted a control experiment in 1851 from which they reported that the raps did not occur if the sisters sat on a couch with cushions under their feet. None of this negative reporting did the Foxes any substantial harm.

Despite Kate developing a serious drinking problem, the sisters continued their careers as professional mediums for another thirty-seven years. In 1888 matters changed irrevocably. In that year a bitter row boiled over between the younger siblings and Leah, who together with leading spiritualists, was concerned that Kate's alcohol intake was harming her children's upbringing. At the same time Maggie, intent on returning to her Roman Catholic faith, suspected that her gifts as a medium were diabolically contrived. Accordingly, when a New York City reporter offered the sisters $1,500 in October 1888 to reveal their methods, Maggie and Kate appeared publicly at the New York Academy of Music.

In a public show of contrition Maggie demonstrated how she could produce raps audible throughout the theatre. Doctors came on stage to verify that the cracking of her toe joints was the source of the sound. Maggie attempted to recant her confession a year later but it was too late. The sisters' reputations were in ruins and in less than five years all three had died in abject poverty.

In 1848 that ignominious end was not anticipated. On the contrary, the events in Wayne County and the Fox sisters' selfless calling were quickly regarded as proof of survival after death and a pathway to eternal life. In the words of one gushing acolyte:

> The humble frame dwelling at Hydesville loomed up into the proportions of a gigantic temple whose foundations are laid in the four corners of the earth, and the rough and rugged path which the bleeding feet of the Hydesville mediums seemed doomed to tread...afforded a transit for millions of aspiring souls into the glorious realms of eternity.[7]

The Foxes had started something that could not be stopped. By 1851 it was estimated that in New York City alone there were 100 mediums demonstrating their newfound calling. Meanwhile, the Hydesville rappings brought the sisters celebrity status and provided the world with a rich source of material, which in the hands of the scholar and the philosopher fashioned the building blocks for a new esoteric system of scientific thought.

---

[7] Hardinge Britten, E., *Modern American Spiritualism*, New York, 1870

Leah, Margaret and Catherine Fox

The next significant exponent of directed mesmeric thought to appear on the scene was Andrew Jackson Davis (1826-1910), the "Seer of Poughkeepsie." At seventeeen Davis attended Professor Grimes' demonstration of Mesmerism and volunteered to be publicly mesmerised but the attempt failed. Afterwards, a Poughkeepsie tailor named Levington tried his hand and successfully put Davis into trance. During the experience Davis feared he was dying:

> ...an eternal midnight clothed my tender spirit, and I was filled with terror. The darkness became more dark and appalling...I found myself revolving in that blackened gloom with an inconceivable velocity!...Down, down I sank, till I immersed myself in that mighty ocean where conflicting elements were swallowed by a mountain wave of darkness...and I sank to the lowest depths of forgetfulness.[8]

Undeterred by this first terrifying foray into the inner worlds, Davis pressed on enthusiastically in developing his powers as a medium and gave many demonstrations of his newfound clairvoyance. He made astonishing claims, including instances of being bodily transported from place to place. On one occasion Davis said that he was taken forty miles into the Catskill Mountains where he met a mysterious stranger carrying a silver cane. David told how the stranger opened the cane to reveal all the secrets of medicine contained in small blocks, each inscribed with the name of a different disease, its curative contained inside. To his chagrin, Davis was not permitted to keep the cane.

This episode is mindful of the mischievous practice described in folklore when fairies for sport toss wayfarers high in the air and whisk them to a far place from which they have to make their own way home. Indeed, as time went by and Davis began diagnosing ailments while in trance (only attaining a recognised medical qualification in 1886), he issued quack prescriptions whose ingredients were more likely to have been found in a witch's medieval cottage than in a New York State pharmacy: the application of a rat's skin behind the ear for deafness and frog's skin for a poisoned finger being examples.

At the age of twenty Davis dictated in trance to his amanuensis, William Fishbaugh, *The Principles of Nature, Her Divine Revelations, and a Voice to Mankind*, which appeared in print in 1847. This work with its ecstatic language and visionary flair bore a distinct Swedenborgian stripe. Like Swedenborg, Davis reiterated the prophesies of the likes of Isaiah, Ezekiel, Malachi, Confucius,

---

[8] Davis, A., *The Great Harmonia*, Bela Marsh, Boston, 1862

Zoroaster and Jesus, proclaiming the imminent coming of a Golden Age, a "rising tide of intelligence that flows to and over all nations, even as an ocean of truth and knowledge" during which "in every continent, nations converse through the medium of the electric fire." In later pages we will examine the resumption of the "Golden Age" theme in 1888, according to legend the seventh year of the New Age of Michael and a period of immense import to occultists in the time of the Ripper. Remarkably, as illustrated in the following passage, the book's contents also presaged principles of cosmic wholeness and the "Implicate Order" that quantum physicists such as Dr. David Bohm would develop one hundred and thirty years later:

> In the beginning the Univercoelum was one boundless and unimaginable ocean of LIQUID FIRE! The most vigorous and ambitious imagination is not capable of forming an adequate conception of the height, and depth, and length, and breadth thereof. There was one vast expanse of liquid substance. It was without forms; for it was but one Form. It had no motions; but it was an eternity of Motion. It was without parts; for it was a Whole. Particles did not exist; but the Whole was one Particle. There were no suns, but it was one Eternal Sun.

In subsequent works Davis inveighed against the social evils of the day, especially those that featured what he regarded as the iniquities of the clergy whose role, he averred, was to keep the lower orders in a state of subjection to those at the top of the heap.

Through such powerful proclamations did Davis become the chief theoretician of a nascent spiritualist movement, an ascendance that was bolstered by the political upheavals in Europe of 1848 and by the explosion of esoteric events in America, notably those initiated by the Fox sisters. Davis and those rapidly drawn to his teachings became regarded as experts on the supernatural; and it was this influential group that provided the first leaders of the spiritualist movement.

Davis continued to strengthen his clairvoyant powers, learning to pass into trance without the need of magnetic devices. He regarded as one of his most important tasks the clairvoyant mapping of what he termed the "Summer-Land," the cosmic realm from which the spirits communicated with those on earth. Fellow spiritualists seized eagerly on the notion of the Summer-Land and, consequently, Davis's occult star could hardly have risen higher. Nevertheless, the Seer of Poughkeepsie did not devote the remaining years of his long life solely to spiritualist matters. Together with his wife Mary, Davis combined his clairvoyant mediumship with a finely honed sense of social justice, particularly in furthering the cause of emancipation for married women.

In Europe spiritualism spread rapidly and was espoused by those from all walks of life and in every stratum of society. In France one of spiritualism's early champions was "Allan Kardec," pen name of translator and educationalist Hippolyte Léon Denizard Rivail (1804-1869). Kardek penned five books, collectively known as the *Spiritist Codification* in which he elaborated on Mystical Spiritualism, in effect setting out an alternative religion founded on the principle of reincarnation. This doctrine is absent from nineteenth-century Anglo-American or Scientific Spiritualism, so named because its adherents believed that phenomena would eventually be explained by scientific empirical investigations.

Somewhat stealing Davis' clothes, Kardec claimed to have discovered a "perfectly coherent picture of the universe" through the outpourings of two young mediums. In his "Spiritist" philosophy Kardec claimed that reincarnation took place in other worlds as well as on earth and that at the end of the reincarnational cycle the travelling soul attains the form of pure spirit.

The public's interest in Kardec's theories and the burgeoning spiritualist movement as a whole caused considerable concern in Europe's high circles. The Russian Court's traditional commitment to the Orthodox Church did not permit the disclosure of the Imperial family's views but many believed that were they permitted to speak freely the Romanovs would support the new doctrine. It did not go unnoticed that Captain Perbikov of the Imperial Navy was allowed to publish openly a spiritualist periodical. Meanwhile, in Austria Imperial Archduke Johann was much alarmed by the spread of spiritualism, lamenting:

> ...that this modern superstition...has fixed its abode in numerous palaces and residences of our nobility, so that in many cities of the monarchy, and especially in Vienna and Buda-Pesth, entire spiritualist societies exist, carrying on their obscure nuisance without any interference.

Johann arranged for Austrian's most eminent spiritualist, Baron Hellenbach, to conduct a series of sittings in the archducal palace with acclaimed American medium, Harry Bastian. By all accounts, the demonstrations were a dismal failure. In Berlin the Kaiser, Wilhelm I, attended a séance in the home of the von Moltke family. Imagine

Wilhelm's extreme discomfort when the medium prophesised (correctly) the coming of great ill-fortune to the Royal House. He immediately forbade any public discussion of psychic matters.

Spiritualism never took such a hold in Britain as it did in the U.S. but it was clearly on society's radar. British spiritualists commonly believed that Queen Victoria, in deep grief over the untimely passing of Albert in 1861 and known also to hold a fascination with the subject of the afterlife, was an early convert to the cause. The rumour circulating in the 1860s was that Victoria's favourite, Scottish ghillie John Brown, acted as medium in séances during which Albert's spirit made an appearance. Spiritualists maintain that Sir Henry Ponsonby and the Dean of Windsor destroyed the evidence for these events in a bonfire after the Queen's death.

Despite Britain's more reserved attitude to spiritualism, its esoteric communities were significantly impacted by the activities of two high profile American mediums: Mrs. Hayden and D.D. Home, who was the only medium never to have been exposed as a fraud.

Mrs. Hayden, wife of a newspaper editor, came to London in 1852 and advertised her services as a medium in *The Times*. She would sit quietly while raps and table movements went on around her. Using an alphabet board, her clients would move their fingers down it and stop where the raps denoted the letters of the message. It was all done tastefully with no signs of the sensationalist characteristics of Hydesville but the results convinced many that Mrs Hayden was truly gifted. One of her converts was Welshman Robert Owen, philanthropic social reformer and one of the founders of utopian socialism and the cooperative movement. Through Mrs Hayden he enjoyed communicating with his friends Shelley, Jefferson and Franklin and, especially, with the Duke of Kent about his plans for social reform. Hayden returned to America in 1853.

Two years later Daniel Dunglas Home (1833-1886) came from New York to London for health reasons. When in 1871 Kate Fox, her reputation still intact, visited England and held sittings some of her séances were co-hosted by Home, one of the most extraordinary mediums in the entire history of spiritualism. Were Home demonstrating his remarkable gifts to witnesses today, his seemingly unbelievable feats would doubtlessly be compared with the exceptional skills of a David Blayne or an Alexandra Duvivier. But if Home was an illusionist he was an exceptionally capable one. A representative of *The Times* attended a séance hosted by Home in November 1871 and published a detailed account in an article, *Spiritualism and Science*, which occupied three and a half columns of leading type.

His parents' third child, Home was born in 1833 in a village near Edinburgh. His mother Elizabeth ("Betsy") was known as a seer in Scotland like her forbears. Home's father was William Home, the illegitimate son of Alexander, 10th Earl of Home. William was an unhappy man who drank to excess and, by all accounts, often raised his hand to his wife. At the age of one Daniel, deemed an overly sensitive child, was passed to his mother's sister Mary Cook for his upbringing, thus putting him out of harm's way of his boorish father.

In 1842, Daniel's aunt and uncle immigrated to New England and settled in Greeneville near Norwich, Connecticut. In 1850, rappings similar to those heard in Hydesville two years earlier began disturbing the Cook residence. Ministers brought to the house to investigate laid the blame for the knockings on teenage Daniel who declared that they were not to be feared but were a gift from God. The rappings not only continued but a table took a spin about the floor despite Mary laying a Bible on it and then her full body weight. Distraught that the neighbours were making complaints, the Cooks banished Daniel from the house. He went to live with friends and by the following year he had conducted his first séance.

Home adopted a peripatetic lifestyle, travelling round New England healing the sick and speaking with the dead. He charged no fees for his services but accepted donations and offers of lodgings from wealthy admirers. Home believed that he had embarked on a "mission to demonstrate immortality."

By 1852 Home was conducting six or seven séances daily. These drew large audiences, including Harvard professor David Wells and the poet and editor of the *New York Evening Post*, William Cullen Bryant, each convinced of Home's credibility. At one séance five men with combined weight of 850 pounds sat on a table, which nevertheless continued moving about the floor. Witnesses observed "a tremulous phosphorescent light gleam over the walls."[9] Home was subjected to numerous investigations, including those conducted by Professor Robert Hare, the inventor of the oxy-hydrogen blowpipe, and John Worth Edmonds, a Supreme Court judge. Both initially sceptical, the pair subsequently declared that Home was genuinely gifted.

Also in 1852 Home demonstrated publicly his powers of levitation. At the Connecticut home of Ward Cheney, a successful silk manufacturer, witnesses described how Home twice levitated. On each

[9] Lamont, P., *The First Psychic: The Extraordinary Mystery of a Notorious Victorian Wizard*. Abacus, 2005.

occasion he floated to the ceiling accompanied by increasingly loud rappings and the din of tables moving violently round the floor amid the sounds of a ship at sea in a storm. Soon after this demonstration Home moved to New York and took an apartment on 42nd Street.

His career as spiritualist *extraordinaire* was not plain sailing. New York City was full of admirers and critics alike. The most voluble among the latter was celebrated author William Makepeace Thackeray. The writer mocked Home's abilities as "dire humbug," describing them as "dreary and foolish superstition" but had to admit that the table turning episodes were impressive.

In 1853 Home embarked on a course of medical studies but abandoned them early in 1854 when he was diagnosed with tuberculosis. Very poorly, his left lung almost entirely wasted away, Home heeded his doctors' advice and relocated to Europe for recuperation, hosting before his departure in late March 1855 in Hartford, Connecticut, his last séance in America.

In England Home continued exercising his remarkable gifts as a medium *sine pari*. He displayed amazing documented abilities, among them levitation, flight, bodily elongation, handling live coals and producing phantom hands. Conan Doyle described him as the greatest medium the world had ever seen. As in the past, Home took no money for his services. In 1857 the Union Club in Paris offered Home £2000, an enormous sum for the day, for a single séance. He refused saying, "I have been sent on a mission. That mission is to demonstrate immortality. I have never taken money for it and I never will."

Although Home was far too much of a gentleman to name names it is known that among the celebrated figures that sought his guidance and proclaimed his extraordinary gifts were Emperor Napoleon, Empress Eugenie, Tsar Alexander, Emperor William the First of Bavaria, and the Kings of Bavaria and Wurtemberg. On his many trips to Russia Home stayed at the home of A.K. Tolstoy whose occult circle included philosopher Vladimir Soloviev, one of the the "god-builders" whom we will get to know better in later pages.

In 1858 Home married Alexandria de Kroll ("Sacha"), the 17-year-old daughter of a noble Russian family in Saint Petersburg. His Best Man was Alexandre Dumas. They had a son, Gregoire ("Grisha"). Sacha fell ill with tuberculosis and died in 1862.

In the year that Sacha died fellows in Cambridge University, under the leadership of Edward White Benson, founded the Cambridge Ghost Club, an organization dedicated to the investigation of paranormal activity. Its early membership included Charles Dickens and Sir Arthur

Conan Doyle. In fact, the Ghost Club was not based on new thinking but was a reboot of a short-lived campus society formed by Benson, Brooke Foss Westcott, Fenton John Anthony Hort and other colleagues in 1851. In a letter of 20 December to John Ellerton, Hort said:

> Westcott, Gorham, C.B. Scott, Benson, Bradshaw, Laurd, etc. and I have started a society [Cambridge Ghost Society] for the investigation of ghosts and all supernatural appearances, and effects, being all disposed to believe that such things really exist, and ought to be discriminated from hoaxes and mere subjective delusions; we shall be happy to obtain any good accounts well authenticated with names. Westcott is drawing up a schedule of questions. Cope calls us the "Cock and Bull Club"; our own temporary name is the "Ghostly Guild."

Benson's son later stated that his father and Ghost Club colleagues were always more obsessed with psychic phenomena than they cared to admit. Reflecting the trend that the paranormal drew disproportionate interest from religious figures, in addition to Benson's future elevation to the Archbishopric two other members of the Ghost Club, Lightfoot and Westcott, subsequently became Bishops while Hort became a Professor of Divinity. The Club was dissolved in the 1870s following Dickens' death. The leading activities of Westcott and Hort in connection with nineteenth-century Bible revision will be addressed in later pages.

Home continued to demonstrate his powers of levitation. On more than one hundred occasions he raised himself aloft in good light to the amazement of witnesses. In one celebrated episode in 1868 witnessed by Lord Adare, Captain Wynne and Lord Lindsay, Home levitated out of the third storey window of one room at 5 Buckingham Gate, London, floated to a window seven feet distant and re-entered the house's adjoining room.

Adare described witnessing another remarkable event. On this occasion Home, holding above his head a glass of brandy, stood by a window and was lifted off the floor by about five feet. While Home was in the air witnesses saw a bright light materialise in the

D.D. Home levitating

glass. Home descended and showed the glass was empty by turning it upside down. He returned to the window, held the glass up and those present heard it re-filling with liquid. All this while, Home was speaking about the brandy saying, "It is under certain circumstances a demon, a real devil, but, if properly used, it is most beneficial." As he said this, the light once more became visible in the glass and he was again raised in the air. "But," Home went on, "if it is improperly used, it becomes *so* (the light disappearing) and drags you down, down, lower and lower," and as he spoke he descended gradually till he touched the floor. Home again raised the glass above his head and drops of brandy that materialised in the air fell into the glass.

Worsening tuberculosis forced Home to retire in 1871. He said that his powers were failing. In this same year he married Julie de Gloumeline, a wealthy Russian whom he also met in Saint Petersburg, and converted to the Greek Orthodox faith. Home died 21 June 1886 and was buried in the Russian cemetery of St. Germain-en-Laye in Paris.

In 1869 the London Dialectical Society, the precursor to the Society for Psychical Research, was formed in Britain to investigate the claims of spiritualism. It examined Home's activities and declared that: "nothing occurred at any of the meetings which could be attributed to supernatural causes." However, the Society's work was roundly criticised as unreliable and unscientific, *The Times* describing one of the committee's reports as "nothing more than a farrago of impotent conclusions, garnished by a mass of the most monstrous rubbish it has ever been our misfortune to sit judgement on."

The vacuum left by the death of a spiritualist of Home's calibre was at least partially filled by the Reverend William Stainton Moses (1839-1892). Educated at Exeter College, Oxford, Moses was ordained as a priest of the Church of England in 1870. Three years earlier he had joined Robert Wentworth Little's new esoteric Christian order, the Societas Rosicruciana in Anglia (S.R.I.A.), and soon afterwards was inducted into another Masonic order, the Swedenborgian Rite.

Moses, yet another cleric obsessed with the supernatural, attended his first séance with Lottie Fowler in 1872 and went on to visit other mediums, including Home. In the same year Moses exhibited his own extraordinary mediumistic powers, which included raps, the evocation of lights, scents, musical sounds, automatic written messages and demonstrations of levitation. He quickly became very well known and went on to co-found the British National Association of Spiritualists in 1873, the Psychical Society in 1875, the Society for Psychical

Research in 1882, and the London Spiritualist Alliance in 1884.

Like Homes, Moses was utterly indifferent to making any kind of financial gain from his spiritualist activities and, being publicity shy, he wrote under the pseudonym, "M.A. (Oxon.)." In 1878 Moses wrote *A Treatise on One of the Objective Forms of Psychic or Spiritual Phenomena*, coining the term "psychography" for the spiritualist concept of channeling messages from the dead via automatic writing.

Subsequently, in his books *Spirit Teachings* and *Spirit Identity* Moses transcribed his automatic scripts from twenty-four notebooks for the period 1872 to 1883. Moses's chief spirit guide signed itself "Imperator +" and said little except to state that he had previously lived as a human in Paris. Madame H.P. Blavatsky, co-founder of Theosophy, believed that "Imperator" was Moses' Higher Self.

On his part, Moses was shocked by Blavatsky's attacks on spiritualism, which he believed was providing evidence of the immortality of the soul. However, he was open minded and listened carefully to what an apparently genuine psychically gifted woman had to say about spiritual matters. Gradually, Moses became receptive to Blavatsky's suggestion that spiritualist phenomena were produced by elemental forces. He converted to Theosophy in 1876.

While Home and Moses were among the leading male mediums of the day, Emma Hardinge Britten (née Emma Floyd, 1823-1899) is regarded as the mother of modern spiritualism. Britten was a tireless propagandist for the movement, travelling all over the United States, Canada, England, Australia and New Zealand where she expounded the truths of spiritualism and associated esoteric topics.[10]

Emma was born in London's East End to a sea captain's family. From an early age she showed impressive gifts as a musician, singer and speaker. At eleven Emma was earning her living as a music teacher. During this year she came to the attention of the mysterious Orphic Society which used Emma as a "child medium."

Emma Floyd

[10] Hardinge Britten, E., .*Autobiography of Emma Hardinge Britten*. Ed. Margaret Wilkinson. Manchester: John Heywood, 1900

Emma was able to predict the futures of people she met, describing what she saw in visions, including information on deceased relatives about whom she had no prior knowledge.

Present day research undertaken by "Dark Journalist," Daniel Liszt, and his cohorts indicates that the Orphic Society's insidious practice was to identify young girls aged around ten with mediumistic potential and to bring them into the inner circle for an approximate five-year period. During this time the girls would be encouraged to develop their skills as trance-mediums so that on "graduation" as fully-fledged seers they could be of life-long service to the ultra-secret Society, many of whose members went on to occupy very high levels of influence at national level in Britain. A case in point was Edward George Earle Bulwer-Lytton, 1st Baron Lytton, a hugely influential man. He served as Secretary of State for the Colonies between 1858 and 1859, and in 1862 was offered the Crown of Greece after the abdication of King Otto but declined it.

By use of their finely honed esoteric faculties, the teenage mediums would be used to infiltrate powerful groups of high standing in areas such as politics, science, philosophy, the Church, spiritualism, Theosophy and the occult. Once in place they were expected to tap into and report back on matters concerning state secrets, cutting edge thinking on the nature of reality, other dimensions and planes of existence, closely guarded secrets of ancient mystical fraternities and other like areas of vital interest to the furtherance of the Society's occult objectives.

Liszt further claims that around 1862 Alice Liddell, the putative model for Charles ("Lewis Carroll") Dodgson's "Alice" character, was brought into the Orphic Society for mediumistic development through psychic enthusiast Dodgson. Later when Alice as the widowed Mrs Hargreaves visited America in the 1932 (having lost her husband Reginald in 1926) she is said to have made veiled allusions about this period. If there is merit in Liszt's claims one is presented with the possibility that it was this act by Dodgson and not over-familiarity that caused the Liddell family to bar him in 1863 from further contact with their 11-year old daughter.

Alice Liddell

It has been suggested that an important physical attribute which enhances psychic ability in a person is hair length: the longer the hair, the more heightened the mediumistic ability. On balance, this trait tends to favour women over men. An example is J. Augustus Knapp's beautiful illustration of the Oracle of Delphi for Manly P. Hall's *The Secret Teachings of all Ages*, in which he depicts the all-knowing Pythoness as wearing waist-length, golden hair.

The remark might appear absurd were it not for a body of opinion among indigenous cultures that connects long hair to psychic capabilities and improved intuition. The renowned Choctaw and Navajo Native American scouts of the Vietnam War, known as the "Code Talkers," attributed their extrasensory capabilities to their long hair. According to these recruits, their intuition dimmed when they were forced under army regulations to trim their hair.

In Carroll's children's stories the figure of Alice was illustrated with considerably longer hair than worn by Liddell at that time. In asking Tenniel to draw his heroine in this way, may Carroll have been seeking to draw attention to a physical characteristic that was keenly sought by the Orphic Society in its quest for outstanding child mediums?

With help from the Society Emma was able to go to Paris in her teens to continue with her music studies. She had ambitions to become an opera singer and while working to that end she earned a living in Paris as a piano demonstrator for the Erard Company. Her hopes were dashed when she became prone to increasing episodes of somnambulism. In a deep sleep she would go out into the wintry Paris streets, climb high points in the city and cry out like a banshee. Tragically, these incessant screaming fits eventually robbed Emma of her fine soprano voice.

It appears that around this time Emma was lured into a "mystic marriage" with a member of the aristocratic Hardinge family. Spiritualist Dr. E.J. Dingwall's researches revealed that while working as a medium in her teenage years Emma had been sexually abused and that, in revenge, she adopted the surname of the man responsible.

Emma's abilities developed quickly. Not as showy or as sensationalist as Home in exercising her gifts in automatic writing, psychometry, healing and prophecy, Emma was no less highly regarded by her admirers. Undoubtedly, Emma was best known for her inspirational speaking addresses during which she would extemporise on topics chosen by her audience. Listeners were impressed by her eloquent and informative style.

Through the mediumship of Miss Ada Hoyt (Mrs. Coan), Emma converted to spiritualism in 1856 while working with a theatre company in America. In this same year Emma provided one of the best-attested cases of early spirit return. During a sitting the spirit of a crewmember from the mail steamer *Pacific* recently lost at sea, disclosed the particulars of the tragedy. Angry that prejudicial details were being made public, the ship's owners threatened to prosecute Britten but all the information was subsequently found to be accurate.

Following this impressive demonstration, Emma's fame grew. She sat as a medium for the wonderfully named Society for the Diffusion of Spiritual Knowledge of New York, practising in the same building as Kate Fox. Working in trance, Emma delivered many well-received lectures on diverse topics such as *The Discovering of Spirits*, *The Philosophy of the Spirit Circle*, *Hades* and *What Is the Basis of the Connection of the Natural and Spiritual Worlds?*

Emma became politically active in 1864. She threw her weight behind the campaign for Abraham Lincoln's re-election, delivering an impassioned lecture on the subject of *The Coming Man; or the Next President of the United States*. So popular was this address that by invitation Emma went on tour and delivered another thirty-two lectures on political themes. The culmination of Emma's career as an inspirational political speaker was a speech she delivered 14 April 1865 in response to President Lincoln's assassination thirty-six hours earlier. Her speech was widely acclaimed by journalists as her greatest achievement as an orator.

In 1866 Emma returned to England where she worked hard on two major works: *Modern American Spiritualism: A Twenty Years' Record* and *Nineteenth-century Miracles*. With financial assistance from a "noble English gentleman" whom she did not name but was well known in the spiritualist community, Emma published *Modern American Spiritualism*, an encyclopaedia of the people and events associated with the early days of the movement.

In October 1870 Emma married mesmeric physician Dr. William Britten and settled in Boston. In 1872 the Brittens started a spiritualist magazine, *Western Star*. It was shortlived, lasting

Emma Hardinge Britten

for just six issues until the devastating fires that raged from 9th-11th November destroyed much of Boston's commercial centre, including the Brittens' offices and Emma's personal property. The couple moved back to New York where they made ends meet by offering their services in "electrical therapeutics."

Behind her public commitment to spiritualist affairs Emma Britten hid an allegiance to the darker side of esoteric undertakings. René Guénon, a French intellectual highly regarded in the domain of metaphysical philosophy, believed her to be a member of the Brotherhood of Luxor, a precursor to the Theosophist movement. Certainly, Britten was continuing her association with the Orphic Society, a secretive community that claimed lineage from alchemy, mediaeval Rosicrucianism and Freemasonry.

Emma knew much more about the Orphic Society's beginnings in 1872 than she had forty years earlier when in service as a child medium. She stated that the Society was an offshoot of the original Cabala, describing it as an "affiliation with societies derived from the ancient mysteries of Egypt, Greece and Judaea, whose beliefs and practices had been concealed from the vulgar by cabalistic methods."

In 1888 Emma would publish an article in which she claimed that the Orphic Society was the result of the organisation by master adepts of "true occultism" into secret associations in England around 1830.[11] Research indicates that the Society was indeed a constituent part of a far wider global network of shadowy occult fraternities, one of which was the secretive Berlin Brotherhood of "natural philosophers" that used drug-induced trances, fumigations, invocations to contact spirits and mirrors consecrated to Hebraic angels.

The Orphic Society's initiates considered themselves "magians," Zoroastrian-style priests with "supernatural" powers. Its members included the Earl of Stanhope (secret agent, and guardian of the mysterious feral child, Kasper Hauser), astrologer and writer Richard Morrison, fellow occultists Frederick Hockley

Lord Edward Bulwer-Lytton

---

[11] *"Occultism in England"* [extract from *Ghost Land*], in *Two Worlds* I, (1888).

and John Cavendish Dudley, Richard Francis Burton, the infamous president of the Cannibal Club and, as noted, politician and novelist Lytton, who in his 1871 novel *The Coming Race* informed the world of the Atlanteans' mysterious and mighty Vril power.

As rumours of the group's existence began to spread outsiders took to calling them the Orphic Circle, a reference to the ancient Greek cult of Orpheus, the transcendental poet and musician who descended into Hades and returned with the secrets of life and death.

At their regular meetings Circle members studied esoteric manuscripts and undertook metaphysical experiments using electricity, magnetism, clairvoyance and even moonlight as ways to explore mankind's true potential. These they combined with scrying, an esoteric procedure first developed by Queen Elizabeth's magus, Dr. Dee, using mirrors, crystal balls and quartz obelisks for "prophecy, revelation, or inspiration."

Through Britten's attachment to the Egyptian mysteries and her friendship with Lytton, an occultist acclaimed in Britain and Europe, there is strong reason to believe that the Orphic Society inspired the later formation of the Alldeutsche Gesellschaft für Metaphysik (All German Society for Metaphysics), a female circle of mediums founded and led by Zagreb-born Maria Orsitsch (Oršić). The society was later renamed the "Vril Gesellschaft" or "Society of Vrilerinnen Women," a movement very highly regarded by Heinrich Himmler's occult circle, which was impressed by the Oršić group's claim to be in contact with Aryan beings living on Alpha Centauri in the Aldebaran system. Oršić's group believed that these extraterrestrials had visited Earth and settled in old Sumeria, the word "Vril" deriving from a Sumerian word "Vri-ll" ("like god" or "God-like"). The significance of this one hundred year chain of unholy alliances will become apparent in later pages.

In the course of her affiliation with the Orphic Society, Britten befriended a mysterious individual who went by the pseudonym "Austria." "Austria" supplied an autobiographical sketch for the *Western Star* that in 1876 was lengthened to form the substance of a novel: *Ghost Land; or, Research into the Mysteries of Occultism*. At this time "Austria" was living in Havana under the alias "Chevalier Louis de B," whom E.J. Dingwall believed was Baron Joseph Henry Louis de Palm, an early member of the Theosophical Society.

Today, the Orphic Society and its lust for prepubescent girls would

---

[12] Hardinge Britten, E., *Modern American Spiritualism*. New Hyde Park: University Books, 1970.

be classified as a paedophile ring; one, moreover, whose members occupied positions of power and influence in the highest reaches of the arts, the church, government and the occult movement. It was a predatory network of a kind that parallels so many observed in the present day, except in Victorian times there was simply no possibility of members being brought to justice, tried and sentenced. Those at the helm *were* the law and their authority protected the Jack Tars in the Society's lower ranks.

The Society went about its business with impunity, secure in the belief that its affairs were rooted in an occult pedigree of ancient and unassailable authority which none may threaten. Its work continued unabated, engendering a line of succession that included the Golden Dawn whose activities and allies at home and abroad will be reviewed in later pages.

Thereafter, as we shall come to understand, the Society's Teutonic foundations became an invisible but irresistible influence upon the very worst of twentieth-century occult-driven enterprise as evidenced in the actions of Hitler's National Socialist Germany.

In 1873, channelling recently deceased Welshman, Robert Owen (1751-1858), Britten expounded on her newly developed Seven Principles, which encapsulated the philosophy of spiritualism. The Principles, designed to help spiritualists navigate between their exoteric and esoteric journeys in life, comprised the Fatherhood of God, the brotherhood of man, the communion of spirits and the ministry of angels, the continuous existence of the human soul, personal responsibility, compensation and retribution hereafter for all the good and evil deeds done on earth, and eternal progress open to every human soul. The Principles remain an essential part of spiritualist belief.

In 1876 Britten edited a book written in 1875 whose authorship is something of a mystery. Present day scholars differ on the writer's identity, some saying Louis de Palm who was writing a follow-up to *Ghost Land*; others Emma herself although the book's style and content suggest the former. Its title (take a deep breath) was: *Art Magic or Mundane, Sub-Mundane and Super-Mundane Spiritism*: *A Treatise in Three parts and Twenty-Three Sections: Descriptive of Art Magic, Spiritism, the Different Orders of Spirits in the Universe Known to be Related to, or in Communication with Man; Together with Directions for Invoking, Controlling, and Discharging Spirits, and the Uses and Abuses, Dangers and Possibilities of Magical Art*.

Emma circulated a prospectus for *Art Magic,* which would "contain the results of a European gentleman's researches into nature's most profound mysteries." Subscribers would pay $5 in advance and the print run would be limited to 500, although Henry Olcott later suggested that far more were printed. Although published as a tome on the fledgling Theosophy movement, the mention of invoking and controlling spirits in *Art Magic* puts the Brittens' work into a distinctly occult framework, a field of magical activity that within a few years would be exemplified by the practices of the Golden Dawn.

This was not an unexpected development considering that in the previous year Emma, taking a direction in her career well beyond the tenets of spiritualism, was elected one of the Councillors at the meeting that founded in New York City the Theosophical Society. The Society was actively interested in powers believed latent in humans, which went beyond mediumship into occult areas such as astral projection. Many of the Society's early meetings were held in Britten's home.

For a while Britten remained in daily contact with the Society's corresponding secretary, Madame Blavatsky, and president, Colonel Henry Steel Olcott, the latter with whom she had shared lodgings many years before. However, it was not long before Britten severed her connections with Blavatsky. This breaking off of relations may not be interpreted as constituting Emma making an equal break with Theosophy because the Brittens continued to maintain an active and continuing interest in occult learning.

In general the critics were not impressed with *Art Magic*, one reviewer dismissing it as a rehash of generally available works. Daniel Dunglas Home said that it was partly rubbish and Andrew Jackson Davis was equally scathing. Nevertheless, the book did influence occult thinking and many subsequent writers on the topic borrowed heavily from it. Today *Ghost Land* and *Art Magic* are regarded as the first English language publications that make a clear distinction between occultism and spiritualism.

In 1878 the Brittens travelled to Australia and New Zealand as missionaries for the spiritualist movement and founded a number of churches and societies. While in Australia, Emma wrote her book *Faiths, Facts and Frauds of Religious History*. Returning to New York in 1879, Britten continued working on her magnum opus, *Nineteenth-century Miracles*, which was eventually published in 1884.

Britten finally achieved success in the magazine business when, living in Manchester, England, in 1887, she founded the Two Worlds Publishing Company in order to produce *The Two Worlds* periodical. The journal was devoted to "Spiritualist, Occult Science, Ethics, Religion and Reform."

Madame H.P. Blavatsky

Colonel Henry Steel Olcott

Britten chose to locate the company in England's northwest region in an effort to offset the dominance of London as the main centre of spiritualism in England. One of Britten's principle objectives in founding the company was to provide a platform through which to encourage the establishment of a national federation of spiritualist groups and churches. Britten served as its editor until she was forced out in a boardroom coup in 1892.

Interestingly, the Olcott circle believed that spiritualist phenomena were not provoked by spirit entities but by living representatives of a secret occult Order of highly evolved men who held mastery over the forces of nature. In his 1875 work, *People from the Other World*, Olcott wrote:

> After knowing this remarkable lady [Blavatsky], and seeing the wonders that occur in her presence…I am almost tempted to believe that the stories of the Eastern fables are but simple narratives of fact; and that this very American outbreak of spiritualist phenomena is under the control of an Order, which while depending for its results upon unseen agents, has its existence upon Earth among men.

Although relying on unseen forces for their results, the members of this "Universal Brotherhood" (named by Blavatsky as the Hermetic Brotherhood of Egypt and known in America as the Brotherhood of Luxor) were based here on Earth. It was not until 1893 that clues emerged as to the putative identity of this Order when Anglican and occultist, Charles G. Harrison, delivered a course of lectures in London that was accompanied by a book now lost. The mysterious Harrison, who has defeated all subsequent attempts at further identification, said that in around 1840 occult groups decided that modern Europe had reached a "point of physical intellectuality"

René Guénon

---

[13] Harrison, C., *The Transcendental Universe. Six Lectures on Occult Science, Theosophy and the Catholic Faith. Delivered before the Berean Society*. Introduction and Notes by Christopher Bamford. Hudson: Lindisfarne Press, 1993.

in its evolutionary cycle, which was predominantly characterized by gross materialism. The adepts argued back and forth about what should be done to halt the decline; some saying that mankind should be told that there is around us a higher invisible world which is every bit as real as our own. Others were aghast at the prospect of taking any action that profaned the ancient mysteries.

Subsequently, according to Harrison experiments were conducted through mediums who, contrary to the expectations of the occult orders, proclaimed that they were being controlled by the spirits of the dead rather than serving as vehicles for insights from cosmic representatives. Consequently, instead of introducing a way through which humankind could become aware of the existence of higher powers and reduce its relentless drive towards materialism, the adepts succeeded only in inculcating a false belief among the masses that humans have the ability to confer with the dead. Irrevocable damage had been done; the genie could not be pushed back in the bottle. It was inevitable that the way was open for unprincipled occultists to step in and manipulate matters to satisfy impure motives.

René Guénon also believed that phenomena associated with spiritualism and Theosophy were produced by occultists acting at a distance for unknown purposes, a line of thinking described as the "provocation theory."[14] However, Guénon went further than Harrison in suggesting that the principals behind this activity were those from within the Inner Circle of the Hermetic Brotherhood of Luxor (the H.B. of L.), a rival group to Theosophy and HPB's "Universal Brotherhood" which was founded in 1870 by Max Theon (discussed in later pages) and brought to the public's attention in 1884.

Guénon said that the H.B. of L. was in close contact with the German occult organizations that inspired the work of the Orphic Society, especially with the mysterious Frankfurt Lodge and its pan-European offshoots. On their part, Olcott and Blavatsky believed that Harrison's adepts were no less than Theosophy's invisible Mahatmas: Koot Hoomi and Morya, who in their communications never had a good word to say about spiritualism.

Nevertheless, these were minority opinions. The march of spiritualism continued unabated, especially in America and Europe where new organizations flourished. One such was the London Spiritualist Alliance, which in 1881 published a newspaper called *The Light*, featuring articles such as "Evenings at Home in Spiritual

---

[14] Guénon R., *Le Théosophisme, histoire d'une pseudo-religion* Enlarged ed. Paris: Editions Traditionelles, 1982.

Séance" and "Chronicles of Spirit Photography."

In 1882 the Society for Psychical Research (S.P.R.) was founded. Essentially, it was a coming together of those groups that were already working independently in investigation of spiritualist matters. Its core membership consisted of Stainton Moses, Henry Sigdwick, Frederic Myers and Edmund Gurney, each a Fellow of Trinity College Cambridge who took their inspiration from the former Ghost Society. The S.P.R.'s loosely worded remit was to examine by purely scientific methods "that large group of debatable phenomena designated by such terms as mesmeric, psychical, and spiritualistic." Inveterate paranormal obsessive Conan Doyle was one of the S.P.R.'s members, as was Charles Dodgson who in a roundabout way provoked the undertaking of this present work. Gurney was found dead in a Brighton hotel on 23 June 1888 with a bottle of chloroform by his side, suicidally depressed after realising that the bulk of the evidence he had used to write a 1,500 page work on psychic research, *Phantasms of the Living*, was false.

In this brief chapter we have gained an insight into the nature and evolution of spiritualism and its associated psychical phenomena by 1888. By this time, spiritualism was walking arm in arm with other, no less controversial esoteric movements, principally Theosophy and its occult tributaries. Before we put these developments under the microscope, we turn to Whitechapel and Jack the Ripper's "first" victim (no specific individual can be categorised with absolute proof as the first).

Chapter 2

Whitechapel

Monday, 6th August 1888

It was the end of a perfect day for London's citizens. The Bank Holiday entertainment attractions had drawn tens of thousands to venues across the capital. At Alexandra Palace the excited crowd had thrilled to watch daredevil Professor Baldwin ascend 1,000 feet in his gaily-coloured hot air balloon before parachuting safely to the ground to tumultuous applause. To the southeast in Crystal Palace, revellers had enjoyed a Grand Fairy Ballet, the madcap antics of aeronaut Captain Dale Keen, an endurance cyclist competing against racehorses, and a monster firework display for a "Grand Fairy Ballet."

It was a quarter to midnight. Londoners were bedding down for the night and Whitechapel's streetwalkers were preparing for business. Laughing drunkenly, Martha Tabram and Mary Ann Connelly ("Pearly Poll") fell out of the Angel and Crown pub in Hanbury Street into a light drizzle, arm in arm with their soldier clients, a corporal in his early thirties and a private barely out of his teens. Plump, dark haired Martha, 5'3" tall, was wearing a black bonnet, long black jacket, dark green skirt, brown petticoat and stockings and well-worn spring-sided boots. We will return to Martha shortly.

Whitechapel in 1888 has been described as a place of unparalleled squalor and desperation, housing London's most deprived citizens in its worst slums. The increasing mechanisation of industrial processes in the second half of the nineteenth century had resulted in large-scale unemployment, mostly affecting the hordes of agricultural workers that had been drawn to the capital at the start of the Industrial Revolution by its promise of plentiful jobs and higher wages.

The poor of London migrated further eastward as the City expanded its role as a financial and commercial centre of world excellence. The social problems that accompanied this growth were exacerbated by the unchecked influx of many thousands of foreign immigrants that began in the late seventeenth-century by the arrival of large numbers of Huguenots fleeing religious persecution in their native France into the Spitalfields area of Whitechapel.

1881 saw the beginnings of a vast Diaspora of Russian and Polish Jews fleeing from bloody pogroms. Many of those in flight made a beeline for London's East End, adding severely to the problems of overcrowding and the attendant social issues brought about by extreme poverty. Their arrival caused great difficulties to the existing and long established East End Jewish communities that saw only too readily the threat to the status quo from their poorer and less literate brethren. The native population, already resentful of the Jews' ability to prosper gave vent to their feelings and the result was a rising tide of anti-Semitism that would suppurate from time to time into open hostilities.

Yiddish theatre actor Jacob Adler wrote, "The further we penetrated into this Whitechapel, the more our hearts sank. Was this London? Never in Russia, never later in the worst slums of New York, were we to see such poverty as in the London of the 1880s."

The population of the East End in 1888 is estimated at 900,000 of which 90,000 were paupers, excluding vagrants and lunatics in asylums. The more transient adult inhabitants of the square mile that framed Whitechapel were crammed into approximately 200 common lodging houses, which provided the barest shelter to eight thousand souls. Those unable to find fourpence for a single bed could sleep on a "line," a webbing of rope stretched across a room, for two pennies (tuppence). By and large, these mean dwellings were the only form of shelter available for the Ripper victims and their sisters of the streets.

Whitechapel in 1888

[15] Adler, J., *A Life on the Stage: A Memoir*, tr. Rosenfeld, Knopf, New York, 1999.

Contemporary observers pulled no punches in describing the reality of the human condition in Whitechapel. Arthur G. Morrison writing in the *Palace Journal*[16] of 24 April 1889 runs riot, depicting Whitechapel as a chthonic pit of sub-human squalor worse even than the seventh level of hell. It was a:

> ...horrible black labyrinth...reeking from end to end with the vilest exhalations; its streets, mere kennels of horrent putrefaction; its every wall, its every object, slimy with the indigenous ooze of the place; swarming with human vermin, whose trade is robbery, and whose recreation is murder; the catacombs of London darker, more tortuous, and more dangerous than those of Rome, and supersaturated with foul life.
>
> Others imagine Whitechapel in a pitiful aspect. Outcast London. Black and nasty still, a wilderness of crazy dens into which pallid wastrels crawl to die; where several families lie in each fetid room, and fathers, mothers, and children watch each other starve; where bony, blear-eyed wretches, with everything beautiful, brave, and worthy crushed out of them, and nothing of the glory and nobleness and jollity of this world within the range of their crippled senses, rasp away their puny lives in the sty of the sweater.

Having got this undisguised distaste off his chest Morrison ploughs on to make a vivid sketch of the East End's piteous "horrible black labyrinth." Many other commentators similarly provided their own first-hand impressions.

We walk in their footsteps. We keep in mind as we walk that Whitechapel as understood by its residents extends some distance beyond the bounds set by the parish authorities of St. Mary and includes much of Aldgate, Spitalfields and a substantial fragment of Mile End. The main road passing through Whitechapel stretches from Houndsditch and the Minories to the London Hospital. This road serves as a crowded omnibus and tramcar route and also accommodates four railway stations.

On the right as we leave the Minories is the Aldgate Meat Market, a row of butchers' shops where hang hundreds of carcases in rows. Dozens of wagons loaded with hides stand in the roadway. Close by in the middle of the road the great hay market is in full swing. It has drawn conspicuous country types in tweed and brogues who appear decidedly out of place in this narrow vesica of territory that overlaps the City of London and Whitechapel.

---

[16] A weekly chronicle published by the People's Palace in Mile End Road. It ran from 1887 to 1895.

Here, too, we find Hill's, the old gabled public house that looks more like a warehouse than a watering hole for thirsty workers. Along the south side of the road is a row of stalls, many of them owned by booksellers described by Morrison as of "misanthropic, gloomy and grim appearance" who fret over the increasing decline in trade. Despite the downturn, the long established premises of George's and Gladding's, beloved by book-hunters for donkey's years, manages to keep ticking over.

Moving on, we pass by a number of long-serving commercial enterprises, among them the Mears and Stainbank bell foundry, established in 1570. Down near the London Hospital opposite the Pavilion Theatre is a terrace of shops called The Mount, so named because of the presence until late in the previous century of a fort constructed for the defence of London.

Whitechapel is abuzz with life. Under the light of a street lamp by a steaming cook shop is a small assembly of onlookers drawn by the patter of a silk-tongued pill seller. By the next lamp another gathering is listening to a young man playing a dulcimer. In later weeks between this spot and the next post along passers-by will find a waxworks show featuring hastily constructed models of the recent victims of a murderous fiend dubbed "Jack the Ripper."

A workhouse in Victorian Britain

Further on is Atlas the Strongman's booth. He is making heavy weather of tearing in half a trade directory. Next, a soapbox preacher who has no sense of when to put the brake on his fire and brimstone harangue is incensing his tiny congregation by insisting they are all going to hell. A large swede tossed from the crowd at the preacher's nose brings a swift and bloody end to the pavement sermon. Before turning off the main road we see an Italian street performer doing tricks with a tamed rat. With the aid of a square bit of rag the rat is made to appear as an old woman, a monk and a stiff, pink-nosed corpse. Then the rat is stood on a board, covered up and made to vanish altogether, turning up in the cap of a startled lad among the onlookers.

Next to Giuseppe's pitch stand a dozen more stalls selling celery, cabbages, comic songs, hairbrushes, ribbons, doorkeys, trousers and tenpenny nails among the grand miscellany of wares. A few yards further along is a woman in a bedraggled skirt standing by a wire cage of lovebirds. She waits forlornly for pennies to be flung down in return for the coloured paper "fortunes" lying in the little box inside the cage.

We pass into Mansell Street, a quiet thoroughfare accommodating as in nearby Great Alie Street and Tenter Street large houses of a shabby-genteel appearance. In their many rooms is conducted a wide array of trades connected with clothing, tailoring, Hebrew bookshops and synagogue paraphernalia. Names such as Isaacs, Levy, Israel, Jacobs, Rubinsky, Moses and Aaron appear on inscriptions in the dusty windows. Toward the end of nearby Leman Street is "Goodman's Fields," where once stood the theatre in which Garrick made his first London appearance and took the town by storm. We regain the corner of Mansell Street and see before us Middlesex Street, first known as Hog Lane with its sunny hedgerows and pleasant houses and, subsequently, as Petticoat Lane renowned for its thievery, squalor and old clothes. We plunge into the crowd. In the near distance we hear the pealing bells of St Mary-le-Bow strike ten. What lies before the the visitor?[17]

Every inch of space in Petticoat Lane's teeming market is crammed with stalls and barrows vying for custom. Feeling hungry we pop into the the Bell pub and spend eightpence on a breakfast of eggs, bacon, black pudding, fried bread and "bubble and squeak" (fried mashed potato and vegetables), which we wash down with a pint of mild and bitter. Suitably nourished, we begin our Petticoat Lane adventure. Costermongers are bawling out their patter.

"No need to walk any further, ladies and gents. Save yer plates of

---

[17] "Sunday Morning in Petticoat Lane," *London as it is*, No. V, published 1877

meat. Everything you want is on the barrer. Gather round and make me an offer," shouts a ruddy-faced coster in a wideawake hat who waves his brawny arms in exaggerated invitation.

"Who'll buy?" others sing out in the lane.

"All the new songs, only a penny!" proclaims a tall thin young man waving a fistful of flimsy song sheets.

"Who'll buy an 'at for a bob, worth three, so 'elp me," a Jewish trader asks while unveiling a pile of "billycocks," a popular felt hat of the day with a low rounded crown like a derby. The billycock perched proudly on top of the heap is decorated with tall peacock feathers.

"Who'll buy?" implores buxom Madame Rose from the door of her wardrobe shop. In her Aladdin's cave of apparel one can buy cheap stockings and silk handkerchiefs in as many brilliant hues as in Jacob's Coat, a scarlet uniform and plumed hat for the next young gentlewoman's coming out Levee, or a dress suit for the Lord Mayor's ball.

A man selling the latest fashion in weekend wear for gents, a black-check cut-away Sunday coat, bellows, "Don't be shy, try it on, turn around and see 'ow it fits like a glove." Past the garment trader are ranks of stalls piled high with all things cheap and cheerful—jewellery, tools, crockery, clothes, cakes and confectionaries.

A carpenter begins a cheerful exchange with a stout stallholder in his sixties. He wants a new saw, screwdriver and hammer and knows he will get what he wants at the prices he can afford to pay if he plays the bargaining game with good grace and humour.

Petticoat Lane in London's East End

We pass by a haberdasher's barrow and observe a young woman buying a second-hand brown linsey frock for one and tuppence, a pocket looking glass, a white handkerchief and a comb. Next to it is a milliner's stall where a passer-by with dark brown hair is eyeing covetously a pretty black straw bonnet with velvet trim. It bears a price tag of two shillings. We move on as the tiny, plump woman begins the bargaining game.

A balding mountebank standing in a doorway taps his pearl handled walking cane on a poster depicting a human lizard swallowing fire. "Step right in," he shouts. "See the spectacle, only a penny."

Another showman is hollering with equal fervour from across the street, "Hi, hi! See the world's strongest man, can break a bar of iron across his knee, only just arrived from Kiev, admission one penny!"

A few yards further on is a man squatting on the kerb with a sack spread out before him. On it is a stock of needles in small packets.

Past the needle seller are stalls offering calico by the yard, sliced bread, smoked fish, fur boas, shawls, hosiery and petticoats. If you want it, you can find it in this chaotic corner of Whitechapel.

"Who'll buy?"

Occasionally, a loud slapping sound rises above the general hubbub. It is coming from a cart belonging to the kamptulicon man. Every few minutes the enthusiastic trader, a man possessed of supernatural lung-power, bangs the roll of floor covering made from powdered cork and rubber against the side of the cart to demonstrate its sturdy qualities. "Who'll make me an offer?" he shouts out with stentorian power.

Next to the kamptulicon seller stands a man in the midst of the slow moving crowd. He is holding aloft a placard bearing facts about the human body. It reveals that the body contains no fewer than 6,500,000 air cells. The placard bearer is spouting forth about the remarkable healing properties of an item of quack medicine that cures all ills. Beyond the quack merchant's pitch an elderly haberdashery stallholder with her head wrapped in a massive shawl is stoking the zinc pail of coke embers she has brought with her to keep warm.

We leave behind Petticoat Lane and its organized chaos. The far end of Middlesex Street becomes Sandys Row where the pavement narrows. We venture into a narrow passage off Gravel Lane and slip on the greasy slime that covers the lumpy cobblestones. We cross Stoney Lane and enter another passage that leads to Harrow Alley, a passageway lined with shops selling second-hand clothes and mouldy saddlery.

Proprietors in yarmulkes stand by laden rails crammed with goods. Here hang old items of militaria, rusted bayonets, bundles of broken spurs, hammerless pistols, mangy busbies, battered lancers' helmets, musty wallets, wooden water bottles, frayed knapsacks and three-cornered hats that Greenwich pensioners used to wear. The visitor struggles to understand how anyone can make a living from selling such unappealing tat.

Artillery Lane, Gun Street and Raven Row, thoroughfares running from the end of Sandys Row, are characterised by ragshops, small beer-houses and an overall dirty, unkempt appearance.

As we walk, we take a peep over a pavement grating and catch a whiff of a sweater's den, one of 2,000 similarly wretched rooms with no ventilation in the East End. Typically, a shirt-maker's den accommodated eight to ten female "finishers" who laboured from 8:00 a.m. to 9:00 p.m. making buttonholes and sewing buttons on shirts made usually elsewhere by better skilled and better paid machinists.

Continuing on our way we can choose to pass through White's Row or Dorset Street into busy Commercial Street whose bustle, busy trade and streetlights provide some neighbourhood cheer. Here we find the Toynbee Hall and Institute and St. Jude's Church.

Our destination is Brick Lane, which we can approach by Fashion Street, Flower and Dean Street, Thrawl Street or Wentworth Street. Feeling brave, we choose notorious Wentworth Street. We see men lounging in doorways smoking, swearing and swigging from bottles. Hard-faced aproned women in stairwells stand in pairs, gossiping and shouting at children who are running about in termite proportions. Heavily painted prostitutes offer the business from every gas lamp lit corner. We know the statistics. Whitechapel in 1888 accommodates around sixty brothels and twelve hundred prostitutes.

From somewhere close by comes the sounds of glass breaking, a scuffle, the overturning of furniture, screams, a cry of "Murder" and, then, silence. No one moves or stops what they are doing to investigate. Whitechapel police will only patrol Wentworth Street in pairs. We arrive in Brick lane in one piece. Morrison describes it as:

> Black and noisome, the road sticky with slime, and palsied houses, rotten from chimney to cellar, leaning together, apparently by the mere coherence of their ingrained corruption. Dark, silent, uneasy shadows passing and crossing—human vermin in this reeking sink like goblin exhalations from all that is noxious around. Women with sunken, black-rimmed eyes, whose pallid faces appear and vanish by the light of an occasional gas-lamp, and look so like ill-covered skulls that we start at their stare. Horrible London?

Yes. Brick Lane is a comparatively cheerful, although not a

patrician, thoroughfare…Here German-Hebrew provision shops display food of horrible aspect; greasy yellow sausages, unclean lumps of batter fried in grease; and gruesome polonies and other nondescript preparations repellent to look upon.

Up close the scene is even more dreadful than the chroniclers' descriptions. Everywhere is filth, foulness and privation. Moving shadows vaguely resembling human form fill Whitechapel's caliginous landscape. We are aware that the East End in this period is housing a hundred thousand paupers: men, women and children whose quality of life is unimaginably wretched.

Clearly, Whitechapel in 1888 was a part of the East End where all possible shades of commerce, industry, social interaction and unimaginable deprivation exist cheek by jowl. Morrison reminds his readers that it was once fashionable to "slum" in the East End's dirty streets. A "civilised" person would walk gingerly through foul byways and alleys and go back West with the conviction that "something must be done." Personally, Morrison was doubtful that anything could be done to save the citizens of Whitechapel from their own worst excesses. He concluded his piece, saying:

> Children must not be left in these unscoured corners. Their fathers and mothers are hopeless, and must not be allowed to rear a numerous and equally hopeless race. Light the streets better, certainly; but what use in building better houses for these poor creatures to render as foul as those that stand? The inmates may ruin the character of a house, but no house can alter the character of its inmates.

Was Morrison being entirely fair? On the surface, Whitechapel was undoubtedly a place of horror but on our walk did we not also detect beneath the filth a glimpse of something perhaps not overtly beautiful but something worthy of pause and a moment or two of reflection? Because, after all, this was a time when there was much to celebrate in terms of human endeavour and scientific advancement.

If one were to arrive in London in autumn 1888 and pick up a copy of *The Times*, more than likely its pages would be reporting on the next "new thing." The visitor might read about Scotsman John Dunlop's promising invention of the first inflatable tyre and the trials he had been conducting with bicycles in Belfast's Cherryvale sportsground.

On another page he might read about Nikola Tesla's amazing invention of the induction motor, a device he constructed after having a Eureka moment while reciting stanzas from Goethe's *Faust* during a stroll in Budapest's city park. *The Times'* reporter did not have the benefit of hindsight and goes on to describe the event as largely unremarkable but today we know that Tesla's discovery was destined to become one of the most important inventions in scientific history.

The same may be said of other remarkable subjects, news of which would have graced *The Times'* inner pages. One such might have been a story about George Eastman's introduction of the box camera, a modestly priced product whose significance would only later emerge and become a boon to families everywhere.

Another article may have described Heinrich Hertz's discovery that radio waves belong to the same family as light waves. Today we know that, once again, it would be left to Tesla's genius to advance Hertz's work and to go on to develop the field of radio communications.

Here one is faced with a startling paradox. While Jack the Ripper was murdering women in the most heinous fashion, discoveries were being made in science and technology that would rapidly change for the better the lives of billions of people across the globe. It follows that a forward thinker in 1888, faced with so many new and exciting possibilities, would have spun mental cartwheels in identifying how they could personally contribute to society in an environment where there was such a tremendous amount of invention and creativity taking place.

It follows also that these new social and technological memes must have created a multitude of problems between science and religion. It is the premise underlying this present work that the circumstances that engendered the Whitechapel murders were deeply rooted in the conflicting demands of the rational and irrational characteristics of late-Victorian living.

It is also my contention that the forces responsible for the slayings skilfully wrapped their activities in this shroud of uncertainty just as surely as a bronchial pea souper draped an impenetrable cloak over Whitechapel's greasy cobblestones. Let us now return to Martha and her final hours.

Chapter 3

Martha

The two pinchpricks paired off. Poll, a tall woman with masculine features and a flushed pallor, made for the parallel Angel Alley with her soldier in tow. The young private and Martha (whom was known to Poll as "Emma") headed for nearby George Yard Buildings, a narrow alley (present day Gunthorpe Street) connecting Wentworth Street and Whitechapel High Street, and populated by what the *East London Observer* described as "people of the poorest description."

About thirty or forty minutes later Poll and her corporal went their separate ways, he setting off in the direction of Aldgate and she towards Whitechapel. According to Poll under interview at the inquest there had been no animosity between the four despite a few sharp words about money, a brief spat which did not, she said, involve Martha.

Between midnight and 2:00 a.m. Mrs Hewitt, resident of George Yard Buildings, was awoken by cries of "Murder!" Such cries were commonplace and Hewitt ignored them. At the same time, beat copper PC Thomas Barrett 226H was questioning a grenadier who was loitering by George Yard. Barrett moved on after the soldier said he was waiting for a friend.

At 3:30 a.m. cab driver Albert George Crow, returning home after a night's work, noticed a body lying on the landing above the first flight of stairs. Unable to see clearly in the dim light, Crow assumed the figure was that of a sleeping vagrant, a familiar enough sight. Needing his bed, Crow passed it by and went into his lodgings.

At 4:45 a.m. dock labourer John Saunders Reeves came down the stairs and saw on the steps the body of a woman lying in a pool of blood. He went off to fetch a policeman and soon returned with PC Barrett on his heels. Barrett observed that the body was that of a middle-aged, plump woman with dark hair and dark complexion. She was lying on her back, tightly clenched hands at her sides. Her clothes were old and worn and, in Barrett's words at the inquest held 9 August, "were turned up as far as the centre of the body, leaving the lower part of the body exposed; the legs were open, and altogether her position was such as to at once suggest in my mind that recent intimacy had taken place."

Although the woman was plainly dead, Barrett called for a doctor. Dr Timothy Robert Killeen of 68 Brick Lane arrived at about 5:30 a.m. Killeen's *in situ* examination was brief but long enough to ascertain the extent of her injuries. She had been stabbed thirty-nine times. Killeen concluded that she had been dead for about three hours and instructed that she should be conveyed to a mortuary. Because of the absence of a mortuary in Whitechapel, the police took the body to the deadhouse in the workhouse infirmary in Old Montague Street.

Because Wynne E. Baxter, Coroner for the South Eastern District of Middlesex, was on holiday in Scandinavia, deputy coroner George Collier opened the proceedings on Thursday 9 August in the library of the Working Lads' Institute, Whitechapel Road.

At this time the identity of the deceased had not yet been established. A woman carrying a baby who attended the proceedings had been taken to view the body and said it was an acquaintance named Martha Turner, an identification which on its own would have provided a very useful clue. However, she was only one of three women who had identified the body, the other two each proffering different names.

Killeen presented his detailed post-mortem findings to the inquest jury. Inside the head he had found an effusion of blood between the scalp and the bone. The brain was pale but healthy. The trunk had sustained at least twenty-two stab wounds. In Killeen's words:

> The left lung was penetrated in five places, and the right lung in two places, but the lungs were otherwise perfectly healthy. The heart was rather fatty, and was penetrated in one place, but there was otherwise nothing in the heart to cause death, although there was some blood in the pericardium.
>
> The liver was healthy, but was penetrated in five places, the spleen was perfectly healthy, and was penetrated in two places; both the kidneys were perfectly healthy; the stomach was also perfectly healthy, but was penetrated in six places; the intestines were healthy, and so were all the other organs.
>
> The lower portion of the body was penetrated in one place, the wound being three inches in length and one in depth...there was a deal of blood between the legs, which were separated. Death was due to haemorrhage and loss of blood.

Killeen disagreed with Barrett that there was evidence that sexual intercourse had recently taken place. He saw no physical signs that there had been any kind of struggle. Killeen suggested that one of the wounds may have been made by a left-handed person but that the others were more likely to have been inflicted by a right–hander. He also believed that two weapons had been used. *The East London Observer* quoted Killeen on this point:

> I don't think that all the wounds were inflicted with the same instrument, because there was one wound on the breastbone which did not correspond with the other wounds on the body. The instrument with which the wounds were inflicted would most probably be an ordinary knife, but a knife would not cause such a wound as that on the breastbone. That wound I should think would have been inflicted with some form of a dagger.

Inspector Edmund Reid of the Metropolitan Police's H or Whitechapel Division was tasked with running the investigation. It was not going to be a quick one. The dead woman was not known to the residents of George Yard Buildings. There were no discernable clues and no evident motive for so grisly a murder. And then there was the singular fact that no one had heard the attack despite its obvious ferocity.

H Division personnel

Reid instructed Barrett to visit the grenadier guard detachment at the Tower of London in the hope that he might recognize the soldier he had seen near the murder scene. The PC drew a blank. Other soldiers in the company were also interviewed but in each case they provided solid alibis.

On 9 August Pearly Poll walked into Commercial Street Police Station and said that she had been in the company of the deceased on Bank Holiday night. She stated that she would know both soldiers if she saw them again and promised she would attend an identity parade at the Tower the next day. However, Poll was a no-show on that day and on the next. In fact, reluctant to get involved she had gone to stay with her cousin, a Mrs Shean who lived near Drury Lane.

Finally, she pulled herself together sufficiently to attend on the 13th a re-scheduled parade at the Tower garrison where were gathered every non-commissioned officer and private who had leave of absence at the time of the murder. Nevertheless, Poll failed to identify either of the men with whom she and Tabram had paired up, exclaiming finally, her arms spread akimbo, "He ain't here!" Poll claimed that the men had been wearing white cap-bands, which were part of the uniform of the Coldstream Guards whose London billet was the Wellington Barracks. She attended an identity parade there on the 15th where she picked out two soldiers but, once again, both had solid alibis.

The murdered woman was formally identified as Martha Tabram on 14 August by her estranged husband, Henry Samuel Tabram of 6 River Terrace, East Greenwich. Martha, the youngest of five children, was born Martha White in the London Borough of Southwark, daughter of warehouseman Charles Samuel White and Elizabeth (née Dowsett). In May 1865 her parents separated; six months later her father died. Subsequently, Martha met Henry Samuel Tabram, a packer at a furniture warehouse. The pair married 25 December 1869. Martha bore two sons: Frederick John Tabram (born February 1871) and Charles Henry Tabram (born December 1872). Martha's heavy drinking, sufficient enough to cause alcoholic fits, put a great deal of strain on the marriage. By 1875 Henry had had enough and moved away but supported his estranged wife with the payment of a weekly allowance of twelve shillings

Martha Tabram

for three years, later reducing the amount to two shillings and sixpence weekly when he heard she was seeing another man. This other man was carpenter, Henry Turner. The pair lived together on and off from 1876 until three weeks before Martha's death. As before, this new relationship was also impaired by Martha's drink problem and her occasional habit of staying out all night. The Census of 1881 was conducted during a period of separation because it recorded Martha and her two sons as being inmates at the Whitechapel Union workhouse casual ward at Thomas Street.

By early 1888 Turner was out of regular employment and the couple were eking out a pitiful income by selling trinkets and other small articles on the streets and by Martha's prostitution activities. For four months they resided at 4 Star Place off Commercial Road in Whitechapel. Around the beginning of July, the pair skipped without paying the rent and separated for the last time just days later. Martha moved to a common lodging house at 19 George Street, Spitalfields, her address at the time of her murder. Collier concluded the inquest on 23 August with a verdict of murder by person or persons unknown. No suspect was ever arrested for Tabram's murder.

Traditionally, due largely to the absence of throat injuries and evisceration Martha Tabram has not been included in the "official" canon of Jack the Ripper's victims: Mary Ann "Polly" Nichols, Annie Chapman, Elizabeth Stride, Catherine Eddowes and Mary Kelly. However, there is significant expert opinion that the general particulars of Tabram's murder (a knife murder upon a Whitechapel "unfortunate" carried out on or close to a weekend or holiday under cover of darkness) indicate a high probability that the Ripper was the perpetrator. I share this opinion.

Although Tabram's murder was a matter of great consternation to police and to the public it was not the first such frenzied attack to have taken place in the area that year. In fact, the assault on Tabram was the fourth. On 25 February Annie Millwood, widow of soldier Richard Millwood, was admitted to the Whitechapel Workhouse Infirmary, which recorded her admission details simply as "stabs." Annie recovered from her wounds and on 21 March was discharged to the South Grove Workhouse, Mile End Road. Ten days later she collapsed at the rear of the building and died where she fell. Reporting on the story, the *Eastern Post* expanded on Annie's knife wounds confirming that she had been admitted to the Infirmary with:

> ...numerous stabs in the legs and lower part of the body. She
> stated that she had been attacked by a man who she did not know and

who stabbed her with a clasp knife, which he took from his pocket. No one appears to have seen the attack, and as far as at present ascertained there is only the woman's statement to bear out the allegations of an attack, though that she had been stabbed cannot be denied.

39-year old machinist Ada Wilson, resident of Mile End, was the next victim. On the night of 27-28 March, Ada was about to retire when she heard a knock at the door. Opening it, she saw a stranger who looked about thirty and stood around 5'6" inches tall. His face was sunburnt and he had a fair moustache. He was wearing a dark coat, light trousers and a wideawake hat.

He demanded money. When Ada refused he drew a clasp knife from his pocket and stabbed her twice in the throat. Ada's screams drew assistance and after Dr. Wheeler of Mile End Road tended her wounds she was sent to the London Hospital. It had been a very vicious assault and press reports commented, "It is thought impossible that the injured woman can recover." Ada was made of strong stuff and, against the odds, pulled through. Her attacker was never traced. The police put the assault down to an attempted robbery.

On the evening of Easter Monday, 2 April, 45-year old widow, Emma Elizabeth Smith, resident at a common lodging house at 18 George Street, Spitalfields, went out. Nine or ten hours later she staggered back into the premises, telling deputy keeper Mrs Mary Russell that she had been attacked and robbed. Her head was injured, her face battered and half of one ear was almost torn off. She complained of severe pains in the lower part of her body.

Mrs Russell took Emma to hospital but she died at 9:00 a.m. from peritonitis. Examination had shown that a blunt instrument had been inserted into her vagina with great force and had ruptured the perineum.

The press reported that Emma Smith had been accosted by "some men" and severely maltreated. The attackers had not yet been apprehended. What actually had taken place?

At about 12:15 a.m. fellow resident at 18 George Street, Margaret Hames, saw Emma with a man at the corner of Farrance Street and Burdett Road in Limehouse. The man was of medium height and wearing a white silk handkerchief around his neck and a dark suit.

Emma, herself, said in hospital that she had been walking home along Whitechapel Road at about 1:30 a.m. when, by St Mary's Church, she saw three men coming towards her. She crossed the road to avoid them but they followed her into Osborn Street where they raped and attacked her, making off with the little money she was carrying. Emma could recall nothing about them except that one was a youth about nineteen years of age.

Hospital records recorded Emma's occupation as charwoman but it was believed that she supported herself at least partly through prostitution. It was known that many years previously Emma had walked away from family and friends for reasons never clarified. All she ever said about her mysterious past was that she had left her husband and broken away from all her early associations.

Lead investigating officer Inspector Edmund Reid noted in his report that Emma's clothing was "in such dirty ragged condition that it was impossible to tell if any part of it had been fresh torn." Every effort was made to find her assailants. Hundreds of people were questioned (including soldiers from the Tower of London garrison) and scores of statements taken. Ships in docks were searched and sailors quizzed. No one was ever brought to justice for the appalling manner in which Emma Elizabeth Smith was murdered.

Detective Constable Walter Dew of H Division (who besides being a part of the Ripper investigation also played a subsequent role in the arrest of the infamous Dr. Crippen) was a lone voice in believing that Emma Smith was the Ripper's first victim. He later wrote:[18]

> Her past was a closed book even to her intimate friends. All she had ever told anyone about herself was that she was a widow who more than ten years before had left her husband and broken away from all her early associations.
>
> There was something about Emma Smith, which suggested that there had been a time when the comforts of life had not been denied her. There was a touch of culture in her speech, unusual in her class.
>
> Once when Emma was asked why she had broken away so completely from her old life she replied, a little wistfully: "They would not understand now any more than they understood then. I must live somehow."

There is no evidence that the assaults on Millwood, Wilson and Smith were connected but in their execution one senses the presence of a gathering force. With the benefit of hindsight, the attacks may be said to represent the foothills of a much larger approaching phenomenon. It was as if the principle of "coming events cast their shadows before" was agitating the ethers. This agitation prompted three violent actions, which, in turn, opened a corridor for the emergence of far more extreme atrocities, beginning with the thirty-nine stab wounds inflicted on Martha Tabram.

---

[18] Dew, W., *I Caught Crippen*, Blackie & Son, 1938

Moreover, in the context of this present study it may be noted that the assaults were also synchronous with three significant occult and political events, two of which connected with matters in Germany and neighbouring regions. This trio of agitations did not take place in a vacuum and, I contend, was not unconnected with contemporaneous and uncharacteristically violent actions in Whitechapel.

Thirteen days before the attack on Wilson, Dr. William Wynn Westcott (no relation to Bible scholar Brooke Foss Westcott), Dr. William Robert Woodman and Samuel Liddell Mathers signed the Hermetic Order of the Golden Dawn (H.O.G.D.) pledge. On 1 March the occult H.O.G.D. was formally established. It is unlikely that the founding year of the H.O.G.D. was chosen indiscriminately. For many years the story did the rounds that the H.O.G.D. was established in 1886 by one Anna Sprengel, the Nuremberg-born putative countess of Landsfeldt and alleged lovechild of Ludwig I of Bavaria and Lola Montez. Sprengel is supposed to have held a Rosicrucian ritual and, subsequently, forwarded documents to Westcott in his capacity as the German-nominated (puppet) head of the H.O.G.D. in Britain. Sprengel's existence has never been satisfactorily proven and one theory is that Westcott dreamed her up as a backstory to confer legitimacy on the Order and on his leadership ambitions.

Today it is believed that the true occult basis for the Order's establishment was documents obtained from Freemason and Rosicrucian scholar, Kenneth R.H. Mackenzie (1833-1886). In turn, some believe that Mackenzie came into possession of the documents from Count Apponyi of Hungary. Besides being a fellow Rosicrucian, Apponyi was also a representative of an extremely secretive Continental European order of Hermetic alchemists referred to in H.O.G.D. circles as the "Secret Chiefs," ("Geheime Oberen" in the German occult tradition).

Mackenzie encrypted certain of these documents using a code from the *Polygraphia*, a cryptographic work written by the 15th century German abbot mentioned earlier: occultist and cipher expert, Johannes Trithemius, an influential figure venerated in esoteric circles. Trithemius claimed that 1888 would be the seventh year of the New Age of Michael, the Angel of the Sun, and an event of great import for those in the late nineteenth century working within the esoteric traditions. He predicted that the dawning of the Age of Gold under the influence of Michael, the angel dedicated to the expansion of human consciousness and freedom, would mark a fundamental turning point in history and inaugurate an exciting change of direction for mankind. It would herald the coming of new arts and an exciting new period of architecture.

Next, the European political scene in the spring of 1888 was a time of turbulent chaos that threatened to engulf the imperial structures in other European power centres. Wilhelm I, King of Prussia for twenty-seven years and Emperor of a unified Germany for seventeen, died 9 March. His son Frederick William, who at the time of succession was suffering from terminal throat cancer, followed him. He spent his ninety-nine days on the throne battling the disease, giving up the ghost in mid-June whereupon his son, Wilhelm, took the Emperor's crown. "Kaiser Willy," Queen Victoria's grandson, was just twenty-nine. 1888 became known as the year of the three Emperors. German schoolchildren of the day delighted in chanting, "Drei Achten, drei Kaiser," ("Three eights, three Emperors").

Victoria was not blind to the increasing frailty of the European imperial structures. At home, too, the Queen could clearly observe how the political and imperial status quo was being tested. Citizens and their deep-pocketed champions were becoming increasingly vocal in their demands for social reform, better wages and safer working conditions. Whilst to the Fenians and anarchists working in tandem with fellow conspirators across the Irish Sea and the English Channel, the House of Hanover was a house of cards that must be toppled.

Thirdly, the intemperate actions of Metropolitan Police Commissioner Sir Charles Warren during the previous November in quelling civil unrest in Trafalgar Square on "Bloody Sunday," an occasion of a march principally held in protest against unemployment and coercion in Ireland, had not helped matters. The death of two unemployed protesters and the hospitalisation of scores more at the hands of troops and police in the heart of London's West End had created uproar. It had reflected as badly upon the Royal Family as on the police. The Queen had not been amused. Any actions by the Establishment that would further fan the flames of hatred and sedition were to be avoided at all costs.

And then a malignant force that would become known to the world as "Jack the Ripper" comes along. Jack's frenzied assault on Martha Tabram signals the moment when life for the British establishment and the monarchy was about to get difficult, just how difficult would not become apparent until the autumn of 1888.

"Bloody Sunday," London, 13 November 1887

Chapter 4

HPB

The second major metaphysical development of the nineteenth century of importance to our narrative is the establishment of the Theosophical Society, founded in New York City in 1875 by Russian émigré Helena Blavatsky, Henry Steel Olcott and William Quan Judge. Blavatsky (often referred to as HPB) was the principle force behind the movement but it should be borne in mind that she was a highly controversial figure who invoked extremes of opinion. It would appear that either one idolizes her as a spiritual guru or dismisses her as a charlatan.

René Guénon was dismissive, stating in his critique of Theosophy[19] that Blavatsky had acquired all her knowledge naturally from other books, not from any supernatural masters. Carl Jung was extremely critical of Blavatsky's work. So too was Agehananda Bharati[20] (monastic name of Leopold Fischer, twentieth-century professor of Anthropology at Syracuse University), who dismissed it as "a melee of horrendous hogwash and of fertile inventions of inane esoterica."

Other well regarded authorities have been kinder. Joscelyn Godwin has stated that there is "no more important figure in modern times" than Blavatsky within the Western esoteric tradition.[21] While admirer Nicholas Goodrick-Clarke[22] noted how Blavatsky's ideas reflected the chief characteristics of Western esotericism identified by the prominent French scholar Antoine Faivre: (a) correspondences between all parts of the universe, the macrocosm and microcosm; (b) living nature as a complex, plural, hierarchical and animate whole; (c) imagination and mediations in the form of intermediary spirits, symbols, and mandalas;

---

[19] Ibid.
[20] Bharati, A., *Fictitious Tibet: the Origins and Persistence of Rampaism,* Tibet Society Bulletin, Vol. 7, 1974
[21] Johnson, K.P., *The Masters Revealed: Madame Blavatsky and the Myth of the Great White Lodge,* Albany: State University of New York Press, 1994
[22] Goodrick-Clarke, N., *Helena Blavatsky*, Berkeley, CA: North Atlantic Books, 2004

(d) the experience of transmutation of the soul through purification and ascent. High praise, indeed.

It is a common misunderstanding that Blavatsky and her colleagues formulated "theosophy," per se. They did not. The term had been in use for centuries ("theosophy" being used as a synonym for theology as early as the 3rd century CE).

In broad terms, theosophy refers to aspects of esoteric Christianity in the Western mystical tradition that focus on the attainment of direct, unmediated knowledge (Gnosis) of the Divine and of the origin and purpose of the Universe. In this wider sense, it is known as Christian theosophy or Boehmian theosophy (the latter after German philosopher and Christian mystic Jakob Böhme, 1575-1624).

Students of theosophy believe that a study of mystical Christian philosophy offers a path to enlightenment and salvation. Theosophy has been described as the most intellectually important of the fashionable esoteric trends of the nineteenth century.

Expert authorities such as Godwin and Faivre tend to differentiate the older tradition of religious illumination from Blavatsky's by referring to the latter with a capital letter as Theosophy, and the former with a lower-case "t." Additionally, followers of Blavatsky's religious system are termed Theosophists, while adherents of the Boehmian tradition are called theosophers.

Webb[23] reflected upon the significance of the Theosophical Movement, noting that as a prototype occult society it bore the capacity to offer new and unfamiliar patterns of thought to those seeking spiritual meaning.

Before proceeding with a potted history of the years preceding Blavatsky's contribution to the founding of the Theosophical Society, it should be remembered that much of what constitutes her life story is not independently verified. Paul Johnson is a very useful source for biographical material on Blavatsky.

Blavatsky was born Helena Petrovna von Han to Russo-German parents on 12 August 1831 at Ekaterinoslav in the Ukraine. Her father was Pyotr Alexeyevich von Hahn, a Captain in the Russian Royal Horse Artillery and a descendant of the aristocratic German von Hahn family. Her mother was self-educated Helena Andreyevna von Hahn

---

[23] Ibid.

[24] Johnson, P., *In Search of the Masters. Behind the Occult Myth*. South Boston, VA: Author, 1990.

(née Fadeyeva), the daughter of Princess Yelena Pavlovna Dolgorukaya. Helena was also part French through her great-great grandfather, a Huguenot nobleman who fled to Russia to escape persecution and thereafter served in the court of Catherine the Great.

Through Captain Hahn's career the family moved regularly from place to place in the Empire. While living in the army town of Romankovo, Helena, at the age of two, lost her younger brother to illness. In 1835 the family relocated to Odessa where resided Helena's maternal grandparents, Privy Councillor Andrei Fadeyev and Princess Helena Dolgoroukov. In this same year Helena's sister, Vera Petrovna, was born.

In the following year Captain Hahn was posted to Saint Petersburg. Liking the city, Helena's mother established her career there as a novelist, writing novels under the pseudonym "Zenaida R-va." She translated Bulwer-Lytton's novels for Russian publication. Helena Andreyevna and her daughters stayed in the city after her husband was posted back to Ukraine in 1837.

Helena gained her first experience with religion when she and her mother joined Fadeyev in Astrakhan. There they befriended members of the Kalmyk community, which practised Tibetan Buddhism. The family returned to Odessa where Helena learned English from a British governess. It was not long before the family were packing their cases yet again, moving to Saratov where a brother, Leonid, was born in June 1840. After a short relocation to Poland the family returned to Odessa where Helena's mother died of tuberculosis in June 1842, aged 28. Helena, Vera and Leonid were sent to live with their maternal grandparents in Saratov where Fadeyev had been appointed Governor.

Young Helena, described by contemporaries as a cosseted, wayward child and a beguiling storyteller, was educated in French, art and music: the subjects necessary for her to find a suitable husband.

Blavatsky in her younger days

While in Saratov she took a holiday in a Kalmyk summer camp where she learned horse riding and some Tibetan. Later, Blavatsky claimed to have found in Saratov the library of her maternal great-grandfather, Prince Pavel Vasilevich Dolgorukov, which contained many books on esoteric subjects. Dolgorukov had entered Freemasonry in the late 1770s and was inducted into the Rite of Strict Observance. There were rumours that he had met with occult luminaries, Alessandro Cagliostro and the mysterious Comte de Saint Germain. It was during this period of her early teens that Blavatsky began to experience visions of a mysterious Indian man, understanding from these encounters that she would meet him later in life.

After yet another family move, on this occasion to Tiflis in Georgia, Helena established a friendship with Russian Freemason, Alexander Vladimirovich Golitsyn, who, she said, kindled her interest in esoteric matters. She also claimed that during her time in Georgia she had her first out-of-body experiences in astral travel.

In July 1849, aged seventeen, Helena married Nikifor Vladimirovich Blavatsky, a man in his forties who was Vice-Governor of Erivan Province in Armenia. She claimed later that she was drawn to this man because of his interest in magic. The couple moved to Sardar Palace where Madame Blavatsky tried repeatedly to escape and return to her family in Tiflis.

Eventually, her husband relented and Blavatsky, fleeing those who were tasked with returning her to the family home in Odessa, bribed a ship captain and acquired a berth to Constantinople, marking the beginning of a nine-year period of travel, possibly financed by her father. Blavatsky's distant relative, Count Witte, said that while in Constantinople Blavatsky joined a circus as an equestrienne before taking up with ageing Hungarian opera-singer Mitrovitch.

There are few proven records of what transpired during Blavatsky's travel years. What is known is that in 1851 Blavatsky travelled to Egypt. Disguised as young Muslim men to circulate unhindered, she and an American friend, Albert Leighton Rawson, roamed around Old Cairo where they learned the techniques of snake charming.

In the city they met celebrated Coptic magician, Paulos Metamon, who showed the pair very curious books crammed with astrolological formulae, occult diagrams and magical incantations. Blavatsky and Rawson failed in an attempt to establish a society for occult research and Metamon advised delay.

The story then goes that after leaving Egypt Blavatsky went to Paris where she served as an assistant to Daniel Dunglas Home. According to

Jocelyn Godwin,[25] Blavatsky also kept company with the city's spiritualist community, including magnetizer Victor Michal who practised crystal gazing with hashish, astral projection and table-turning and was familiar with Séidism (the teachings of The Old Man of the Mountain, chief of the "assassins" of Lebanon). Michal reported that Blavatsky was a marvellous subject to magnetize but that her bouts of anger on coming out of trance became all too much for him.

Significantly, according to Rawson's memoirs[26] Blavatsky during her stay in Paris astonished Freemason Thevenot, Grand Secretary of the Grand Orient of France, with her knowledge of all the secrets of the degrees in one branch to the 33rd and in another to the 95th.

During her short stay in Paris Blavatsky was friendly with the Leymarie family, followers of Allan Kardec's reincarnational school of spiritualism. She, herself, was not an ardent believer and explained that she was sent from Paris to America to:

> ...show the fallacy of the Spiritualistic theories of "Spirits." But how could I do it best? I did not want people at large to know that I could produce the same thing at will. I had received ORDERS to the contrary, and yet, I had to keep alive the reality, the genuineness and possibility of such phenomena in the hearts of those who from Materialists had turned Spiritualists and now, owing to the exposure of several mediums fell back again, returned to their skepticism.[27]

And:

> I am here, in this country sent by my Lodge, on behalf of Truth in modern Spiritualism, and it is my most sacred duty to unveil what is, and expose what is not.[28]

In speaking of exposure, Blavatsky is referring to her belief that in their communications spiritualists did not commune with the spirits in the afterlife but either with the elemental forces of earth, fire, air and water or with the etheric larva-like "shells" discarded by the dead. Such psychic shells, she believed, were able for a time to imitate the personalities of the individuals that had cast them off. It would be several years before Blavatsky commenced her mission "to unveil what

---

[25] Godwin ibid.

[26] Rawson, A.L.,"Mme Blavatsky: a Theosophical Occult Apology." *Theosophical History* 2/6 (1988), 209-20. (First ed. 1892)

[27] Note in HPB's *Scrapbook*, published in BCWI,73.

[28] Letter to Prof. Hiram Corson, 16 February 1875, quoted in BCWI,1v.

is and expose what is not" in earnest.

Her next port of call in 1851 was England where Blavatsky claimed she met the "mysterious Indian," a Hindu whom she referred to as the Master Morya. A "Master" in the occult and metaphysical sense denotes a superhuman being concerned with guiding humanity along the right path towards spiritual enlightenment. They are said to reside in a higher dimension of the earth plane, symbolically located in remote high regions such as Tibet but can and do appear in human form when circumstances demand.

According to Blavatsky's account, Morya said he had a special task for her that required a trip to Tibet. Accordingly, she made her way to Asia via America where she met with the Native American communities of Quebec in the hope of meeting their shamans but was instead robbed of her luggage, an act she attributed to the negative influence of Christian missionaries. Blavatsky then travelled south to New York where she made lifelong friends, journeyed down through the Andean region and subsequently took a boat to Ceylon and then Bombay. She spent two years in India, allegedly following Morya's instructions before attempting to pass into Tibet and being denied entry by the British colonial authorities.

Blavatsky returned to England in 1854 having, she claimed, survived a shipwreck off the Cape of Good Hope. On her arrival she suffered hostility as a Russian national due to Britain's engagement in the Crimean War.

She soon left England and took a berth to the U.S. Blavatsky visited New York City, Chicago, Salt Lake City and San Francisco from which she sailed to India via Japan, making stops en route in Kashmir, Ladakh and Burma before making a second attempt to enter Tibet. She claimed that on this occasion she was successful; entering the country in 1856 accompanied by a Tartar shaman who was attempting to reach Siberia and wanted help from a Russian citizen. Blavatsky gave no account of her time in Tibet, except to say that the shaman and she visited Leh and spent time with a Tartar community.

Blavatsky then travelled back to Europe, spending time in France and Germany before returning in 1858 to her family then living in Pskov. She claimed that while in Pskov she began exhibiting paranormal abilities. These were of a kind that was quite familiar in the Foxes' cottage with much rapping, creaking and furniture moving of its own accord and what were described as the sound of "astral bells."

In 1864, while riding in Mingrelia, Blavatsky fell from her horse and sustained a spinal fracture. After waking from a coma lasting several months, she claimed that she had gained full control of her paranormal abilities. Having recovered sufficiently, Blavatsky travelled to Italy, Transylvania and Serbia, in the latter reportedly studying the Kabbalah with a rabbi.

Three years later she resumed her travels, spending time in the Balkans, Hungary, Venice and Florence. Blavatsky also claimed that in this period she fought alongside Giuseppe Garibaldi at the Battle of Mentana.

Responding to a message from Morya, Blavatsky travelled to meet him in Constantinople from where they reportedly journeyed overland to Tibet through Turkey, Persia, Afghanistan and India, entering Tibet via Kashmir. Once in Tibet, Blavatsky stayed at the home of Morya's friend, Master Koot Hoomi, one of the Mahatmas that would later inspire the founding of the Theosophical Society.

Blavatsky claimed that while in Tibet Morya and Koot Hoomi helped her to develop and control her psychic powers. She said that among the powers displayed by her teachers were clairvoyance, clairaudience, telepathy, the ability to control another's consciousness, the dematerializing and rematerializing of solid objects, and bilocation.

Tibet during the nineteenth century was closed to Europeans and one struggles to understand how Blavatsky could have travelled its interior. However, her supporters have pointed out that traders and pilgrims were able to access the country freely. Blavatsky's Asian appearance and the fact of her being accompanied by Morya may have facilitated her passage into the region. Moreover, one scholar of Buddhism, D.T. Suzuki, did state in her defence that her advanced knowledge of Mahayana Buddhism was consistent with her having studied in a Tibetan monastery.

Nevertheless, there were those among Blavatsky's contemporaries who poured cold water on her having entered Tibet. In his lectures on *The Transcandental Universe* C.G Harrison said that Blavatsky had by magical means been incarcerated in an "occult prison," a psychic condition which made her believe that while staying in Khatmandhu she was physically present and active in Tibet. Occult prison is a certain operation of ceremonial magic conducted by an adept wherein a wall of psychic influences is constructed around one considered to have become in some way dangerous. It is a form of spiritual sleep during which the "prisoner" experiences fantastical visions. The unnamed informant who disclosed the affair to Harrison is believed to have been Charles Massey who would go on to become a principal of the fledgling Theosophical Society.

Reportedly accompanied by Mitrovitch, Blavatsky set off for Greece via the Suez Canal. She boarded the SS *Eumonia* bound for Egypt on which she suffered her second ocean calamity. On 4 July 1871, the ship exploded off the Greek island of Spetsai carrying 400 passengers. According to Count Witte, Mitrovitch saved Helena's life at the expense of his own. Blavatsky was one of only 16 survivors. For years there were rumours that Blavatsky had a deformed child by Mitrovitch but it has been established that the father was Estonian, Baron Meyendorf, keen spiritualist and friend of Daniel Dunglas Home.

Arrriving in Cairo "in a wet skirt and without a penny to her name,"[29] Blavatsky soon picked herself up. With the help of a woman named Emma Coulomb Blavatsky established, twenty years after her first attempt with Albert Leighton Rawson, the *Société Spirite*, which was based largely on the Spiritist philosophy of Allan Kardec. According to Blavatsky, after two weeks during which a madman with a gun ran amok in a meeting she wrapped up the society, disgusted that the mediums enlisted in the group's service cheated and drank to excess. Others believe that the *Société Spirite* continued its work. Diplomat and spiritualist James M. Peebles spoke in 1874 of the Society and its meetings held in Cairo's Oriental Hotel. He stated that it had fine writing mediums and other forms of manifestations, adding that the lady whose husband keeps the hotel is a spiritualist. This was a reference to Coulomb who would become Blavatsky's housekeeper in India in 1880 and later one of her most vociferous opponents.

Blavatsky went to live in Boulak near the Museum and sought contact only with Paulos Metamon whose magical practices had earned him a strange reputation in Egypt. High officials laughed at him in public but dreaded him in private. Isma'il Pasha, the Khedive (Turkish Viceroy to Egypt), better known as Ismail the Magnificent, consulted him on more than one occasion but ignored Metamon's advice for him to resign. With hindsight it might have been better for Pasha to heed Metamon's counsel to spare him the embarrassment of being unceremoniously forced out of

Allen Kardec

---

[29] *The Memoirs of Count Witte*, tr. and ed. A. Yarmolisky, London, 1921

office by the British in 1879.

Leaving Egypt, Blavatsky went on to Syria, Palestine and Lebanon. In this period she met with writer Lidia Pashkova, a source that provided independent verification of Blavatsky's travels during this time. On Morya's instructions Blavatsky travelled in July 1873 to New York City, having in the previous year spent time with her family in Odessa and made trips to Bucharest and Paris. In New York Blavatsky took up residence in a women's housing cooperative on Manhattan's Lower East Side where she earned a living sewing and designing advertising cards. Her presence in the U.S. began to attract attention. She was interviewed by Anna Ballard of New York's *Sun* newspaper, the piece reporting for the first time details of Blavatsky's time in Tibet. Soon afterwards she inherited a considerable fortune consequent to her father's death, enabling her to move into an upmarket hotel.

In 1875 Blavatsky married Georgian, Mikheil Betaneli. This was a bigamous relationship because her first husband was still alive and kicking. However, her refusal to consummate the marriage provided Betaneli with grounds for divorce and he returned to Georgia.

Blavatsky became interested in a news story about William and Horatio Eddy, two brothers who held séances in their small family-owned inn, the Green Tavern, in Chittenden, Vermont. Visitors from around the world came to witness the unusual goings-on, which included displays of levitation and musical instruments that appeared to play on their own (a ruse later exposed as a trick by magician Chung Ling Soo).

William and Horatio Eddy

At Chittenden Blavatsky met reporter Colonel Henry Steel Olcott who was investigating the brothers' activities for the *Daily Graphic*. Olcott was soon impressed with the Russian's own abilities in manifesting spirit phenomena. The pair clicked and became close friends, giving each other the nicknames "Maloney" (Olcott) and "Jack" (Blavatsky). The *Daily Graphic* published an article about Blavatsky that attracted considerable attention, and Olcott discussed her in his 1875 work, *Spiritualism, People from the Other World*. Soon Blavatsky was instructing her new friend in occult matters.

"Maloney" and "Jack" decided that their new ideas needed a much wider audience. To this end, on 17 April 1875 they published a circular letter in the Boston-based spiritualist publication, *The Spiritual Scientist*, setting out HPB's mission. At Blavatsky's request, Olcott signed the letter: "For the Committee of Seven, the Brotherhood of Luxor." Olcott understood from Blavatsky that this was a group of seven Adepts that belonged to the Egyptian group of the Universal Mystic Brotherhood. Blavatsky spoke of this American Order in *Isis Unveiled*:[3]

> What will…astonish American readers is that in the United States a mystical fraternity now exists which claims an intimate relationship with one of the most powerful of Eastern Brotherhoods…the Brotherhood of Luxor…its faithful members have the custody of very important secrets of science…Mackenzie describes it as having "a Rosicrucian basis, and numbering many members" (*Royal Masonic Cyclopaedia*). But in this, the author is mistaken: it has no Rosicrucian basis. The name Luxor is primarily derived from the ancient Baloochistan city of Looksur…which gave its name to the Egyptian city.

HPB's statement appeared to indicate imperfect knowledge of the contemporary occult scene because Mackenzie's remark probably referred to Max Theon's Hermetic Brotherhood of Luxor. HPB was not all wrong. Theon's Order did indeed not have a Rosicrucian basis and claimed descent from Egyptian occultism as practised around 2450 BC.

The American Brotherhood of Luxor was not destined to establish a lasting existence, instead soon fading away but not before sewing the seeds of other like-minded movements such as AMORC (Ancient and Mystical Order of the Rose Cross), the OTO (Ordo Templi Orientis) and the Hermetic Order of the Golden Dawn. Historian of Theosophy

---

[30] Blavatsky, H.P., *Isis Unveiled*, 2 vols, New York, Bouton, 1877

David Board has argued that the establishment of an American Brotherhood of Luxor was inspired by yet another British occult group: the English Brotherhood of Light, established in 1873 by Irish born Captain Francis George Irwin (1828-1892). We will return both to Theon's H.B. of L. circle and Irwin's Society in Chapter 8.

Blavatsky and Olcott set up house together in a number of rented apartments in New York City, their lifestyle largely funded by income from Olcott's activities as a lawyer (despite the fact that Blavatsky was now independently well off from her father's money). Early in 1875 Olcott began studying occultism with an Egyptian adept known as "Tuitit Bey," with Blavatsky serving as the vehicle for the channeled teachings. Olcott learned about the elementals and nature-spirits, which he believed were the real agents of spiritualist phenomena rather than the spirits of the dead. Later that year, reportedly at the behest of Tuitit Bey, Blavatsky and Olcott established the Miracle Club in New York where they hosted and delivered lectures on esoteric themes.

Through this group the pair met Irish-American spiritualist William Quan Judge with whom they shared mutual interests, so much so that at a Club meeting on 7 September 1875 Blavatsky, Olcott and Judge agreed to found an esoteric order. The man who would become the first librarian of the Society, Charles Sotheran, suggested the name "Theosophy." Sotheran knew Blavatsky and admired her intellectual prowess though he was not an admirer of her occult dabblings. On occasions when Sotheran saw that Blavatsky's occult practices interfered with the work of the Society he would tackle her head on which led to many fractious scenes, breakups and reconciliations.

The term Theosophy derives from two Greek words, meaning "divine wisdom." Theosophists would forever argue about how to define the Society but Blavatsky herself insisted that its purpose was not an attempt to establish a new religion but to initiate a spiritual process that would distill out the universal mother doctrine which the guardians of the ancient Mystery Schools had kept secret from the profane for thousands of years. Blavatsky revealed that these guardians whom she called "mahatmas" or "masters" had told her that the time was ripe to spread the word through carefully chosen vessels (such as herself). Officially, the Society based itself upon three objectives:

- To form a nucleus of the Universal Brotherhood of Humanity, without distinction of race, creed, sex, caste or colour.

- To encourage the study of Comparative Religion, Philosophy and Science.

- To investigate the unexplained laws of Nature and the powers latent in man.

However, it was evident that for Blavatsky and her associates in the "Brotherhood of Luxor" there was an additional objective that was equally important, namely the replacement of the illusions of spiritualism by the higher knowledge of occultism.

The Blavatsky circle also shared another precious ideal, one that they did not discuss with occultists outside the Society's inner core. This was no less than the abolition of Christianity in favour of libertarian humanism. Member Emma Hardinge Britten shared this ambition. In promoting this highly radical objective, Blavatsky and her peers had no problem with Jesus whom HPB called "the great Socialist and Adept, the divine man who was changed into an anthropomorphic god," but were quite unable to see any positive correspondences between the Nazarene master and the "racist" Hebrew god of the Jewish Scriptures.

Between 7 September and the date of the Society's inauguration on 17 November Olcott busied himself with organising the new movement in New York. On 20 September Blavatsky provided insight into its founding principles in a letter to Russian psychic researcher Aksakov:

> It will be composed of learned occultists and cabbalists, of philosophes *Hermétiques* of the nineteenth century, and of passionate antiquaries and Egyptologists generally. We want to make an experimental comparison between Spiritualism and the magic of the ancients by following literally the instructions of the old Kabbalahs, both Jewish and Egyptian.

On the Society's inauguration Olcott was appointed chairman; Judge, secretary; and Blavatsky a corresponding secretary. Although the Theosophical Society was not founded with Blavatsky at its helm she was regarded as its chief theoretician and leading public figure. Notwithstanding that Emma Hardinge Britten was one of the Society's principal members, on the whole spiritualists were not drawn to the new movement, judging Theosophy as unscientific, occultist and cultish.

The Society taught that humanity had gone beyond its lowest point of spiritual myopia and was now proceeding on a path to a more enlightened race. Blavatsky said that if the Society were allowed to continue with its work without hindrance, "Earth will be a heaven in the

---

[31] Solovyoff, V.S., *A Modern Priestess of Isis*, Abridged and tr. Walter Leaf, London, Longmans, 1895

twenty-first century in comparison with what it is now!" It is fact that Blavatsky's movement appealed to those who felt threatened by Darwin's ideas. In her opinion, Indian religions were grounded in an evolutionary cosmology that complemented Darwinian thinking. Furthermore, Blavatsky believed that the Eastern doctrine of reincarnation offered an optimistic spiritual perspective at a time when gloomy Victorian society tended to emphasise the beckoning horrors of eternal damnation facing those that disdained Christian values.

According to Goodrick-Clarke,[32] the Theosophical Society "disseminated an elaborate philosophical edifice involving a cosmogony, the macrocosm of the universe, spiritual hierarchies, and intermediary beings, the latter having correspondences with a hierarchical conception of the microcosm of man."

In Blavatsky's opinion Europe and America were imprisoned by two false faiths: exoteric Christianity and material science. With this in mind, she began a short time after the founding of the Society to sketch out her spiritual philosophy for a book. Blavatsky tentatively titled the work *The Veil of Isis* but renamed it after discovering that it had been used for an 1861 Rosicrucian work by W.W. Reade. Her book was published in 1877 in two volumes, comprising more than 1,300 pages, as *Isis Unveiled: A Master-Key to the Mysteries of Ancient and Modern Science and Theology*.

In *Isis Unveiled* Blavatsky proclaimed Theosophy as "the synthesis of science, religion and philosophy," aligning her opus with Hermetic and Neoplatonic doctrines, the only possible keys to the absolute Universal Powers in science and theology. Blavatsky did not claim to have written every word and acknowledged the contributions from Sotheran, Rawson, Alexander Wilder (pioneer of holistic medicine), and especially from Olcott. Blavatsky said that while undertaking the work she felt as if her body was playing host to a second consciousness, "the lodger who is in me" which, she maintained, inspired and guided her writing. In constructing this seminal Theosophical work, Blavatsky quoted

William Quan Judge

---

[32] Ibid.

extensively from other esoteric texts including, said Olcott, those to which she had had no prior access. Olcott was in no doubt that Blavatsky looked up her references "from the astral light." Olcott described Blavatsky's writing style:

> Her pen would be flying over the page, when she would suddenly stop, look into space with the vacant eye of the clairvoyant seer, shorten her vision as though to look at something held invisibly in the air before her, and begin copying on her paper what she saw. The quotation finished, her eyes would resume their natural expression...

Isis Unveiled was very badly written despite Wilder's insistence on Blavatsky cutting out hundreds of pages. Marked by an extreme anti-Christian slant, the book attracted considerable negative press criticism, much of it highlighting instances of quoting from more than 100 works without acknowledgement. Nevertheless, the book was a commercial success but despite it selling out its print run of 1,000 in just one week, Blavatsky turned down her publisher's request for a sequel.

Opinion is divided on the merits of *Isis Unveiled*. Many are convinced that Blavatsky was an out-and-out plagiarist accusing her, for example, of filching heavily from the novels of Lytton, a highly regarded personality of the day whom Blavatsky used to praise regularly in extravagant terms. It has been argued that Lytton was the "master of my dreams" to whom she made reference in her diary. Emma Hardinge Britten twisted the knife when she said that the whole work came from the manuscripts of Baron de Palm.

Overall, present day scholarship tends to regard *Isis Unveiled* as a milestone in the history of western esoteric study. Among her supporters Goodrick-Clarke, never at a loss for laudatory words where HPB was concerned, described it as an important work that represented an original synthesis connecting disparate ideas brought together for the first time:

> The underlying theme among these diverse topics is the existence of an ancient wisdom-religion, an ageless occult guide to

---

[33] Olcott, H., *Old Diary Letters*, vol.1., New York and London, 1895
[34] Ibid.
[35] Joseph Henry Louis Charles, Grand Cross Commander of the Order of the Holy Sepulchre and Knight of various other orders. He joined the Theosophical Society soon after its inception. He was the first person to be cremated in the United States.
[36] Ibid.

the cosmos, nature and human life. The many faiths of man are said to derive from a universal religion known to both Plato and the ancient Hindu sages. The wisdom-religion is also identified with Hermetic philosophy as "the only possible key to the Absolute in science and theology." Every religion is based on the same truth or "secret doctrine," which contains "the alpha and omega of universal science." (It) will become the religion of the future.

Isis Unveiled also set out Blavatsky's thoughts on spiritualism, which she regarded as unsophisticated and uncosmopolitan. She was no kinder to Darwin, stating that his theories of evolution dealt only with the physical world at the expense of the spiritual. Its success did not, however, re-ignite public interest in the Theosophical Society, which by the autumn of 1876 had become largely inactive despite the establishment of new lodges throughout the U.S. and in London. In fact, the Theosophical Society was at this time regarded more as a literary body that was prone to acts of crankiness (an example being Blavatsky's sponsorship of Baron de Palm's cremation in May 1876).

In July 1878 Blavatsky gained U.S. citizenship. Two years later Olcott, abandoning his wife, travelled with Blavatsky to India where the Theosophical Society was aligned with Arya Samaj, a Hindu reform movement with whom the pair shared a mutual spiritual perspective. Olcott secured work as a U.S. trade representative to India. Soon after their arrival a pair of Mahatmas appeared in order to present startling new esoteric teachings about the nature of man and the history of the cosmos. Some believe that the "Mahatmas" were a cover for a group of Sikh, Buddhist and Sufi notables who were protesting against the British Empire, a symbol of Western arrogance and native exploitation.

In *Old Diary Leaves* Olcott described encounters with one of the "masters" around Blavatsky who was a young Cypriot named Ooton Liatto. On the first occasion, Liatto visited Olcott in his apartment and in an extraordinary display of otherworldly powers made his bedroom disappear into a cube of empty space in which appeared fantastical landscapes and Elementary forms, some as "horrid to see as the pictures in Barrett's 'Magus.'"

Despite British colonial administrative opposition and accusations of fraudulent paranormal practices, Theosophy spread rapidly in India. Well before the culmination of this process Blavatsky, diagnosed with Bright's disease (a kidney condition more commonly known today as chronic glomerulonephritis and which, coincidentally, afflicted the Ripper's penultimate victim Catherine Eddowes), left India in 1885 to return to Europe.

In London Blavatsky found her hands full trying to quell mounting internal discontent among members within the higher echelons of the Theosophical Society. Many were very uncomfortable with Blavatsky having opened a branch of the Society in India and there was much talk of establishing counter movements.

Consequently, some broke away to participate in the occult work of the Hermetic Brotherhood of Luxor and the Hermetic Order of the Golden Dawn while, in the meantime, arguments were raging between Alfred Percy Sinnett on the one hand and the joint forces of Edward Maitland and Anna Kingsford on the other. Sinnett played no small part in the dissemination of Theosophism. He was the editor of the influential Anglo-Indian paper, *The Pioneer*, and his two books—*Esoteric Buddhism* and *The Occult World*—introduced Theosophy to Europe for the first time.

Like Theon, Kingsford eventually voted with her feet, quitting the Society in 1884 to establish the Hermetic Society. Kingsford was a remarkable figure in her own right among late nineteenth-century esoteric Christian thinkers and we will return to consider in Chapter 8 her place in Britain's occult establishment.

There then came a hammer blow to HPB's standing and reputation. Madame Coulomb re-emerged and claimed that Blavatsky, her husband and she were engaged in a partnership of deceit in Cairo after the 1871 shipwreck. Evidently wanting to damage the Russian, Coulomb passed damaging letters from HPB to the editor of the *Madras Christian College Herald*. Only too pleased to lash out at what he regarded as Theosophy's pagan practices, the editor published in 1884 articles exposing as conjurer's trickery Blavatsky's production of genuine "phenomena."

These articles provided the Society for Psychical Research with just the ammunition they had been seeking to challenge Theosophical "phenomena." They invited Blavatsky to submit to an independent test of her paranormal abilities. Blavatsky did not think much of the S.P.R., calling it the "Spookical Research Society," but agreed to the examination process. The S.P.R.'s investigator, Richard Hodgson, made short shrift of his work, swiftly concluding that Blavatsky's Theosophical mystique was transparently fraudulent.

This became obvious when he was shown the Shrine, a wooden box in which was supposed to appear "apports," materialised objects such as flowers and messages from the Mahatmas. He was told the Shrine was entirely solid but a blow from his hand on the back of the box released a secret trapdoor. The game was up. Threatened with exposure, Blavatsky retracted her paranormal claims and accused the Coulombs of plotting with Christian missionaries to destroy her and her work.

Blavatsky went back to Europe to lick her wounds but she was not down for long. During the next four years she immersed herself in writing three books: *The Secret Doctrine* (1888-1889), *The Key to Theosophy* (1889) and *The Voice of the Silence* (1889*). The Secret Doctrine* was her 1,500-page magnum opus. Unable to persuade a company to publish it, Blavatsky established the Theosophical Publishing Company and brought out *The Secret Doctrine* in two volumes: the first in October 1888, the second in January 1889. Blavatsky claimed that the book constituted her commentary on *The Book of Dzyan*, a religious text written in Senzar. However, most scholars of Buddhism that have examined *The Secret Doctrine* maintain that *The Book of Dzyan* was Blavatsky's fictional creation.

Like *Isis Unveiled*, *The Secret Doctrine* and its esoteric cosmology appealed to a wide readership but it was a work that featured a much darker side of Blavatsky's personal philosophy. In its densely written pages one discovers commentaries on highly controversial cultural and anthropological issues that were later to be exploited by extremist ideologies. In particular, the book's second volume sets out Blavatsky's theory that humankind evolved over several millions of years to its present day form through seven "root-races." Blavatsky believed that the purest and most highly evolved of these were the Aryans, which, she said, constituted the latest, seventh sub-race of the Atlantean civilisation. According to Blavatsky's spirit-sight, the Aryans, surviving the mighty cataclysm that destroyed Atlantis, invaded Europe and Asia and won supremacy over other races. Predicting the demise of the "failures of nature," Blavatsky wrote:

> Mankind is obviously divided into god-informed men and lower human creatures. The intellectual difference between the Aryan and other civilized nations and such savages as the South Sea Islanders, is inexplicable on any other grounds. No amount of culture, nor generations of training amid civilization, could raise such human specimens as the Bushmen, the Veddhas of Ceylon, and some African Tribes, to the same intellectual level as the Aryans, the Semites, and the Turanians.
>
> The "sacred spark" is missing in them and it is they who are the only inferior races on the globe, now happily, owing to the wise adjustment of nature which ever works in that direction, fast dying out. Verily mankind is "of one blood," but not of the same essence. We are the hot-house, artificially quickened plants in nature, having

in us a spark, which in them is latent. Thus will mankind, race after race, perform its appointed cycle pilgrimage. Climates will, and have already begun, to change, each tropical year after the other dropping one sub-race, but only to beget another higher race on the ascending cycle; while a series of other less favoured groups—the failures of nature—will, like some individual men, vanish from the human family without even leaving a trace behind.

There are no prizes for guessing which 20th century group found the most inspiration in these teachings. Conventionally, historians date the beginnings of the Nazi movement to the years immediately after the Great War. We will see in later pages that Vatican sources indicate that it was seeded much earlier, its progenitors driven by just the kind of extreme racist thinking that flowed from Blavatsky's self-guiding pen.

In the winter of 1891 Blavatsky contracted the influenza virus and died in Annie Besant's house on the afternoon of 8 May. The date is commemorated by Theosophists as White Lotus Day.

We turn to the untimely death of the Ripper's next victim, Mary Ann "Polly" Nichols, who was killed on the feast day of Saint Raymond, the patron saint of midwives, children and pregnant women. Raymond was a missionary imprisoned by Moslems for attempting to convert the poor. His lips were pierced and his mouth shut up with a padlock. As these pages turn we may wonder how many in the highest positions of power in Britain were similarly silenced regarding their knowledge (and tacit complicity?) in connection with the Whitechapel murders.

Madame Blavatsky and Henry Steel Olcott

Chapter 5

"Polly"

Thursday, 30 August 1888

Echoing peals of thunder herald the streak and crackle of lightning. Driving rain pummels Whitechapel's dark streets. Despite the rain and cloud, the night sky retains a dull reddish afterglow from two fires in the docks that earlier drew large crowds to watch the firefighters at work.

Middle-aged prostitute Mary Ann "Polly" Nichols is getting a soaking, not an uncommon experience for a Whitechapel streetwalker. A passer-by would recall seeing her walking along Whitechapel Road at around 11:00 p.m.

Polly passes out of sight and turns into Osborn Street, a short thoroughfare that leads to the crossroads with Brick Lane, Wentworth Street and Old Montague Street. Approximately ninety minutes later Polly is observed leaving the Frying Pan pub in Brick Lane.

At 1:30 a.m., Friday the 31st, Polly is turned out from lodgings at 18 Thrawl Street, a five-minute walk from Brick Lane via Wentworth Street, for lack of fourpence for a bed.

For about six weeks Polly had shared a room at the Thrawl Street common lodging house with elderly married woman, Ellen Holland. Polly then moved out for a week to a lodging house in Flower and Dean Street but had returned on this fateful night to Thrawl Street at 1:20 a.m., the worse for drink and sporting a new black straw bonnet trimmed with black velvet.

Polly does not seem too put out to be turned away by the lodging house deputy. Cheerily, she asks him to keep the bed while she goes out to earn the doss money. She turns away, laughing. "I'll soon get my doss money," Polly cries. "See what a jolly bonnet I've got now!"

Just before 2:30 a.m. Ellen Holland, returning to her lodgings after seeing the fire that had broken out earlier that morning at Shadwell Docks, meets Polly at the corner of Whitechapel Road and Osborn Street. Polly is unaccompanied and very drunk.

The friends speak for a few minutes until the clock at St. Mary's

Church across the road strikes the half-hour. Mrs Holland tries in vain to persuade Polly to return with her to Thrawl Street but her friend is determined to earn her fourpence. She is confident of success.

Polly boasts, "I have had my lodging money three times today, and I have spent it...it won't be long before I'll be back," implying that her new bonnet will soon draw a paying customer.

They part. Mrs Holland watches her friend weaving a drunken path eastwards along the Whitechapel Road. She will never see Polly in life again.

Pickford's meat carter Charles Lechmere (also known as Charles Allen Cross, the name he gave to both the police and the coroner, and the one used in this chapter) of Doveton Street, Bethnal Green, was walking towards Baker's Row on the northside of Buck's Row, a gloomy cobbled thoroughfare (present day Durward Street) that narrowed before widening out past the local board school. It was about 3:40 a.m. Cross was approaching the end of the narrow stretch when he saw something on the pavement on the opposite side of the street. At first glance he thought it was a length of tarpaulin and then saw that it was a body with skirt raised almost to the stomach lying by the gated entrance to Mr Brown's stables. The spot was about 150 yards from the London Hospital and 100 yards from Blackwall Buildings.

Another carter on his way to work, Robert Paul of Foster Street, Bethnal Green, came by and saw Cross standing uncertainly by the body. The latter approached him and tapped him on the shoulder, saying, "Come and look over here. There's a woman lying on the pavement." Cross went to the body and felt the hands. They were cold. "I believe she's dead," he said.

Paul was not so certain. Her face and hands were indeed cold and Paul crouched down to detect any signs of life. He touched her breast and imagined he noticed slight movement. "I think she's breathing," he said, "but very little if she is." He suggested propping her up but Cross would not touch her. In the gloom neither man noticed her wounds, or even the terrible gash to the throat that had almost severed her head from her body.

These were two men who, despite the circumstances, wanted to waste no time in getting to work. Paul said that he would fetch a policeman except that he was running late, while Cross said he was in the same predicament. They agreed that the most expedient option was to press on and tell the first policeman they saw of their find. To preserve the woman's modesty, they pulled her skirt down towards her knees and then, indifferently, set off.

In Baker's Row at the junction of Hanbury and Old Montague Streets they met PC Jonas Mizen 55H and told him of what they had seen. Cross told Mizen, "She looks to me to be either dead or drunk, but for my part, I believe she's dead."

Cross and Paul then continued on to work while Mizen went to inspect the body. In Buck's Row Mizen saw PC John Neil 97J, who while approaching on his beat from the opposite direction had already come upon it.

Neil's lantern light afforded the officer a closer look at the woman than Cross and Paul had managed. She was lying on her back lengthways on the pavement. Her hands, one touching the stable gate, were resting by her sides. Her legs were slightly apart and her eyes were wide open. Her right arm above the elbow was still warm to the touch. At the side of the body lay a black straw bonnet trimmed with black velvet.

Hearing another officer passing the end of Buck's Row from nearby Brady Street, Mizen flashed his lantern which summoned to the scene PC John Thain 96J.

"Here's a woman has cut her throat," said Neil. "Run at once for Dr Llewellyn."

Meanwhile, Mizen had arrived at the stable gate and Neil sent him for an ambulance and to get further help from Bethnal Green Police Station.

While waiting Neil had a good look around then crossed the road and rang the bell to a wharf. The manager, Walter Purkis, appeared at an upper window and in answer to Neil's questions said that he and his wife had neither seen nor heard anything untoward.

Neil was then joined by Sergeant Kirby who woke Mrs Green at New Cottage immediately to the east of the stable. She, too, had heard nothing. Neil examined the road with his lantern and saw no trace of wheel marks or any clue that might help the investigation.

Dr Rees Ralph Llewellyn of 152 Whitechapel Road arrived just before 4:00 a.m. Llewellyn made an initial assessment. He pronounced the women dead. Noting that her body and legs were still warm, he estimated that she had not been dead for longer than thirty minutes.

This preliminary investigation revealed that her throat had been cut twice from left to right. Her abdomen had been mutilated with one deep jagged cut, a wound that was surrounded by other, less severe incisions. There were three or four cuts to her right side that Llewellyn determined had been made with violent downward movements by a knife with estimated blade length of 6-8 inches. The abdominal injuries were made post mortem, the killer needing no longer than five minutes or so to carry them out.

Meanwhile, news that a murder victim may be close by brought to the scene three horse-slaughterers from the neighbouring Barber's knacker's yard in Winthrop Street, together with an increasing trickle of other sightseers. Seeing their arrival, Llewellyn decided that the body should be moved. "Move her to the mortuary," he told the police officers. "She is dead and I will make a further examination of her there." Llewellyn then left the scene and Sergeant Edward Badham conveyed the body to the mortuary. Neil, Mizen and Kirby accompanied the body while Thain waited for Inspector John Spratling.

On Spratling's arrival, Thain showed his superior where the body had lain, by which time the blood was reduced to tracings between the cobbles because it was being washed away by one of Mrs Green's sons who worked at the stables. Spratling then hurried on to the mortuary to find it locked up, the ambulance carrying the victim's body in the yard left unattended. While awaiting mortuary keeper Robert Mann, Spratling occupied his time making a description of the woman. Mann arrived between 5:00 a.m. and 5:20 a.m. and moved the body into the mortuary

Resuming his investigation of the body, Spratling lifted the woman's clothes and discovered that her abdomen had been ripped open from as high as the breastbone to expose her intestines. Dr Llewellyn, called out for a second time, was appalled at the extent of the woman's injuries. "I have seen many terrible cases," he later told the press, "but never such a brutal affair as this."

Llewellyn expressed surprise about the lack of blood present: "about enough to fill two large wine glasses, or half a pint at the outside," which suggested that she was not killed at the scene. However, it had been observed after Llewellyn's departure from Buck's Row that a copious amount of blood from the wounds had soaked into the victim's clothes and hair, making it far more likely that she died instantaneously from a swift slash to the throat. PC Thain noted that there was a "mass of congealed blood" about six inches in diameter beneath the body when it was lifted, some of which had run towards the gutter. This blood had apparently trickled from the wounds in the throat.

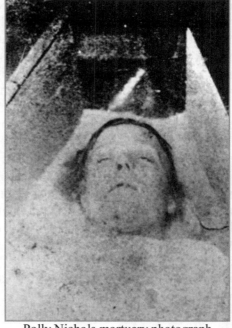

Polly Nichols mortuary photograph

In the mortuary Dr Llewellyn made his second investigation of the body prior to conducting a formal post-mortem. Dr Llewellyn left no official records of this assessment or the subsequent post-mortem but his preliminary mortuary findings can be summarised from the Metropolitan Police records signed by Inspector John Spratling and dated 31 August 1888.

The woman's throat had been slit from left to right by two distinct cuts on the left side. The windpipe, gullet and spinal cord were cut through. A bruise was evident on both the right lower jaw and left cheek, attributed to the pressing down of a thumb. The abdomen had been cut open from the centre of the bottom ribs along the right side and under the pelvis to left of the stomach. The wound there was jagged. The omentum (coating of the stomach) was cut in several places. The private parts had suffered two small stabs. All the wounds appeared to have been inflicted with a strong bladed knife, supposedly by a left-handed assailant. Death would have been almost instantaneous.

On 19 October Inspector Donald Swanson noted in the record, "At first the Doctor was of opinion that the wounds were caused by a left-handed person but he is now doubtful."

On Saturday morning, 1 September, Dr Llewellyn set to work on the post-mortem. Today his report can only be pieced together by comparison with contemporary newspaper records. Information additional to the facts gleaned from Llewellyn's preliminary mortuary examination can be summarised as follows.

A bruise along the lower part of the jaw on the right side of the face might have been caused by a blow from a fist or by thumb pressure. The circular bruise on the left side of the face may have been caused by pressure exerted by fingers. Detailing the two incisions in the throat, both made left to right "with great violence," one was about four inches long beginning on the left side of the neck immediately below the ear and running about an inch below the jaw. The other was eight inches long and encircled the throat. It ran about an inch below the first incision and terminated at a point about three inches below the right jaw. This cut had severed both carotid arteries and all the tissues down to the vertebrae. The abdominal injuries had been inflicted with a knife wielded violently and downwards.

Replying to questions at the inquest, Llewellyn said that the murderer "must have had some rough anatomical knowledge, for he seemed to have attacked all the vital parts. The murder could have been executed in just four or five minutes."

Initially, identification of the victim was a challenge. The body bore no distinguishing marks apart from a small scar on the forehead and three missing teeth. She was a middle-aged woman not more than 5'2" or 5'3" tall. She had a dark complexion, brown eyes and dark brown hair that had begun greying. Her personal belongings—a comb, a piece of looking glass and a white pocket-handkerchief—provided no clues as to identity.

Similarly, her clothing gave nothing away. She was wearing a reddish-brown Ulster coat with seven large brass buttons that had seen better days, a newish brown linsey frock, a white chest flannel, two petticoats: one woollen and one flannel, a pair of brown stays, a pair of black ribbed woollen stockings, a pair of men's side spring boots cut on the uppers with steel tips on the heels, and a black straw bonnet trimmed in black velvet.

However, the deceased's identity became known after less than twenty-four hours when it was learned that a woman matching her appearance had been living in a common lodging house at 18 Thrawl Street. Brought to the mortuary, Ellen Holland identified the body as that of her former roommate, "Polly."

Additional corroboration was provided after the police examined the woman's petticoats and found on them the mark "Lambeth Workhouse, P.R.," (P.R. standing for Prince's Road). Mary Ann Monk, an inmate of the Lambeth Workhouse, was taken to Old Montague Street on the evening of the 31st August and named the victim as Mary Ann Nichols, confirming that Nichols had been a resident at Lambeth as late as May that year. With this information police traced on 1 September Mary's father, locksmith Edward Walker, and husband, William Nichols. Both identified her body.

Polly's adult life had been marked by one unhappy episode after another. Aged eighteen, she married printer's machinist William Nichols. Between 1866 and 1879 the couple had five children: Edward John, Percy George, Alice Esther, Eliza Sarah, and Henry Alfred.

Polly had been dismayed to discover that her husband was bedding Rosetta Walls, the nurse who assisted at the confinement for the birth of Henry Alfred. Polly's father, Edward Walker, claimed that William walked out on his wife in 1880 after this indiscretion but Polly claimed to have proof that their marriage had continued for at least three years afterwards. In his turn, William claimed that his wife had deserted him. Police reports say they separated because of Polly's drunkenness. Legally bound to support his estranged wife, William supported Polly with a weekly allowance of five shillings until 1882 when he learned that she had turned to prostitution. By law one spouse was no longer required to provide financial support if the other had turned to earning money by illicit means.

Thereafter, Polly lived in very difficult circumstances. She went from workhouse to boarding house to common lodging premises, breaking this cycle when she went to live with her father until after a year they quarrelled and parted. Her father said that his daughter lived for a while with a blacksmith named Drew in the Walworth district of the East End.

In 1888 Polly hit rock bottom. At the start of the year, after being found sleeping rough in Trafalgar Square, she was placed in Lambeth workhouse. She then took a job in domestic service with the Cowdry family in Wandsworth but left after two months, absconding with clothing belonging to her employers worth three pounds and ten shillings.

At the inquest on 1 September Edward Walker said, "I don't think she had any enemies, she was too good for that."

Polly was murdered just a few days after her forty-third birthday. Saint Raymond recovered from the torture inflicted upon him for his missionary work. After paying his ransom he returned to Spain. Polly was not given the opportunity to strike a redemptive bargain. As she tottered drunkenly down Whitechapel Road watched by her friend Mrs Holland, little did Polly know that the price of securing her doss money was to be her life.

Polly had been killed within the jurisdiction of the newly established J or Bethnal Green Division, and Inspector Joseph Helson was called upon to lead the inquiry. Together with Smith and Tabram, Nichols was the third "unfortunate" to have been murdered in the Whitechapel area. And so it was that Helson must have considered himself fortunate that Scotland Yard asked seasoned police officer Inspector Frederick George Abberline to assist in the search for Polly's murderer. 45-year old Abberline (tentatively identified by Vanderlinden and Rumbelow in this picture) was a man of medium height and stature with mutton chop moustache and side-whiskers that contrasted with thin receding hair on top.

Man, left, with cane may be Abberline

Abberline's record of service was hugely admired by his colleagues. His knowledge of the East End was second to none. He had served twenty-five years in the Metropolitan Police, fourteen of which spent in Whitechapel. With this impressive track record, Abberline was deputed by his superiors to co-ordinate the work of divisional detectives.

Both Helson and Abberline were convinced that Polly had been murdered on the spot where she lay. Dr. Llewellyn who at first held that Nichols was murdered elsewhere and then brought to Buck's Row eventually admitted his mistake and concurred with police opinion. Nevertheless, despite all the experience and resources that were invested in the search for assailant, Mary Ann "Polly" Nichols' killer was never brought to justice.

Polly was buried in the City of London Cemetery, Ilford, Thursday, 6 September. The coffin was fashioned from polished elm and bore the inscription: "Mary Ann Nichols, aged 42; died August 31, 1888." The mourners included Polly's father, her husband and her son, Edward John.

In recent years there have been efforts to finger Charles Cross as the perpetrator and, by extension, for the other Ripper murders. At the inquest Robert Paul was asked if the other man (Cross) had identified himself. "No sir," he replied, "he merely said that he would have fetched a policeman but he was behind time. I was behind time myself."

The presumption has always been that Robert Paul arrived in Buck's Row shortly after Charles Cross had come upon her body. Those who argue that Cross was the assailant insist that Paul interrupted him in the act of trying to cover up some of the wounds he had just inflicted in his attempt to do murder.

Supporters of this theory suggest that on hearing Paul's approach Cross, thinking on his feet, chose to stay at the scene and feign shock rather than try to flee and thereby draw suspicion to himself. On 3 September Paul told the London *Evening Standard*:

> It was exactly a quarter to four when I passed up Buck's-row to my work as a carman for Covent-garden market. It was dark, and I was hurrying along, when I saw a man standing where the woman was.
>
> He came a little towards me, but as I knew the dangerous character of the locality I tried to give him a wide berth. Few people like to come up and down here without being on their guard, for there are such terrible gangs about. There have been many knocked down and robbed at that spot.

The man, however, came towards me and said, "Come and look at this woman."

I went and found the woman lying on her back. I laid hold of her wrist and found that she was dead and the hands cold. It was too dark to see the blood about her. I thought that she had been outraged, and had died in the struggle.

I was obliged to be punctual at my work, so I went on and told the other man I would send the first policeman I saw. I saw one in Church-row, just at the top of Buck's-row, who was going round calling people up, and I told him what I had seen, and I asked him to come, but he did not say whether he should come or not. He continued calling the people up, which I thought was a great shame, after I had told him the woman was dead.

The woman was so cold that she must have been dead some time, and either she had been lying there, left to die, or she must have been murdered somewhere else and carried there.

If she had been lying there long enough to get so cold as she was when I saw her, it shows that no policeman on the beat had been down there for a long time. If a policeman had been there he must have seen her, for she was plain enough to see. Her bonnet was lying about two feet from her head.

Those who favour Cross as the murderer argue that Paul's account contradicts Cross's. Cross said he had been walking along the opposite side of Buck's Row when he observed something lying in the gateway. He had gone as far as the "middle of the road" when he saw that what was lying in the gateway was, in fact, "the figure of a woman." He said he was still standing in that same position when Robert Paul arrived. However, Robert Paul reported that Cross was actually "standing where the woman was." Presented with this contradiction, it is an easy task to visualise that Cross had just murdered Mary Nichols and was in the act of inflicting additional wounds on an already lifeless body when he was interrupted by Paul's appearance.

The reality is that there is very little evidence to substantiate Cross's guilt. Those who seek to paint him as the Ripper point to the fact that he gave a false name to the police and to the inquest, arguing that he would only do this if he had something to hide. But the fact that Cross gave his correct address and place of employment *and* appeared as a witness at the inquest rather deflates this argument. It follows that Cross must have either been a very cool customer or he was innocent of any involvement in Nichols' death or in any of the subsequent Ripper murders.

Another strand of the argument for identifying Cross as the Ripper was that he was a local man, which was one of the principle theories in attempts to sketch a profile of the Ripper. Cross lived only a few streets to the east of Buck's Row and he worked as a carman at Pickford's in Broad Street, thirty or so minutes to the west of Buck's Row. All this is little more than conjecture and the case against Cross remains unproven.

If Charles Cross was not what he seemed that was equally the case with many high profile individuals in Britain, Europe and America in the late nineteenth century. Historian Roger Shattuck referred to the period 1885-1914 as the "Banquet Years" during which "Bohemia," the land described as having no geography but whose capital is Paris witnessed a great outpouring of esoteric activity.

Esteemed figures in the arts, politics, science, industry, law, literature and, in particular, religious affairs bowed to the idols of rational enterprise in the open, yet worshipped the dark gods of occultism behind closed doors. In seeking fresh meaning and direction in the esoteric philosophies, these diverse personalities were swept along in what became known as the "Occult Revival." Its exponents dived headlong into Theosophy, secret societies, astrology, the Tarot, geomancy, magical practices, and religious fanaticism such as exemplified by the heretical priest Abbé Boullan.

In later pages we will shine a light on the British wizards of the occult establishment. In then meantime, let us mine for alchemic gold the shafts and seams of the occult underground of continental Europe.

Chapter 6

The Occult Underground

The emergence of spiritualism in the early nineteenth century appeared to catalyse a tremendous outpouring of occult fervour in the West. In fact, the study and application of the occult to endow the practitioner with supernatural powers had always existed in one form or another. The following timeline[37] provides a snapshot of the evolution of occult and esoteric philosophy during the last two millennia:

1st Century AD—various groups adopted a Gnostic position, which emphasised the individual arriving at personal knowledge of God.

46—according to one version of its mystical beginnings, the Rosicrucian order was created when Alexandrian sage, Ormus, and his six followers were initiated by Mark, and thereafter fused the principles of Christianity with the Egyptian mysteries.

1st-3rd Century—composition of the *Testament of Solomon*, an early grimoire (a magical "textbook").

6th century—the earliest extant book on Jewish esotericism and the Kabbalah, the *Sefer Yetzirah*, is edited. The Kabbalah is a mystical philosophy that originated in Judaism. It seeks to explain the relationship between an unchanging, eternal, and mysterious *Ein Sof* (infinity) and the mortal and finite universe (God's Creation).

1118—King Baldwin II of Jerusalem grants the Knights Templar, an order initiated in 1111 by Bernard of Clairvaux, a place to live within the sacred enclosure of the Temple on Mount Moriah on the site where King Solomon had once built his Great Temple. Hugh de Payens is chosen as the Order's first Grand

---

[37] A helpful source for timeline content is to be found at:
https://www.golden-dawn.com/eu/displaycontent.aspx?pageid=71-

Master. According to legend, the Knights Templar in Jerusalem sought and found the Holy Grail, the Ark of the Covenant, the True Cross, the Shroud of Turin, and guarded the Jesus and Mary Magdalene bloodline.

ca. 1150—corresponding with the period of the first Crusades alchemy took root in Spain, brought there by Arabian Moors.

13th century—the appearance of three grimoires: i) *The Picatrix* (*The Goal of the Sage* [in sorcery]), a major influence on magical thinking in the West; ii) *Sefer Raziel HaMalakh* (Book of Raziel the Angel), a Kabbalistic work primarily written in Hebrew and Aramaic; and iii) *The Sworn Book of Honorius*, supposedly the product of a conference of magicians who decided to condense all their knowledge into one volume. Elizabethan magus John Dee possessed a copy.

1206—alchemist and philosopher Albertus Magnus born. Magnus claimed to have succeeded in creating the Philosopher's Stone, passing it to his pupil Thomas Aquinas who destroyed it believing it to be diabolical.

1214—Roger Bacon, alchemist, occultist and Franciscan friar, born. Also known as Doctor Mirabilis ("wonderful teacher"), Bacon places emphasis on experimentation.

1232—i) Abraham Abulafia, founder of ecstatic Kabbalah, born in Sicily, ii) Raymond Lull born, an alchemist with immense physical and mental energy. Lull's works include *Alchimia Magic Naturalis* and *De Secretis Medicina Magna*.

1330—Alchemist Nicolas Flamel born. Reputed to have succeeded in making the Philosopher's Stone.

1378—According to the *Confessio Fraternitatis*, Christian Rosenkreutz, reputed founder of the Rosicrucian tradition, is born. Aged just sixteen, Rosenkreutz travels to Arabia, Egypt and Morocco where he meets sages of the East, who reveal to him the "universal harmonic science."

1450s—the grimoire, *Book of Abramelin*, written. German Jew, Abraham of Worms, reveals in the work Abramelin''s magical and Kabbalistic secrets. In 1888 Samuel Liddell MacGregor Mathers, a founder member of the Hermetic Order of the Golden Dawn, imports Abramalin's magic into the Order and, later, Aleister Crowley incorporates it into his mystical system of Thelema.

1462—Johannes Trithemius born, becoming a famous scholar, magician, alchemist and Benedictine abbot.

1486—i) Celebrated magician Heinrich Cornelius Agrippa born in Cologne; ii) the witch hunters's bible, *Malleus Maleficarum,* is published.

1493—Legendary alchemist, physician, astrologer and occultist Paracelsus (Philippus Aureolus Theophrastus Bombastus von Hohenheim) born, later tutored by Trithemius.

1527—John Dee, noted Welsh mathematician, astronomer, astrologer, geographer, occultist, and consultant to Queen Elizabeth I, born. Becomes a student of Flamel's work.

1561—Francis Bacon, English philosopher, statesman and scientist, born. For Bacon, alchemy was a major field of experimental science. Some claim that Christian Rosenkreuz is a pseudonym for Bacon.

1574—Robert Fludd, physician, philosopher and mystic, born.

1575—Jakob Böhme, philosopher, mystic and theologian, born.

1614—the first Rosicrucian manifesto, *Fama Fraternitas*, published followed in 1615 by the *Confessio Fraternitatis*.

1688—Emanuel Swedenborg, Swedish scientist, philosopher, Christian mystic and theologian, born.

1717—United Grand Lodge of England of Freemasonry is formed.

1776—Adam Weishaupt founds the Order of Illuminati of Bavaria.

1780—Asiatic Brethren (Fratres Lucis [Brothers of Light] or Ritter des Lichts [Knights of Light]) founded by Hans Heinrich von Ecker und Eckhoffen. The Order's theosophic doctrines are later incorporated into the Hermetic Order of the Golden Dawn.

1795—Richard James Morrison (Zadkiel) born, "resuscitator" in 1870 of the Most Ancient Order of the Suastica (The Brotherhood of the Mystic Cross).

1803—Edward George Bulwer-Lytton born: novelist, poet, playwright, politician and pivotal figure in 19th century occultism. Believed to have introduced Eliphas Levi to ceremonial magic.

1809—Frederick Hockley born, a, highly connected and influential British occultist, scryer, Freemason and member of the Societas Rosicruciana in Anglia.

1809—Baron de Palm (Joseph Henry Louis Charles) born. Became Grand Cross Commander of the Order of the Holy Sepulchre. He joined the Theosophical Society in its earliest days and became the first person to be cremated in the United States.

1810—Eliphas Levi (Alphonse Louis Constant) born. Levi demonstrated in 1861 to his mentor, Bulwer-Lytton, the magical evocation of Apollonius.

Such personalities and milestones in metaphysical development exerted their pull upon the nineteenth-century's occult acolytes more powerfully than any mesmeriser's magnet. Of those occultists at work in 1888 who followed these traditions and whose influence was felt in the Ripper's day, these (with year of birth) are of special interest:

1816—William Alexander Ayton, modern alchemist, member of Hermetic Brotherhood of Luxor and, later, the H.O.G.D.

1823—Emma Hardinge Britten, spiritualist and occultist.

1824—Edward Maitland, humanitarian writer and occultist.

1828—i) Francis George Irwin, Freemason, and correspondent to A.E. Waite, William Wynn Westcott and Kenneth R.H. Mackenzie; ii) William Robert Woodman, member of the Societas Rosicruciana in Anglia (S.R.I.A.) and co-founder of the Hermetic Order of the Golden Dawn.

1833—Kenneth R.H. Mackenzie, co-founder in 1866 of S.R.I.A.). Later, reportedly receives Rosicrucian initiation from Count Apponyi and, allegedly, material for the *Cipher Manuscripts* with which the Golden Dawn is founded.

1846—Anna Kingsford, founder with Edward Maitland of the "Perfect Way," an expression of esoteric Christianity.

1848—i) Max Théon (possibly born Louis-Maximilian Bimstein), Polish Jewish Kabbalist and occultist, founder of the Hermetic Brotherhood of Luxor; and ii) William Wynn Westcott, esotericist, ceremonial magician, coroner, Freemason and co-founder of the Golden Dawn.

1854—Samuel Liddell MacGregor Mathers, British occultist and co-founder of the Golden Dawn.

Our Continental neighbours were no less enthusiastic than their British and American counterparts in their desire to ride the occult merry-go-round in the late nineteenth century. By the 1880s anyone from the occasional dabbler to the serious occultist was guaranteed a new form of –ism, -ology or –osophy with which to satisfy an appetite for sensationalist phenomena or hidden knowledge. The late James Webb's exhaustive research[38] is once more the principle source for our review of the leading actors within the occult underground movement.

In Russia leading theological mystic Vladamir Soloviev (1853-1900) was expounding his Kabbalist philosophies and his ideas for a religious renaissance. Drawn to both speculative mysticism and to the traditional practice of Judaism as a cornerstone of an ideal Universal Church, Soloviev claimed that at the age of nine while attending a church service he experienced his first vision of the divine Sophia, the goddess of wisdom. He visited England in 1875 to further his studies in occultism and mystical teachings. While studying the Zohar texts in the British Museum Soloviev experienced his second vision of Sophia (his third and final vision occurring in the desert outside Cairo). Subsequently, Soloviev was of the firm belief that a marriage between esoteric study and mystical Judaism was destined to reconcile all opposites: East and West, heaven and earth, male and female. Soloviev's work attracted a number of other thinkers, including philosopher Vasily Rozanov (1856-1919).

Rozanov, dubbed the "Rasputin of the Russian intelligentsia" because of repeated references to the phallus in his writings, edited an anti-Semitic work that featured an essay from an "S.D-sky." This anonymous contributor writes of assisting Rozanov in proving Jewish involvement in a horrific murder that could have come from the pages of the Jack the Ripper "how-to" book. It concerned the 1911 murder of a Christian youth named Andrusha Yushchinsky who some believed was the victim of human sacrifice. The essay examines the connections between the thirteen wounds on Yushchinsky's head and the Zohar text, drawing particular attention to the purported shapes and characters of Hebrew letters when lines

Vladamir Soloviev

---

[38] ibid.

are drawn from one stab wound to the next. S.D-sky also seeks to demonstrate his claim that Jewish translators of the Zohar censored passages that illustrate the Hebrews' ancient practice of human sacrifice (the underlying implication being that the barbarity had survived into the twentieth century). Extreme views such as these fed a growing belief among Russians that the Jews of the world were assembled in a secret satanic cabal that was profoundly anti-Christian.

These feelings also contributed to the *fin de siècle* rediscovery of Lucifer and Mephistopheles: romanticised fallen angel and satanic demon respectively, and to the resurgent popularity of the gothic works of Goethe and Edgar Allan Poe. Such sentiments may help to explain, for instance, why the acclaimed Russian baritone Feodor Chaliapin, the man who in 1914 would enjoy the honour of singing *Don Quichotte* privately for Pius X in Castel Gondolfo, instigated in the late 1880s a three-decade campaign to bring to the stage a truly satanic Mephistopheles in Gounod's *Faust*.

Also active in Russia in the 1880s, a period when it was attracting increasing numbers was the illegal and antinomian cult of the Khlysty. Its members (Khlysts) believed that to gain salvation one needed firstly to plumb the depths of sin. Sin was said to be necessary for salvation because without sin there could be no repentance, and without repentance there could be no salvation. The word "Khlysty" refers to the whips that sect members used upon themselves in their rituals. The cult has been compared with Tantric Buddhism and Sabbatean-Frankist Judaism.

One can trace the Khlysty's beginnings to 17th-century Siberia where army deserter Daniil Filippovich declared that he was a living god and that there is no barrier between the individual and the divine. Filippovich declared his follower Ivan Suslov as his Christ. Unsurprisingly, the authorities took a dim view of such blasphemy. They crucified Suslov at the Spassky Gate and hung his body on the wall of the Kremlin. Filippovich was exiled. According to the Khlysts, Suslov's body rose from the dead only to be tortured, flayed, and re-crucified before

Chaliapin as Mephistopheles

---

[39] Antinomianism is any view which rejects laws or legalism and is against moral, religious or social norms.

rising yet again in 1718 and ascending to heaven.

In its early days, the cult stressed asceticism and self-denial. Alcohol, marriage and swearing were forbidden. Children (the product of sex) were called "sins." People could marry but the women were known as "spiritual wives" and no sex was allowed. This changed with the arrival of Khlyst leader Radaev and his followers or "line." Radaev taught that chastity is a sin because it was rooted in pride.

Secret Khlysty cells existed throughout pre-revolutionary Russia. It was especially common in the factories of the Perm district. Each cell was normally led by a male and a female leader (the "Christ" and the "Mother of God," respectively). The cells themselves were referred to as "Arks" among members and messages were carried between them clandestinely in order to facilitate communication. Because the groups were illegal, members were encouraged to be especially devout and active in their local Orthodox churches in order to maintain secrecy and deflect suspicion.

Khlysty meetings were held in forest clearings and secret dugouts beneath barns. The meetings would begin with singing and drumming around a bonfire. By using the power of dance, members sought a state of mystical rapture they called "radeinie" (frenzy), which was seen as necessary for possession by the Holy Spirit. They whipped themselves with birch-branches and spoke ecstatically in what they called "the Language of Jerusalem." Intoxicated by the state of "radeinie," the group would collapse into indiscriminate sexual orgy. They described this phase of the ritual as "using sin to drive out sin."

In 1910, Sofia Ivanovna Tyutcheva, a governess of the Grand Duchesses of Russia, accused Grigori Rasputin of having been a Khlyst. She made her accusation because she was horrified that the monk was allowed access by the Tsar to the nursery of the Grand Duchesses when the four girls were in their nightgowns. Ripperologists are familiar with the old saw that Rasputin wrote a manuscript in French, allegedly found in his basement after his assassination in 1916, which names Russian physician Alexander Pedachenko as the Ripper. The story appears to crumble when one considers

Khylsts "using sin to drive out sin"

that Rasputin's house neither had a basement, nor could he read or write French.

Late nineteenth-century Poland was also a major component of Europe's occult underground, a movement that had been principally engendered by poet Adam Mickiewicz (1798-1855) and artist-musician Józef Oleszkiewicz (1777-1830). When the two Poles met in St. Petersburg, Oleszkiewicz was Grand Master of the Martinist Order in Russia. He taught Mickiewicz the Cabala who thus set on his European travels nourished with traditional knowledge.

In Paris Mickiewicz met Lithuanian Andrei Towianski and together they established a mystical group with support from Amschel de Rothschild. After the death of Mickiewicz in 1855 Towianski and Mickiewicz's wife, Celina, organized the circle of the *Oeuvre de Dieu* in Paris whose principles were closely connected with those of the *Oeuvre de Miséricorde* of Eugène Vintras, so much so that the Norman prophet proclaimed Towianski as the Messiah.

This deep association between the two cults was promoted among the circle of Poles that followed the teachings of notorious priest, Abbé Boullan. Following Boullan's death in 1893, the Poles returned to their homeland and established a Mariavite Church with a membership numbering 500,000, which before its excommunication in 1906 was employing rituals based on the sexual mysticism of Boullan. We will learn more about Vintras and Boullan shortly.

Events in Germany were no less indicative of the European occult scene. In July 1884 the first German Theosophical Society was established at Elberfeld. Two years later Wilhelm Hubbe-Schleiden founded Die Sphinx, which focused on spiritualism and paranormal phenomena. In the same period Franz Hartmann founded a broader theosophical movement devoted to the works of Rosicrucian initiates, Paracelsus and Jakob Böhme. Together with Alfredo Piedu and Countess Constance Wachmeister, a close friend of Blavatsky, Hartmann founded a monastery at Ascona, which would quickly evolve into one of the most influential European metaphysical academies of excellence.

Guido von List, an early exponent of Viennese Ariosophy and revered in his native Vienna as a mystical nationalist guru, published in 1888 in two volumes his first novel *Carnutum*, a work inspired by a memorable Summer Solstice party. Carnutum was a Roman city sacked by Marcomanni tribes in 375 CE. The novel invited all true Germans to look to the archaeology and folklore of their homeland and behold the clear and discernible remains of a theocratic Ario-German state wisely governed by priest-kings and high Gnostic initiates.

This novel established List as an important figure in the Austrian Pan-German movement associated with Ritter Georg von Schonerer, an outspoken anti-Semitist in the Hapsburg Empire, and Karl Wolf, a Pan-German parliamentary deputy. Twenty years later List would offer Germans a new religion he called Wotanism, which emphasised the initiation of man into natural mysteries based on the principles of the Edda and the runes. Wotan was identified as a magician and necromancer who performed ritual acts of self-torture in order to win the magical gnosis of natural mysteries, thereby gaining shamanistic and psychical powers. In reconstructing this ancient gnosis, List turned to theosophical thought but, more significantly in terms of the influence his teachings would exert upon the founder members of National Socialist Germany, he began writing thick volumes on the subject of sexology and eugenics, combining racial doctrines with occult notions derived from his increasingly bizarre interpretations of Teutonic mythology.

However, it was in Paris in 1888 that one would have observed the greatest activity coursing round the labyrinths of the occult underground, the city being the confluence of all the European esoteric sub-streams. By this time the supernatural had thoroughly permeated Parisian artistic society and its prominent astronomers, painters, musicians and writers. This was the Bohemian Age and, increasingly, its activists resorted to drink and drugs to reach for their vision of Nirvana. The English expression of this phenomenon was the Aesthetic Movement whose chief gurus, Oscar Wilde and W.S. Gilbert, exemplified the Cult of the Beautiful. The City of Love was awash with those struggling to peer through the veil in a search for something they could not put a name to but felt that they must have in order to be in tune with the voguish appeal of the mysterious occult underground.

A case in point was Eugène Vintras (1807-1875), one time foreman at the cardboard box factory at Tilly-sur-Seine and, later, founder of the *Church de l'Oeuvre de la*

Guido von List

Miséricorde (Work of Compassion). He described a visit to his workshop by an old beggar who addressed him as "Pierre-Michel," the name that Vintras initially took during his ministry before re-styling himself as "Strathaniel" meaning "herald of God." Vintras gave the man some money but did not see him leave the house. He then saw that the ten sous he had given the supplicant had been left on his writing-table.

After this first encounter with the old man, Vintras met him twice more on the day he was visiting a Mme. Bouche, firstly while on his way to her house in St. Sulpice in Paris and then later that day in her home. On the second appearance Vintras said that the man glowed with a strange light and lifted himself off the ground before revealing himself as the archangel Michael.

The "Michael" figure told Vintras that before the dawn of the approaching Golden Age Paris-Ninevah would be punished together with London-Babylon. He told Vintras, "I saw a great number of flames surrounding Paris and heard an innumerable multitude of cries, of which some were 'To arms!' others 'Fire, fire!'" Mankind's only hope, said Michael, was the redeeming power of the Virgin. Vintras subsequently reported other visitations including Christ, Mary and St. Joseph. Webb notes the similarity between these apocalyptic visions and those experienced by Françoise Mélanie Calvet (Sister Mary of the Cross, 1831-1904), the most dramatic of which foretold that in 1864 Lucifer and his army of demons would leave the environs of hell to destroy the faith of human beings.

Abbé Josephe-Antoine Boullan (1824-1893) was a Vintras disciple. One can date the beginnings of his heretical activities from 1856 when he met Sister Adèle Chevalier at La Salette-Fallavaux, a commune in southeastern France where in 1846 two children, Maximin Giraud and Françoise Mélanie Calvat, beheld a Marian apparition that became known as Notre-Dame de La Salette. In 1842 Adèle, blind, a victim of pulmonary

Eugène Vintras

---

[40] Ibid.

congestion, abandoned by doctors as a hopeless case, claimed to have been miraculously cured after hearing messages from a mysterious voice instructing her to come to La Salette. The news of her cure soon spread throughout the diocese and the Bishop of Soissons delegated his Vicar General to conduct an investigation. His report was clear and precise: "After careful consideration of the circumstances which led to the recovery of sight and the healing of the lungs, I do not hesitate to believe in a supernatural intervention by the Mother of God." Subsequently, the monks of La Salette asked the Bishop of Grenoble for permission to entrust Adèle into the care of Boullan who was well known for his interest in mystical theology.

Boullan's ears pricked up, met Adèle and immediately placed great store in her supernatural gifts. He decided to travel to Rome to present the details of the miracle to the Pope and the Sacred College, despite the fact that he was already burdened by a prior mission concerning a Miss Mary Roche. Like Adèle, Roche claimed to have been entrusted with a divine mission to impart prophecies of a grave nature. One concerned the forthcoming violent death of the Pope, another referred to King Louis-Philippe who, if he did not follow Roche's advice, would die at the hands of his advisers to make way for Henry V (Henri, Count of Chambord, legitimist pretender to the French throne 1844-1883).

Despite these onerous responsibilities, the association between Boullan and Adèle prospered. In 1859, subsequent to Boullan claiming that he had received an instruction from the Virgin to found a religious society, he and Sister Adèle received permission from the Bishop of Versailles to form the *Oeuvre de la Réparation des Âmes*. At the dictation of "divine beings," Adèle wrote down the rules of the Society. The establishment of the Society's premises in Sèvres became a shroud to conceal the increasingly amorous relationship between its founders. Moreover, rumours quickly spread about strange practices by which Boullan sought to heal nuns in the order who had suddenly become afflicted with diabolical diseases. Boullan exorcised one who was tormented by the Devil by spitting in her

Abbé Josephe-Antoine Boullan

mouth. Another had to drink a mixture of his and Adèle's urine, while a third was ordered to eat poultices made from faeces.

In addition, Boullan was accused of conducting bizarre sexual rites. During one particularly heinous act in 1860 Boullan is alleged to have murdered on a sacrificial altar the child he fathered with Adèle.

Complaints were filed with the police and the Bishop of Versailles, especially concerning the money Boullan was making with his bizarre "healing" methods. An investigation was opened against Father Boullan and Sister Chevalier who were accused of fraud and indecency. The Court of Versailles dismissed the latter but sentenced Boullan and Chevalier to three years in prison on the former, which they served at Rouen between 1861 and 1864.

Despite these inconveniences, Boullan continued exercising his miracle cures, one of which had him summoned to the capital by the Archbishop of Paris to explain his claim that he had cured a bout of epilepsy using a part of Christ's seamless robe. The Church was relentless in bearing down on their troublesome priest, on one occasion the Holy Office taking measures to imprison Boullan for a second time. During this new period of incarceration Boullan whiled away his time in drawing in a pink notebook a confession of faith whose text is so shocking that it is customary to speak of it only in whispers.

Unaccountably, Boullan was absolved yet again and he returned to Paris where he continued with his un-Christian activities, recognising during the course of his deviant practices that his personal heresies and the tenets of Vintras's *Church de l'Oeuvre de la Misericorde* contained many points of similarity. Thus it was that in 1875 when the Church finally defrocked him, Boullan celebrated Vintras's passing by naming himself as his successor although most in the Work refused to accept his self-ordination. Regardless of this prejudice, Boullan partnered with an architect dedicated to finding the elixir of life and continued to claim miracle cures, which he achieved by placing consecrated hosts over women's ovaries and by the magical use of precious stones.

In the late 1880s French novelist and art critic J.K. Huysmans (1848-1907) appeared on the scene. Oscar Wilde revealed that the mysterious and corrupting book given to the hero in *The Picture of Dorien Grey* was Huysmans' 1884 novel *À Rebours* in which the central character, Des Esseintes, is the personification of perversity. While researching material for his novel *Là-Bas*, which would deal with the subject of Satanism in contemporary France, Huysmans befriended

---

[41] Griffiths, R., *The Reactionary Revolution: the Catholic Revival in French Literature*, New York, Frederick Unger, 1965

Boullan. In 1893, two years after the book's controversial publication, Huysmans accused Marquis Stanislas de Guaïta and his occult circle of orchestrating Boullan's death by black magic. Huysmans' charge of magical murder revealed the existence in Paris of a deeply rooted occult scene that demanded further investigation. Stanislas de Guaïta was not Boullan's only enemy in Paris's thriving occult underground. Among his other antagonists were his former secretary, Oswald Wirth, and fellow-occultist, Joséphin Péladan.

Swiss artist, author and astrologer Wirth is perhaps best remembered for creating, under de Guaïta's guidance, a Tarot pack consisting solely of the twenty-two major arcana, known as the *Arcanes du Tarot Kabbalistique*. Wirth first met Boullan in 1879 at Châlons-sur-Marne where the visiting cleric performed a miracle cure. Seeing an opportunity for occult advancement, Wirth entered into correspondence with the cleric. With the help of another unfrocked priest, Abbé Roca, Wirth immediately began to wrest from Boullan his most secret doctrines. Firstly, the two conspirators managed to persuade Boullan to divulge his theory of "mystical unions" by which the sex act could be consecrated as a magical rite of spiritual regeneration. Digging further, Wirth and Roca were aghast to discover that Boullan conducted magical rites by coupling with *humanimaux*: beings half-animal, half-human to which he believed he could give pure human form by using these occult practices

Wirth wrote to Boullan in 1886 and declared his intention to lay charges of black magic practices before a tribunal of occultists headed by de Guaïta. Wirth claimed that the tribunal merely condemned Boullan to public denunciation but this version was refuted by Huysmans who when in Lyon after Boullan's death in 1893 saw a letter signed by de Guaïta condemning the Abbé to "death by the fluids." Others dismiss this bizarre claim, maintaining that Boullan died of natural causes from "angina pectoris" (coronary heart disease).

De Guaïta's actions were a classic case of pupil turning on master. Unbeknown to Wirth and Roca, the Marquis had been making secret overtures to Boullan for some

Marquis Stanislas de Guaïta

time. De Guaïta had probably been introduced to Boullan in 1885 by another prominent occultist, the Marquis de Saint-Yves D'Alveydre whom we shall meet shortly. A year later De Guaïta managed to wheedle his way into Boullan's home for a fortnight's stay. While there he filched the manuscript of the Vintrasian *Sacrifice de la Gloire Melchisedéch*, which the Abbé regarded as the supreme occult text.

Boullan later wrote to Huysmann saying that immediately after a subsequent visit to de Guaïta's premises he felt himself in the grip of a heart attack. By means of her bread and milk ritual, seeress Julie Thibault discovered that de Guaïta had attacked Boullan using magic gleaned from the Vintrasian manuscript. Boullan managed to make it to his altar where by repeating the ritual of the *Sacrifice of Melchisedech* he fended off de Guaïta's remote attack.

By all accounts Huysmans was a credulous individual, always ready to believe what he read or heard. His pal, journalist and occult dabbler Jules Bois was similarly naïve. Bois printed off documents given by Boullan to Huysmans, which indicated that at every court of Europe black magic evocations were practised, and that Prussia crushed France in the Battle of Sedan in 1870 because of her superior evocatory powers.

Bois also published an article describing Stanislav de Guaïta's magical methods of murdering from afar. He accused de Guaïta of volatilizing poisons and directing them into space. He added that the Marquis was assisted in these satanic practices by a familiar spirit that he kept confined in a cupboard.

After Huysmans weighed in and retold these accusations in an interview he gave to *Le Figaro*, de Guaïta challenged him to a duel. The Marquis chose as his seconds his friend Maurice de Barres and the poet Victor-Emile Michelet. De Guaïta's letter of challenge, which the seconds delivered by hand to Huysmans at his office at the Ministry of Interior, said "I intend to demand satisfaction, not with the occult weapons which you pretend to fear, and which I do not employ, but honourably, and sword in hand."

Acknowledging that he had bitten off more than he could chew, Huysmans retracted his accusations whereas his rash friend Bois stepped them up by several notches.

The affair culminated in Bois having to fight *two* duels, one with de Guaïta and another with Spanish-born nobleman Gérard Encausse, better known in magical circles, then and now, as "Papus." On an interesting side-note, Bois's second was Paul Foucher, Victor Hugo's nephew.

Bois survived both encounters: the first with de Guaïta in which shots were exchanged with no injuries to either man, the second with skilled swordsman Papus who, a genial sort, gave his opponent a slight nick in the forearm. Apparently, they walked off the field the best of friends.

Papus was a regular member of the Parisian Theosophy scene and used these connections as a stepping-stone to advance to an exploration of more distinctly alchemical and magical topics. To this end, Papus founded with Lucien Chamuel in 1888 the Librairie du Merveilleux and its revue *L'Initiation*.

Stanislas de Guaïta (1860-1898) and Joséphin Péladan (1858-1918) were the leading occult masters in Paris of their day. De Guaïta hailed from a noble Italian family from which he derived his title "Marquis." The family relocated to France and it was in their castle residence in Moselle that Stanislas was born.

From a young age de Guaïta studied metaphysics and the Cabala. He moved to Paris where his luxurious apartment became a meeting place for poets, artists and writers who were attracted to esoteric learning. In the 1880s de Guaïta published two collections of poetry: *The Dark Muse* (1883) and *The Mystic Rose* (1885).

Péladan was born in Lyon into a profoundly Catholic family. His father was a schoolteacher who edited a fanatically Catholic and royalist publication called *Le Châtiment* and published annually his *Annales du Surnaturel*, a list of miracles and prophecies. Péladan senior even proposed forming a new cult based on a so-called sixth wound suffered by Christ, which was caused, he said, by the blow of the Cross on Jesus' shoulder when he stumbled and fell on the way to Calvary. He regarded this wound as the most heinous because the Cross was heavy with the sins of the world.

As if this high strangeness in the family was not enough for young Joséphin he was also heavily influenced by his older brother Adrien, a homeopathic physician and student of the Kabbalah who introduced his sibling to mystical literature. Adrien was a very smart teenager who learned Chinese at the age of sixteen to meet the entrance requirements for a new Chair at the University of Lyon. Joséphin idolised his brother and when Adrien died in 1885, accidentally poisoning himself with one of his homeopathic compounds, he chose to accuse a Protestant chemist in Leipzig for his death

Péladan studied at Jesuit colleges at Avignon and Nîmes but after failing his baccalaureate he moved in 1882 to Paris and accepted a job from Arsene Houssaye as a literary and art critic

Gérard Encausse ("Papus")

Joséphin Péladan

Eliphas Lévi

Having made the bizarre claim that a Babylonian king had bestowed the appellation "Sâr" on his family (Assyrian word for king and in Hebrew "angelic prince"), Joséphin styled himself Sâr Mérodack Péladan, "Mérodack" being the Chaldean god associated with Jupiter. The title is also used in certain Martinist Orders to designate a Martinist Lodge Master or Unknown Superior Initiator.

The Marquis was influenced by the writings of prominent occultist l'Abbé Alphonse-Louis Constant, alias Eliphas Lévi, who was initiated into Rosicrucianism by Edward Bulwer-Lytton in 1854. He stated once, "Sorcery exhibits all the defects of its wild drunkenness, all the luxury of its arrogant infamy, all the pomp of its criminal emptiness." Jules Bois alleged that de Guaïta practised astral travelling although Wirth said that the Marquis never indulged in practical magic of any kind.

De Guaïta and his actress wife Suzanne Gay were both drug users. The Marquis himself was addicted to cocaine and morphine (Edouard Dubus called him a "fanatical morphinomaniac") and was a habitual user of hashish (enjoying its "unique and supermundane intoxication…a foretaste of the heavenly bliss of the Elect").

De Guaïta became further interested in occultism and Rosicrucian philosophy after reading Joséphin Péladan's instantly successful 1884 novel *Le Vice Suprême*, which recommended the salvation of man through the study and application of the occult magic of the ancient East. Péladan's book was the first in a planned series, which the author called *La décadence latine*.

Overwhelmed by the novel's deep trove of perversity and occult riches, de Guaïta immediately sought Péladan's acquaintance and invited him to stay at his apartment. The pair initially clicked although de Guaïta found Péladan's arrogant temperament difficult to stomach. Together with Papus, Péladan and de Guaïta aligned themselves with *Les Compagnons de la Heirophonie*, the inner circle of French occultists dedicated to restoring the western Mystery tradition.

In 1884 de Guaïta and Péladan decided to reconstitute the secret society of the Rosicrucian Brotherhood with the help of Papus. Since its establishment in the seventeenth century, the Brotherhood had been regarded as the principle repository of ancient secrets. In taking the steps to achieve this lofty objective, Péladan conferred upon himself on the death of Adrien the title of Grand Master of the Rose-Croix. Adrien had been initiated into a near obsolete branch of Freemasonry that claimed succession from the legendary Rosicrucians.

In 1888 de Guaïta and Péladan revived the *Ordre Kabballistique de la Rose Croix* comprising a council of twelve members, six of them being unknown "so that the order could be resurrected in case of decay." Its teachings were primarily concerned with the classical occult disciplines of the Kabbalah, Tarot, Astrology, Alchemy, Theurgy, Numerology, Divination and Rituals. Initiations consisted of three degrees and one secret fourth degree. In 1890 de Guaïta was claiming that the Order had more than one hundred adherents, which was certainly a highly exaggerated figure. The six hidden "Chiefs" never existed.

Soon Péladan's high-handed activities became a source of great annoyance among his fellow Rosicrucians. The last straw was Péladan's decision to publish as Sâr Mérodack three randomly conceived mandates, which he termed collectively his *Acta Syncelli*. Péladan sent one to Cardinal Archbishop of Paris, describing its author as the Grand Master of a hidden Catholic elite and heir to the secrets of the Rosicrucians and, sinisterly, the Holy Vehm, a German assassin group formed with Papal backing in the thirteenth-century. Péladan's absurd diktat decried the introduction of bullfighting in the Rue Pergolese in Paris, a "place of corruption where women go in search of orgasm and where they obtain orgasm."

Another mandate Péladan directed to all those working in the graphic arts, urging artists to submit to his will in aesthetic matters. Péladan was obsessed by things artistic, telling artists, sculptors and musicians of his day (men only, he did not believe that the arts were a place for women): "Artist, you are a priest: Art is the great mystery and, when your effort leads to a masterpiece, a ray of the divine shines down as on an altar…Artist, you are a magus. Art is the great miracle and proves our own immortality."

Péladan's third mandate was a condemnation of a female member of the Rothschild family for her proposal to demolish a chapel in her recently acquired château of Beaujon.

Assailed on all sides by his opponents including his fellow Rosicrucians for his witless actions, Péladan took a different tack and in August 1891 founded the *Ordre de la Rose-Croix Catholique et Esthétique du Temple et du Graal*. He claimed that his new Order had links with a number of serious players on the German occult scene, including the Holy Vehm and the Illuminatus of Bavaria. Péladan was also believed to have been under the influence of the Counts of Chambord, pretenders to the throne and promoters of the myth that Louis XVII escaped in 1795 at the age of ten from pre-execution imprisonment in the Paris Temple.

De Guaïta died young, blind, sick and mentally unstable. Péladan, on the other hand, was made of sterner stuff and continued to practise his synthesis of Catholicism and esoteric learning with energy and enthusiasm. In fact, one of the main reasons why Péladan had been moved to found the *Ordre de la Rose-Croix Catholique et Esthétique du Temple et du Graal* was because of what he perceived as de Guaïta's increasing separation from their joint quest to reconcile Catholicism and the occult.

Earlier mention was made of our concluding character in this representative exploration of the European occult underground: the Marquis de Saint-Yves D'Alveydre (1842-1909), an enormously influential French esoteric scholar. Born in Paris, Saint-Yves started his career as a physician at a naval academy in Brest. After becoming ill he gave up his career and in 1863 relocated to Jersey where he became friends with the exiled Victor Hugo. He returned to France in 1870 to fight in the war with Prussia and was invalided out.

Saint-Yves' is perhaps best remembered for his ideas on social reform. He revived the term synarchy, first used by 18th century English clergyman Thomas to denote joint rule or sovereignty. Saint-Yves' reshaped the concept to describe a conservative political-theological philosophy that would supposedly result in a more harmonious society. He based this thinking on his idealised view of life in medieval Europe and also on his ideas about successful governments in India, Atlantis and Ancient Egypt.

To make synarchy a viable political ideology requires that for the greater good the man and woman in the street assent to being governed by those occupying the "higher" levels of society. Far from creating an "us and them" society rooted in fundamental conflict, Saint-Yves argued that social differentiation within distinctly defined hierarchical structures is precisely the model that is necessary to maintain lasting cooperation between social and economic groups—synarchy as opposed to anarchy. Specifically, Saint-Yves, influenced by Plato's *The Republic* and by Martinist principles, envisioned a European society with a government comprising three councils representing economic power, judicial power and the scientific community, the whole bound by an overarching metaphysical governing chamber.

Marquis de Saint-Yves D'Alveydre

Having reached the conclusion that the Rosicrucians successfully fulfilled the role in mediaeval Europe, Saint-Yves assigned to synarchic government an important contribution to esoteric societies populated by oracles that safeguard and, when necessary, influence matters from behind the scenes.

In 1885 when Saint-Yves was supposedly visited by initiates from the East, he declared that synarchy was associated with "ascended masters" who inhabit the mythical subterranean realm of Agartha and with whom he professed to communicate telepathically. Something had led Saint-Yves to believe a synarchist world government was transferred to Agartha at the start of the Kali-Yuga era around 3,200 B.C. This concept was later developed by Zam Bothiva (Cesare Accomani) and the Fraternité des Polaires in France and, more significantly, by the occult membership of the Thule-Gesellschaft in the Nazi era.

Here we emerge, blinking, from the crowded depths of the European occult underground, a chaotic space filled cheek by jowl with assorted spiritualists, table rappers, mesmerists, Theosophists, Hermeticists, psychics, clairvoyants, occultists, magicians, mystic "masters" and many more students of thaumaturgy betwixt and between. Despite their different labels, these occult actors ploughed on in common purpose in the autumn of 1888 in pursuit of their personal ideal of a lasting, inner treasure.

Maybe some among them found their Grail prize. None today may know but the question provides food for thought. In a shocking twist on the classic quest adventure story—the good guy endures many trials to achieve illumination—did Jack believe that he had been similarly tasked so that he might attain his own concept of immortality? The idea is horrifying but that doesn't make it implausible. In fact, the more one dwells on the notion, the more one might begin to see patterns taking shape that lead one to confront very dark areas of possibility at play behind the Ripper murders.

Our re-appearance into the light-bathed surface world is necessarily brief. There remains much more to be said about the unholy state of occult shenanigans that were at work beneath the visible canopy of late nineteenth-century affairs in English society.

Firstly, we shall review the untimely demise of the Ripper's third victim, Annie Chapman, who died on the Catholic feast day in the Julian calendar of Saint Adrian, the patron saint of soldiers and butchers.

Chapter 7

"Dark Annie"

Whitechapel, 1:50 a.m., Saturday, 8 September 1888

Annie Chapman, familiarly know as "Dark Annie," stepped unsteadily out of Crossingham's Lodging House at 35 Dorset Street, Spitalfields, a stone's throw from the chandlery at No. 27 owned by Mary Kelly's landlord, John McCarthy. Annie had been coming and going all evening but this was to be the last time she would see these premises.

She had been staying at No. 35 for about four months where she paid eightpence for a double bed but until earlier that day had not visited the lodge during the past week. Deputy lodge-keeper Timothy Donovan remembered Annie as an inoffensive woman who never caused them any trouble and was on good terms with the other lodgers.

Annie had reappeared at No. 35 between two and three on the Friday afternoon. She asked Donovan if she might be allowed to sit downstairs in the kitchen. He asked where she had been all week and Annie replied, "In the infirmary."

Over the next few hours Annie came and went. Donovan's nightwatchman, John Evans, informed the inquest that once during the evening Annie sent out one of the lodgers to fetch a pint of beer before venturing out again, presumably to find a punter but this is speculation.

At about 1:30 a.m or 1:45 a.m. Annie was sitting in the kitchen, enjoying the warmth, eating potatoes and gossiping with the other lodgers. Donovan sent Evans to ask for her lodging money. Annie came up to the office, saying, "I have not got it. I am weak and ill, and have been in the infirmary...but don't let it [my bed]; I shall not be long before I am in." Donovan was unyielding. "You can find money for your beer," he said, "and you can't find money for your bed."

Annie was not upset by the rebuff; she would get the money. She left the office and stood for a while in the doorway, presently saying to Donovan, "Never mind, Tim, I shall soon be back. Don't let the bed." With that, Evans saw Annie off the premises and watched as she walked, slightly the worse for drink, through Little Paternoster Row into Brushfield Street and, finally, towards Spitalfields Church.

Annie was wearing a long black coat that came down to her knees, a black skirt, two bodices, red and white striped woollen stockings, lace-up boots and a white cotton neckerchief with a broad red border. Tied around her waist with string was an empty large pocket. Under her skirt she wore two petticoats. On the middle finger of her left hand were three brass rings, recently acquired. In her pockets were a piece of muslin, a small-tooth comb, another comb in a paper case and a scrap of an envelope containing two pills.

A little before 6:00 a.m. Annie's mutilated body was discovered in the backyard of 29 Hanbury Street, a three-storeyed house that had originally been built for Spitalfields' weavers. Three stone steps led from the back door of No. 29 down into the yard, which was about five yards by four, in some places bare earth, in others roughly paved with flat or round stones. Wooden palings about five and a half feet high fenced it off on both sides from the adjoining yards. Standing on the steps, an observer would have seen three or three and a half feet to their left the palings that separated the yard from neighbouring No. 27.

In the far left-hand corner opposite the back door was Mrs Richardson's woodshed. In the far right-hand corner was a privy (an outside toilet). The entrance to the cellar, which contained Mrs Richardson's workshops, lay to the right of the back door. Annie's last resting place was just three or four hundred yards away from her Dorset Street lodgings. She was lying on the ground near a doorway in the back yard. Like Polly Nichols, Annie had been terribly mutilated.

Annie's would be the only murder perpetrated by "Jack the Ripper" not committed during the hours of darkness. On the 8th the sun rose at 5:23 a.m. and on this busy market morning there were already plenty of people around. Mrs Richardson's son, John, had been in the back yard shortly before 5:00 a.m. to cut away a loose piece of leather from his boot.

Thirty minutes later carpenter Albert Cadosch entered the yard at 27 Hanbury Street. He heard voices in the neighbouring yard followed by the sound of something falling against the fence. The person who discovered the body was market porter John Davis, described in the press as a small, elderly man with a pronounced stoop. He rented a room in the attic of No. 29 where he lived with his wife and three sons.

Annie Chapman in 1869

For much of the night of 7th-8th September Davis could not sleep. From three to five he lay awake and dozed until the clock at Spitalfields Church struck 5:45 a.m. The strike of the clock and the light coming through the large weaver's window told him it was time to get up for work at Leadenhall Market. Davis's wife made her husband a cup of tea and then he went downstairs to the backyard. On his way down he saw that the street door was wide open and thrown back against the wall. That was not unusual. At the time of Annie's murder, No. 29 accommodated seventeen permanent residents and there were others who regularly came and went to assist with businesses conducted on the premises. The back door was closed. Davis opened it and stood at the top of the steps leading into the yard. What he saw shook him rigid.

In the yard to his left between the steps and the wooden fence adjoining No. 27 was the body of a woman sprawled upon her back. Her head was towards the house, her feet towards the woodshed. Davis noticed that her skirts had been raised to her groin. He did not wait to investigate further. Hurrying through the passage, he stumbled out of the front door and into the street. There, two packing case makers, James Green and James Kent who worked for Joseph and Thomas Bayley of 23A Hanbury Street, were standing outside their workshop waiting for fellow workmen to arrive. Also there passing through Hanbury Street on his way to work was boxmaker Henry John Holland. Their attention was seized by a wild-eyed old man (Davis) who suddenly burst from the doorway of No. 29, crying out, "Men, come here!"

The first officer on the scene was Inspector Joseph Luniss Chandler of H Division who found the victim lying on her back, her left arm resting on her left breast, her right arm lying down her right side, her legs drawn up and her clothes thrown up above her knees. In Chandler's tersely written report, he said:

> I at once proceeded to No. 29 Hanbury Street, and in the back yard found a woman lying on her back, dead, left arm resting on left breast, legs drawn up, abducted, small intestines and flap of the abdomen lying on right side, above right shoulder, attached by a cord with the rest of the intestines inside the body; two flaps of skin from the lower part of the abdomen lying in a large quantity of blood above the left shoulder; throat cut deeply from left and back in a jagged manner right around throat.

Chandler sent for Dr. George Bagster Phillips, the divisional police surgeon, and to the police station for further assistance and an ambulance. Constables quickly arrived on the scene and Chandler directed them to clear the passage. He also covered the body with a piece of sacking to keep it free from any interference pending the doctor's arrival. In the absence of divisional head of CID, Edmund Reid who was on annual leave, the initial task of heading the investigation fell to Chandler with assistance from Detective Sergeants Thick and Leach. Accordingly, H Division was anxious to secure Abberline's expertise. In fact, that morning Abberline had already been instructed to assist in this latest Whitechapel murder.

Dr. Phillips arrived at 6:30 a.m. Then in his fifties, Phillips had been the local divisional surgeon for many years. Metropolitan Police officer Walter Dew who besides his involvement in the hunt for Jack the Ripper later arrested Dr. Crippen knew Phillips well, describing him as a man with an outmoded sense of dress and style who looked as if had stepped out of a century-old painting.

Phillips described the body as he saw it on his arrival in the back yard of the house at 29 Hanbury Street. The left arm was placed across the left breast. The legs were drawn up, the feet resting on the ground, and the knees turned outwards. The face was swollen and turned on the right side. The tongue protruded between the front teeth but not beyond the lips. The tongue was much swollen. The front teeth were perfect as far as the first molar, top and bottom. The stiffness of the limbs was not marked but was evidently commencing.

As with Polly Nichols, Chapman had sustained horrific injuries. Her throat was cut from left to right, and she had been disembowelled with her intestines thrown out of her abdomen over each of her shoulders. The morgue examination subsequently revealed that part of her uterus was missing. Chapman's protruding tongue and swollen face led Dr Phillips to think that she may have been asphyxiated with the handkerchief that was found tied around her neck. He did not consider that it had been tied on after the throat was cut. Phillips estimated time of death at 4:30 a.m. or before, thereby contradicting the testimony of Richardson, Long and Cadosch. However, Victorian methods of estimating time of death, such as measuring body temperature, were crude and Phillips highlighted at the inquest that the body could have cooled more quickly than normally expected. On the wooden paling between the yard in question and the next, smears of blood corresponding

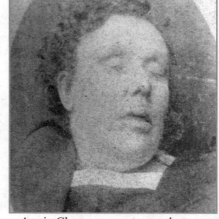

Annie Chapman mortuary photo

to where the head of the deceased lay were to be seen. These were about fourteen inches from the ground and immediately above the part where the blood from the neck lay.

The instrument used at the throat and abdomen was the same. Phillips concluded that it must have been a very sharp knife with a thin narrow blade at least 6-8 inches in length, probably longer. He said that a bayonet or a sword could not have inflicted the injuries. They could have been made by an instrument such as a medical man used for post-mortem purposes, seeing that ordinary surgical cases might not contain such an instrument.

Those used by slaughtermen, well ground down, might also have caused them. Phillips thought the knives used by those in the leather trade would not be long enough in the blade. He said that the deceased had been dead at least two hours and probably more when he first saw her but it was right to mention that it was a fairly cool morning and that the body would be more apt to cool rapidly from having lost a great quantity of blood.

There was no evidence of a struggle having taken place. Phillips was positive the deceased entered the yard alive. As there was no blood trail leading to the yard, Phillips was certain that Chapman was killed where she was found. He concluded that she suffered from a long-standing lung disease, that the victim was sober at the time of death and had not consumed alcoholic beverages for at least some hours before it.

In the same police ambulance that had been used for Nichols (actually a handcart), Chapman's body was conveyed later that day to Whitechapel mortuary.

Phillips believed that the murderer must have possessed anatomical knowledge to slice out the reproductive organs in a single movement with a blade 6-8 inches long. However, experts strongly dismissed the suggestion that the murderer possessed surgical skill.

Whether this opposing opinion was based on deductive reasoning or a desire to avoid a suggestion that upstanding members of the medical profession could commit such a heinous crime (and, by implication, in Nichols' murder) is open to question. As Annie's body was not examined extensively in Hanbury Street, it has also been suggested that the uterus was removed by mortuary personnel who made money on the side from selling organs as surgical specimens.

Local coroner Wynne Edwin Baxter appeared to have been thinking along similar lines when he reflected in his inquest summing up on the possibility that Chapman was murdered deliberately to obtain the uterus. He based this remark on the fact that an American had made inquiries at a London medical school for the purchase of such organs. Baxter said:

The body had not been dissected, but the injuries had been made by someone who had considerable anatomical skill and knowledge. There were no meaningless cuts. The organ had been taken by one who knew where to find it, what difficulties he would have to contend against, and how he should use his knife so as to abstract the organ without injury to it...The conclusion that the desire was to possess the missing abdominal organ seemed overwhelming.

The *Lancet* vehemently rejected Baxter's suggestion, pointing out "certain improbabilities and absurdities" and adding that it was "a grave error of judgement." The *British Medical Journal* was equally scathing, reporting that the American physician who requested the samples was a highly reputable doctor, unnamed, who had left the country eighteen months before the murder. Stung by the criticism, Baxter dropped the theory and never referred to it again. *The Chicago Tribune* claimed the American doctor in question was from Philadelphia, while author Philip Sugden[42] later speculated that the man was long-time Ripper suspect, Francis Tumblety.

Chief Inspector Donald Swanson of Scotland Yard was placed in overall command a few days after the murder, which was quickly linked to similar murders in the district, particularly that of Mary Ann Nichols the week before. Swanson reported that, "an immediate and searching enquiry was made at all common lodging houses to ascertain if anyone had entered that morning with blood on their hands or clothes, or under any suspicious circumstances."

Items belonging to Annie recovered from the yard at No. 29 comprised two pills for her lung condition, part of a torn envelope, a piece of muslin and a comb. The three brass rings that she had been wearing earlier were not recovered, either because she had pawned them or because they had been stolen. All the pawnbrokers in the area were searched for the rings without success.

The envelope bore the crest of the Sussex regiment and was briefly tied to Ted Stanley, a man-friend of Annie's who pretended to be an army pensioner. This clue was discounted when police discovered at Crossingham's lodging-house that the envelope was one Annie had taken from there to keep her pills in.

The press claimed that two farthings were found in the yard but they are not mentioned in extant police records. Edmund Reid is said to have mentioned them at an inquest in 1889, and the acting Commissioner of the City Police, Major Henry Smith, referred to them

---

[42] Sugden, P., *The Complete History of Jack the Ripper*, Robinson, 1994.

in his memoirs, which are known to have been unreliable and beefed up for dramatic effect. Smith claimed that medical students polished farthings so they could be passed off as sovereigns to unsuspecting prostitutes, a theory that suggested the perpetrator was a medical student. However, it has been pointed out that the price of a prostitute in the East End was likely to have been much less than a sovereign.

Efforts were quickly made to identify the victim, including taking residents from the many common lodging houses in the district to the mortuary. Tim Donovan was one such person brought to see the body, recognising it as that of a woman whom he knew by the name of Annie Siffey.

Forty-seven year-old Chapman, also known as Sievey or Sivvey as well as Siffey, had in life been a forlorn little prostitute broken by her unyielding life on the streets of Whitechapel. She had lived a nomadic life, comprising short stints in Spitalfields' common lodging houses interspersed with long hours on the streets in search of her next client and a few pennies for her purse.

She was 5' tall and plump with pallid complexion, blue eyes, dark brown wavy hair (which earned her the soubriquet "Dark Annie"), a large thick nose, and two teeth missing in her lower jaw. Overall, her unprepossessing appearance had not made her an attractive proposition to punters.

She was born Eliza Anne Smith in September 1841: father, George Smith, described on marriage certificate as a Private, 2nd Battalion of Lifeguards; mother, Ruth. George and Ruth married 22 February 1842 in Paddington. Annie had three sisters: Emily Latitia (b.1844), Georgina (b.1856) and Miriam Ruth (b.1858). A brother, Fountain Smith, was born in 1861. By all accounts, Annie did not get along with her sisters.

Annie's years of toil in the desperate and uncertain game of survival in London's East End had taken its toll. She was under-nourished and, worse, the post-mortem indicated that she suffered from tubercular meningitis, a fatal disease of the lungs and brain exacerbated by the degenerative effects of syphilis. Annie's friend, charwoman Amelia Palmer, described her as an industrious woman when sober but who drank heavily on occasion. Palmer said at the inquest, "I have seen her often the worse for drink." Donovan reiterated Annie's fondness for drink, saying that Annie was generally drunk on Saturdays.

Amelia last saw Annie alive on Friday the 7th. At about 5:00 p.m. they met in Dorset Street. "Aren't you going to Stratford today?" Amelia asked. "I feel too ill to do anything," said Annie. Ten minutes later Annie was still standing in the same spot when Amelia came upon her once more. "It's no use giving way," Annie said, "I must pull myself together and get some money or I shall have no lodgings."

There had been a time when Annie's future seemed to have better promise. In May 1869 she married coachman John Chapman and together they resided for a time with Annie's mother at Brompton near Knightsbridge before establishing a home at Brook Mews in Bayswater.

By 1881 they had relocated to Berkshire where John had attained a position as coachman to farm bailiff, Josiah Weeks. Children followed: Emily Ruth in 1870, Annie Georgina in 1873 and John, born crippled, in 1880. Emily Ruth died of meningitis when she was twelve. In 1888 son John was said to be in the care of a charitable school (described in some reports as the Cripples' Home), while Annie Georgina was travelling with a performing troupe or circus in France.

Shortly after the tragic death of Emily Ruth the marriage was on the rocks. Police records indicate that Annie's drinking was to blame but John could also over-indulge, and it is also likely that the misfortunes of the children placed tremendous strain on the relationship. Consequently, the couple lived apart for three or four years during which John paid Annie a weekly allowance of ten shillings.

According to the inquest testimony of Amelia Farmer, in 1886 Annie was lodging at 30 Dorset Street, Spitalfields "with a man who made iron sieves" after which some took to calling Annie, Mrs. Sievey and its variations.

The death of her husband at forty-two from "cirrhosis of the liver, ascites [abdominal swelling caused by fluid accumulation in the peritoneal cavity] and dropsy" on Christmas Day, 1886, robbed Annie of her last vestiges of financial security. She only became aware of her husband's passing when the termination of her weekly allowance put an end to the postal order made payable at Commercial Road Post Office. She made inquiries and one of John's relatives told her of the news. Annie took it badly. Amelia remembered how Annie often seemed out of sorts when speaking of her children and how "since the death of her husband she has seemed to give way altogether."

It appears that the sieve maker's interest in Annie evaporated when he learned of the termination of the allowance. Annie was now alone and living on her wits, sometimes receiving help from relatives. She made a little money doing crochet work, making antimacassars and selling flowers, going to Stratford on Fridays to sell her wares.

She told her brother two weeks before she died when they met in Commercial Street that she was not doing anything and needed money for lodgings. Fountain gave her two shillings. Soon after midnight on the 8th she came in the lodge saying that she had been to Vauxhall to see her sister. A fellow lodger told a newspaper after the murder that Annie had gone to "get some money" and that her relatives gave her fivepence, which she quickly spent on drink. If Annie did go on to Stratford after meeting with Amelia at five o'clock on the previous day it would appear that any money she might have made from selling her wares had been spent.

Donovan said that Annie's only regular visitor was a man he knew as "the pensioner." This person is something of a mystery in Annie's life. Donovan told the inquest that the pensioner regularly came to the lodging house on Saturdays and stayed with Annie until the following Monday. He sometimes dressed like a dock labourer; at other times he sported a more gentlemanly appearance. His attitude to his relationship with Annie was covetous, reportedly instructing Donovan to turn away any other men whom she tried to bring into the lodging house.

The "pensioner's" name was Ted Stanley and he lived in Osborn Place, Osborn Street, Whitechapel. One thing is certain: Stanley was not a pensioner, being described at the inquest as a bricklayer's labourer. It was subsequently learned that Stanley led a double life for it is known that on the night of Polly Nichols' death he was on duty at Fort Elson, Gosport, with the "2nd Brigade Southern Division, Hants Militia." Evidently, Stanley was very anxious that this information should not become public knowledge, making the intriguing remark to Baxter at the inquest, "Am I bound to answer this question? ['Are you a pensioner?']…What I say will be published all over Europe."

More details emerged concerning Annie's weeklong absence from the lodging house. On Sunday 3 September Amelia Palmer met Annie in Dorset Street and noticed a bruise on her right temple. "How did you get that?" she asked. Annie opened her dress, saying, "Yes, look at my chest," indicating a second bruise. Annie elaborated no further, instead saying to Amelia, "If my sister will send me the boots I shall go hopping [hop-picking]."

The following day Amelia saw Annie near Spitalfields Church. Annie said she felt no better and Amelia, observing just how very pale her friend looked, urged her to enter the casual ward for a day or two. Amelia asked Annie if she had had anything to eat that day. Annie said no, just a cup of tea. Amelia gave Annie tuppence but told her not to spend it on rum. On the day of the murder Ted Stanley came to No. 35 to follow up a rumour he had heard from a shoeblack that Annie had been killed. Once this fact had been verified he marched right out again and, thereafter, involved himself as little as possible in the investigation and markedly played down the extent any relations he might have had with Annie. On 14 September 1888 Stanley made a statement at Commercial Street Police Station. Five days later he appeared as a witness at the inquest. He insisted repeatedly that he had visited Annie no more than twice and flatly denied ever telling Donovan to bar any other men she wanted to bring into the lodging house. Nevertheless, it was revealed that the circumstances in which Annie received her bruises featured one of Stanley's visits. A few days before her death, Annie had been in a fight with fellow lodger, Eliza (Liza) Cooper. According to Donovan it was the only altercation he recalled Annie having been involved with. The details he imparted were sketchy.

Cooper, a hawker by trade, gave her own version at the inquest. Liza said that conflict arose when Annie, having brought Stanley onto the premises on Saturday 1 September, asked fellow lodgers if anyone had a spare piece of soap. She was referred to Liza who loaned her one, which Annie handed to Stanley so he could get cleaned up. The following day Liza asked Annie for the return of the soap and received the diffident reply, "I will see you by and by." On the following Tuesday, the 4th, when the two women were in the lodging house kitchen, Liza asked once more for her soap, to which Annie threw down a halfpenny on the table, saying, "Go and get a halfpennyworth of soap." Annie's brusque response provoked an argument that re-erupted the next day at the Brittania pub on the corner of Dorset Street and Commercial Street. On this occasion Annie slapped Liza's face and said, "Think yourself lucky I did not do more." Liza's response was to strike Annie in the left eye and chest.

Liza was obviously being economical with the truth of the matter, presumably in an effort to downplay her involvement. It became evident during the taking of witness statements that the fight could not have taken place as late as the 4th. Ted Stanley recalled seeing Annie with a black eye on Sunday 2 September and Annie showed her bruises to Amelia Palmer the next day. We also have Donovan's testimony that Annie was not seen at the lodging house in the week before her death. He said that the fracas occurred about Tuesday, 28 August, and that two days later Annie was sporting a black eye from the encounter. "Tim, this is lovely, ain't it?" Annie had said to him breezily about her shiner.

As for the location of the fight, John Evans, speaking at the inquest only two days after Annie's death, confirmed that it took place in the lodging house kitchen on 30 August. The post-mortem revealed that Liza's wallop to Annie's face was actually to the right temple, not to the left.

Evidence indicated that Chapman might have been killed as late as 5:30 a.m., an observation that concurred with Elizabeth Long's sighting of Annie alive around that time. She had died in the enclosed back yard of a house occupied by seventeen people, none of whom had seen or heard anything at the time of the murder. The passage through the house to the backyard was not locked as the residents used it at all hours, and the front door was wide open when the body was discovered.

John Richardson said that he had often seen strangers, both men and women, in the passage of the house.

Baxter opened the inquest on 10 September at the Working Lad's Institute, Whitechapel. Dr. Phillips' inquest deposition of 13 September contains the fullest description of the appearance of Annie Chapman's body in the backyard of 29 Hanbury Street:

> I found the body of the deceased lying in the yard on her back, on the left hand of the steps that lead from the passage. The head was about 6 in. in front of the level of the bottom step, and the feet were towards a shed at the end of the yard. The left arm was across the left breast, and the legs were drawn up, the feet resting on the ground, and the knees turned outwards. The face was swollen and turned on the right side, and the tongue protruded between the front teeth, but not beyond the lips; it was much swollen. The small intestines and other portions were lying on the right side of the body on the ground above the right shoulder, but attached. There was a large quantity of blood, with a part of the stomach above the left shoulder...The body was cold, except that there was a certain remaining heat, under the intestines, in the body. Stiffness of the limbs was not marked, but it was commencing. The throat was dissevered deeply. I noticed that the incision of the skin was jagged, and reached right round the neck.

Phillips had conducted the post-mortem examination at the Whitechapel Mortuary in difficult circumstances. On arriving, he discovered that two nurses from the Whitechapel Union Infirmary had already stripped and partially washed the corpse before laying it on the table for his examination.

There were distinct marks of one or more rings on the proximal phalanx of the ring finger. An abrasion over the head of the phalanx suggested that the killer had wrenched the rings from her finger. The throat had been ferociously severed from left to right; in fact, Phillips intimated that the murderer had attempted and failed to cut off the woman's head. He observed two distinct clean cuts on the left side of the spine, parallel to each other and half an inch apart. Phillips remarked, "The muscular structures between the side processes of bone of the vertebrae had an appearance as if an attempt had been made to separate the bones of the neck."

Phillips believed that the woman had been partially suffocated before death and that death had resulted from syncope: the sudden loss of blood supply to the brain caused by the injury to the throat.

He held that the abdominal mutilations had been inflicted after death. Phillips was very reluctant to go into detail at the inquest about the exact nature of these injuries. However, an unsigned piece in the *Lancet* of 29 September summarised Phillips' observations and indicated why he thought he had detected professional skill in their execution:

> The abdomen had been entirely laid open; that the intestines, severed from their mesenteric attachments, had been lifted out of the body, and placed by the shoulder of the corpse; whilst from the pelvis the uterus and its appendages, with the upper portion of the vagina and the posterior two-thirds of the bladder, had been entirely removed. No trace of these parts could be found, and the incisions were cleanly cut, avoiding the rectum, and dividing the vagina low enough to avoid injury to the cervix uteri. Obviously the work was that of an expert—of one, at least, who had such knowledge of anatomical or pathological examinations as to be enabled to secure the pelvic organs with one sweep of a knife...

Chief Inspector Swanson also summarised the mutilations in his report of 19 October:

> Examination of the body showed that the throat was severed deeply, incision jagged. Removed from, but attached to body, & placed above right shoulder were a flap of the wall of belly, the whole of the small intestines & attachments. Two other portions of wall of belly & "Pubes" were placed above left shoulder in a large quantity of blood. The following parts were missing: part of belly wall including navel; the womb, the upper part of vagina & greater part of bladder.

At the inquest Mrs. Elizabeth Long testified that she had seen Chapman talking to a man at about 5:30 a.m. just beyond the back yard of 29 Hanbury Street. Mrs. Long described the man as over forty and a little taller than Chapman, with dark hair and of foreign "shabby-genteel" appearance. He was wearing a deerstalker hat and dark overcoat. It is likely that Long was the last person, other than the murderer, to see Chapman alive.

Newspaper reports referred to a suspect nicknamed "Leather Apron." What prompted the stories was the discovery by police under a tap in the yard at 29 Hanbury Street of a leather apron belonging to John Richardson. His mother had placed it there after washing it. Consequently, Richardson was investigated by the police before being eliminated as a suspect. Somehow the story of the apron fed rumours that the perpetrator was a local Jew called "Leather Apron."

The police were admonished in the press for not disclosing particulars on this line of inquiry. *The Manchester Guardian*, for example, reported: "Whatever information may be in the possession of the police they deem it necessary to keep secret...It is believed their attention is particularly directed to...a notorious character known as 'Leather Apron.'"

Other newspapers joined the fray, resorting in the absence of police updates to writing fantasy pieces based on crude Jewish stereotypes. The *Star* reported that police were looking for a man who had ill-treated "fifty women." The women described him as aged 38 to 40, 5'4" tall with black hair and small black moustache, thickset with an unusually thick neck, and wore a dark close fitting cap. His small, glittering eyes and lips that were usually parted in a grin gave him an excessively repellent appearance. He always carried a knife and got his nickname from a leather apron he always wore. He was said to be a slipper maker by trade but at that time was out of work. No one knew his name. The *East London Observer* described him in grossly unflattering terms:

> His face was not altogether pleasant to look upon by reason of the grizzly black strips of hair, nearly an inch in length, which almost covered his face, the thin lips too had a cruel sardonic kind of look, which was increased if anything by the drooping dark moustache and side whiskers. His hair was short, smooth and dark, intermingled with grey, his head was slightly bald on top, his head was large and was fixed to the body by a thick, heavy looking neck. He appeared splay footed and spoke with a thick guttural foreign accent.

In fact, there was no mystery as to the identity of the local man who was widely known as "Leather Apron." Since the hunt for Polly Nichol's killer, police had been investigating a claim among local prostitutes that they were living in fear of Polish Jew, Jack Pizer, a boot-finisher known as "Leather Apron." It was on record that, for some time, Pizer had been pressing Whitechapel whores to pay him protection money and beating up those who refused. His habit was to peer inside public house windows at night to select his victims and accost them once they were outside. It was reported that he always carried a sharp knife that he used for leather trimming and with which he menaced his victims.

Although the police knew the man they were seeking was Pizer they reportedly had no idea where to find him. It is important to stress that they sought Pizer for his alleged attacks on women for money and not because there was any evidence that he might have stepped up his activities to include murderous assaults.

There was local gossip that Leather Apron had been seen walking with Nichols in Baker's Row on the morning of her murder but this account was not corroborated. In a report of 7 September Helson wrote, "There is no evidence whatever against him," and Abberline said twelve days later, "There was no evidence to connect him with the murder [of Polly Nichols]."

It seems that Helson and Abberline's men did not ask enough of their uniformed colleagues for information about Pizer's whereabouts. If they had put the question to Sergeant William Thick they would have quickly received the intelligence they sought. On September 10, Thick made the arrest of the notorious John Pizer, alias "Leather Apron." Thick's successful apprehension was hardly surprising seeing that he and Pizer lived just streets apart and had known each other for years. Thick knew the extent of the deep feelings of local hostility directed against Pizer and went to 22 Mulberry Street shortly after 8:00 a.m. on 10 September and took him into protective custody before the mob could find him and deliver their own brand of justice.

Pizer had been in hiding, believing that if he ventured outside he would be torn to pieces by angry citizens. Under questioning at Leman Street police station, Pizer said he was unaware that he was known locally as "Leather Apron." He readily accepted that he had in the past worn a leather apron home from work but said he had not done so for a while because he was unemployed.

Pizer was soon cleared of any involvement in the Whitechapel murders, his brother and other relatives confirming his alibi for the night Annie Chapman was murdered. His alibi for the night of Polly Nichol's murder also checked out. Pizer did eventually receive compensation from at least one newspaper that had defamed him but it was not as substantial a sum as some have claimed.

Police made other arrests. Ship's cook William Henry Piggott was detained after being found in possession of a bloodstained shirt while making misogynist remarks. He claimed that he had been bitten by a woman and that the blood was his. He was investigated and released. Swiss butcher Jacob Isenschmidt matched the description of a bloodstained man acting strangely and seen by public house landlady Mrs Fiddymont on the morning of the murder. He wore a large ginger moustache and had a history of mental illness. He was detained in a mental asylum. German hairdresser Charles Ludwig was arrested after he attempted to stab a man at a coffee stall shortly after attacking a prostitute. Isenschmidt and Ludwig were both exonerated after another murder was committed while they were in custody.

Annie Chapman was buried 14 September 1888 in great secrecy. None but the undertaker, police and relatives of the deceased knew anything about the arrangements. Her body was placed in a black-draped elm coffin bearing the words: "Annie Chapman, died Sept. 8, 1888, aged 48 years."

Annie's life was ended. Just beginning was a world of pain for those at the highest levels within the police and in government (as well as, it must not be ignored, for the three subsequent victims of the Ripper). Home Secretary Henry Matthews and his subordinate, Chief Commissioner of the Metropolitan Police, General Sir Charles Warren, did not enjoy harmonious relations. The pair fundamentally disagreed about the extent of the Home Secretary's authority over police matters.

Warren had instigated a sweeping program of reforms throughout the London police service, to an extent that elements within the press were accusing him of moulding the police into a military force that had more interest in curtailing free speech and anti-government rallies rather than effective prevention and detection of crime on the ground. Warren felt embattled and looked to his superior for support for his initiatives but Chapman's murder quickly brought new pressures that widened the gulf between the two men.

Warren was also in conflict with senior colleagues in the force. The most serious row had concerned relations in the early months of 1888 between Warren and James Monro. Monro had been filling two roles: Assistant Commissioner in charge of CID and head of a four-man unit designated Section D that was wholly engaged in political intelligence work and which reported directly to the Home Office. Ex-military man Warren simply could not get his head around the fact that he had no authority over this second part of his subordinate's duties. The Commissioner's continuous efforts to meddle in the political work increasingly exasperated Monro who finally resigned his post on 31 August, the day that Polly Nichols died.

Monro's successor as head of CID, Dr. Robert Anderson, brought with him twenty years experience in intelligence work for the Home Office but he was in such poor health that Dr. Gilbart Smith of Harley Street immediately prescribed him two months' sick-leave to recover his strength. Anderson knew that two months was out of the question but he told an evidently unhappy Matthews that he could not commence his duties until he had recuperated for one month in Switzerland. And, of course, just one week after Anderson's departure Chapman was murdered, leaving the Metropolitan Police seriously short of the high level skills and experience it needed to deal with what was quickly recognised as a serious and growing problem in Whitechapel.

Thankfully, Abberline was on hand to provide a first-rate coordination role in the East End and he worked hand in glove with

Chief Inspector Donald Swanson, who on 15 September was deputed by Scotland Yard to oversee the investigation.

Subsequent to Chapman's murder, Warren would remain in post for just two more months before submitting his letter of resignation to a beleaguered Matthews on 8 November, the day prior to the Ripper's final and most gruesome murder. One can imagine Warren breathing a sigh of relief at this release from a nightmare investigation that was going nowhere under his command. He did, after all, have other pressing matters. Only four years earlier in his capacity as a Master Freemason, Warren had founded with eight brother masons the Quatuor Coronati Lodge No. 2076 in London. It was formally inaugurated in 1886. The drive to found this new Lodge came from the upsurge in the Victorian era to research the origins of Freemasonry and its connection with the Temple of Solomon. But it appears that the Lodge's ranks were becoming populated with those who shared little interest in the nuts and bolts, evidence-based Temple research agenda that had initially brought together its nine founding fathers.

On the face of it, the Quatuor Coronati Lodge was not established as a society that was of interest to occultist enthusiasts. Members presented papers on all aspects of fundamental Masonic research, which were published in their annual Transactions. Nevertheless, in addition to papers provided by Warren and his co-founders on somewhat prosaic matters there were contributions submitted on the esoteric themes of the Kabbalah and Hermeticism by Dr. William Wynn Westcott and the Rev. A.F.A. Woodford, men who in early 1888 co-founded the deeply occult Hermetic Order of the Golden Dawn. With dubious bedfellows in the lodge such as Westcott and Woodford, one cannot help wondering if Warren felt in late 1888 that he was fighting wars on multiple fronts: one against the Whitechapel murderer, the other against unwelcome lodge members who wished to steer its affairs in directions that were anathema to its founders.

Or may it have been the case that Warren empathised with occult sentiments much more than he might have cared to reveal? So many across the world were being swept up by the mystical tsunami that characterised the latter period of the Age of Enlightenment; why should Warren have been any less mesmerised in his search for hidden knowledge than thousands of other seekers who were similarly engaged?

In the following chapter, *The Occult Establishment*, we will focus on many such instances of cross-pollination between the Masonic, esoteric and occult societies across the British metaphysical landscape when the Whitechapel murders were building to a terrifying climax in the autumn of 1888.

Chapter 8

The Occult Establishment

By the 1880s the transatlantic network of streams that fed the occult underground had permeated the highest strata in British society. Pillars of the establishment from all walks of life bathed in their waters and emerged with renewed fervour with which to indulge their occult ambitions. In this chapter's review of Britain's crowded occult environment in 1888 we are firstly reminded that it owed its beginnings to ancient European magical traditions, predominantly those at work in the Germanic regions. René Guénon, an opponent of spiritualism and Theosophy, wrote, for example, of the prevalence in Germany of secret societies outside Freemasonry that were rooted in the Hermetic, Kabbalistic and Rosicrucian traditions and which worked with magical evocations and magnetism.

One such society was Hans Heinrich von Ecker und Eckhoffen's Fratres Lucis (Brothers of Light), also known as Ritter des Lichts (Knights of Light), a group predominantly concerned with alchemical rituals. Unlike older German societies such as Gold- und Rosenkreuz (the Gold and Rosy Cross, rumoured to have possessed the Golden Fleece), Fratres Lucis was open to Jewish members. Ecker's group attracted many high profile members, especially after he reorganised it in Vienna into the Asiatic Brethren. After Ecker's death in 1791, the Asiatic Brethren had an uneasy time in a country that was essentially Christian orientated and which refused in the main to accept the validity of Masonic lodges that admitted Jewish members.

Another was the Loge St. John de L'Aurore Naissant established in Frankfurt am Main and chartered in 1807 by the Grand Orient of France while Germany was under Napoleonic occupation. Its name translates in English as the Lodge of the Rising Dawn. Its Hebrew name was the Chabrath Zereh Boqer Aour, which appeared in the mysterious *Cipher Manuscripts* with which the Hermetic Order of the Golden Dawn was founded. It attracted Jews and Christians, some of whom had been members in the Asiatic Brethren. These various names were all a bit of a mouthful and so the lodge was simply known as the Jewish Lodge.

After Napoleon was defeated, the German authorities put one obstacle after another in the way of the Jewish Lodge and to all outward appearances it withered on the vine. However, there are indications that it survived, its members believing that they alone in secret conclave guarded the eternal flame of the true Rosicrucian lineage.

In a lecture Westcott claimed that Bulwer-Lytton revealed he had been admitted as a Frater of the German Rosicrucian College at Frankfurt am Main, which was closed in 1850. Students of Egyptian Freemasonry have suggested that the date of Lytton's initiation was between 1841 and 1843 (probably very soon after the publication in 1842 of his celebrated occult novel, *Zanoni*) when a branch of the Asiatic Brethren was still operating in Frankfurt. Lytton did reveal to Rosicrucian scholar Hargrave Jennings that he possessed "the cipher sign of the 'Initiate,'" adding that the Rosicrucian Brotherhood remained in existence but not by a name outsiders would recognise.

In his observations upon the German occult scene, Guénon referred to "Austria's" novel *Ghost Land* in which "Louis," its autobiographical subject, speaks of his association as a boy medium with "the German branch of a very ancient secret order, the name and distinctive characteristics of which neither I nor any other human being is privileged to mention." In the absence of permission to give a name to the group Louis calls them the Berlin Brotherhood, which we referenced in our discussion on Emma Hardinge Britten and her affiliation with the sinister Orphic Society.

Ghost Land describes how the lodge's work revolves around scientific experiments conducted with the aid of drugs, vapours, aromal essences, magical spells, dancing and spinning around in whirling Dervish-style, staring into crystals or other glittering substances and the eyes of snakes and running water; in fact, by the use of any method that lifts one's spirit into the superior world by which to gain occult objectives. Louis describes with beautiful lyrical flair an early experience with attaining a state of "lucidity":

> Like a mountain bearing down upon my shoulders, columns of fiery cloud-like matter seemed to stream from the professor's fingers [a reference to a character in the book named Felix von Marx], enter

---

[43] MacIntosh, C., *The Rosicrucians: The History, Mythology, and Rituals of an Esoteric Order,* Red Wheel Weiser, 1998.

[44] Guénon, R., *L'Erreur Spirite*, 2nd ed. Paris: Editions Traditionelles, 1952.

my whole being, and finally crush me beneath their terrific force into a state where resistance, appeal, or even speech was impossible. A vague feeling that death was upon me filled my bewildered brain, and a sensation of an undefinable yearning to escape from a certain thraldom in which I believed myself to be held, oppressed me with agonizing force.

At length it seemed as if this intense longing for liberation was gratified. I stood, and seemed to myself to stand, free of the professor's crushing hand, free of my body, free of every clog or chain but an invisible and yet tangible cord which connected me with the form I had worn, but which now, like a garment I had put off, lay sleeping in an easy-chair beneath me. As for my real self, I stood balanced in the air, as I thought at first, about four feet above and a little on one side of my slumbering mortal envelope; presently, however, I perceived that I was treading on a beautiful crystalline form of matter, pure and transparent, and hard as diamond, but sparkling, bright, luminous and ethereal. There was a wonderful atmosphere, too, surrounding me on all sides.

Above and about me, it was discernible as a radiant, sparkling mist, enclosing my form, piercing the walls and ceiling, and permitting my vision to take in an almost illimitable area of space, including the city, fields, plains, mountains, and scenery, together with the firmament above my head, spangled with stars, and irradiated by the soft beams of the tranquil moon. All this vast realm of perception opened up before me in despite of the enclosing walls, ceiling and other obstacles of matter that surrounded me. These were obstacles no more.

I saw through them as if they had been thin air; and what is more I knew that I could not only pass through them with perfect ease, but that any piece of ponderable matter in the apartment, the very furniture itself, if it were only brought into the solvent of the radiant fire mist that surrounded me, would dissolve and become, like me and like my atmosphere, so soluble that it could pass, just as I could, through everything material.

I saw, or seemed to see, that I was now all force; that I was soul loosed from the body save by the invisible cord which connected me with it; also that I was in the realm of soul, the soul of matter; and that as my soul and the soul-realm in which I had now entered, was the real force which kept matter together, I could just as easily break the atoms apart and pass through them as one can put a solid body into the midst of water or air.

Transcendental experiences such as these were keenly sought by occult practitioners who wished to obtain cosmic powers with which to achieve impossible possibilities. For dedicated exponents of the magical arts spiritualism, Theosophy and other similarly esoteric branches were little more than sideshows to the real business of serious occultism.

Lytton, for example, attended séances out of curiosity but his refusal to come out in support of the table-rapping community upset spiritualists. He believed that phenomena were not generated by the spirits of the dead but by elemental forces or by the power of the mind. Lytton preferred ceremonial magic, which produced phenomena incompatible with the scientific precepts of the day but which were decidedly not generated by the spirits of the departed. On the contrary, occultists like Lytton and Eliphas Levi sought help from other invisible forces, contact with which was a dicey business but worth the risk for the attainment of magical powers. Lytton and his kind occupied an occult world of the imagination from which by magic, sex, drugs and meditation one can conjure up "forms more real than the living man."

But attain them at what price? We should remind ourselves that occult practitioners had no compunction in involving young children, especially females in their activities. In *Ghost Land*, Louis describes the travails of a young girl named Constance who is a captive medium of the Berlin Brotherhood:

> As the months glided on, I found that the spirit of the poor victim [Constance] had been trained to become a "flying soul," and was, at most of the séances I attended, liberated for some purposes which I could only guess at…These soon began to affect her health and spirits. She pined away like a flower deprived of light and air. Frailer and more ethereal grew that slight, sylph-like form; more wan and hollow waxed the once tinted cheek and lips day by day. Her large blue eyes became sunken and hollow…the phantom of the victim presented unmistakable tokens of being a sacrifice, and that an unpicked one, to the dark magicians with whom she was so fatally associated…
>
> There was no speculation in the fixity of the lustrous eyes; but the look of hopeless sorrow and blank despair, which had grown to be a permanent expression on her waking features, was even more piteously depicted on the magnetic shade. She did not see me, touch or know me but the bruised spirit fled…to do the bidding of the remorseless men that had possessed themselves of her helpless soul.

There is no evidence that Lytton personally participated in these sordid practices but his worldview was decidedly elitist and synarchic. He believed that creation is a hierarchical construct, writing in *Zanoni*, "The wiser the few in one generation, the wiser will be the multitude in the next!" The author elaborates on this in a very revealing passage in

Zanoni featuring a Chaldean initiate named Mejnour. (In his works Lytton referred not to a Rosicrucian esoteric tradition but to a far older illustrious order that dates back to Pythagoras and the ancient Chaldean magicians.) Mejnour tells Zanoni that he wishes to:

> ...form a mighty and numerous race with a force and power sufficient to permit them to acknowledge to mankind their majestic conquests and dominion; to become the true lords of this planet, invaders perchance of others, masters of the inimical and malignant tribes by which at the moment we are surrounded; a race that may proceed, in their deathless destinies, from stage to stage of celestial glory, and rank at last among the nearest ministrants and agents gathered around the Throne of Thrones. What matter a thousand victims if one convert to our band.

Presented with these words in 1933, not knowing that they were written in the first half of the nineteenth century, one would have been forgiven for thinking that they were an extract from Chancellor Hitler's new Nazi party manifesto. But, of course, Hitler and his acolytes were deeply occultist; they did not have to search too far back in Germany's esoteric past to find the provenance and extreme racialist sentiments by which to drive their policies of subjugation and mass sacrifice.

The story of nineteenth-century esotericism is, thus, the emergence of German-centric occult dominance whose influence and power is disseminated by a small number of high-level adepts with exceptionally careful planning and an eye to the long game. In Britain the occult charge was led by a caucus of senior establishment figures spearheaded by the master, Lytton. It is a scenario that is supported by the events underpinning the geopolitical scene in Europe.

The rapid handovers of imperial power in Germany during 1888 took place soon after the dissolution of the League of Three Emperors, an alliance between Austria-Hungary, Germany and Russia. The dissolution occurred as a consequence of Russia's refusal to renew the League for the third time. Chancellor Bismarck had cleverly engineered its formation fifteen years earlier to neutralize disagreements between Austria-Hungary and Russia over spheres of influence in the Balkans and to isolate Germany's principle enemy, France. After the dissolution of the League, Bismarck struck a separate accord with the Tsar and his government but it pained the Chancellor to see that this new accord did not stop Alexander making closer ties with France.

Queen Victoria could see as well as any astute statesperson that the break up of the League, Russia's change of policy and the new dynamic in Germany's imperial leadership were shaking Europe to its foundations, very possibly bringing it a step closer to all-out war.

The BBC's excellent 1974, 13-part television documentary, *The Fall of Eagles*, revealed that six weeks after his succession twenty-nine year old Wilhelm confided to Tsar Alexander and Bismarck at Peterhof that he hated his grandmother. He despised Victoria's presumption in regarding herself as the absolute head of all the members of the Coburg tribe and its tributaries. She was a meddlesome old crone, he said, who loved nothing more than to sew discord and conflict among the other great powers on the continent for England's benefit. Well, that would change, Wilhelm had sworn, by God it would. At which point in the conversation, Tsar and Chancellor had looked each other in the eye and knew that Wilhelm's arrival on the throne was destined to rock Europe to its foundations. The ageing Bismarck was glad he would not survive to see it while Alexander, mindful of the assassination of his father seven years earlier by republican forces, was equally fearful of the increasing aspirations of Russian peasantry.

Historians have argued that in the build-up to this cycle of occult intrigue and social upheaval the task of inventing a "Hitler" was already underway. English Freemasons were concerned that they were losing their leading position of influence in Europe at a time when French Freemasonry was growing in power; while masons in Italy were using London to launch revolutions across the Continent. At the same time Karl Marx, living in England in the 1850s, was achieving successes in influencing an increasingly disaffected and restless workforce.

To remedy this paradigm shift in power and aristocratic control, over the next twenty to thirty years English Freemasons organized secret societies to be placed in strategic positions in nations throughout Europe to influence the adoption of political, financial and educational policies that would benefit Great Britain. Some of these groups such as the Fabian Society, established in 1884, operated strictly on political and socio-economic lines, while others reverted to eastern mysticism and occult practices such as practised in Blavatsky's Theosophical Society and, in 1888, the newly founded Hermetic Order of the Golden Dawn. All that was needed to complete the stratagem was the creation of an appropriate political force led by a charismatic leader to combat the spread of communism among the working classes.

It is a notable fact that Adolf Hitler (born 20 April 1889) was conceived in the weeks prior to the murder of Martha Tabram. Those who seek meaning in such coincidences might say that Hitler's conception was a sign from the dark gods that they were about to roll up their sleeves and hurl evil into the world, the like of which had never been seen before.

The League of the Three Emperors: Francis Joseph, William I, and Alexander II

So, the game was afoot. There was to be a copious sewing of Teutonic occult ideals in Britain through the establishment of several esoteric orders. The gardeners that would broadcast the seeds were predominantly from within the mysterious Orphic Society with which, as we have seen, Emma Hardinge Britten enjoyed close relations as she progressed from a spiritualist perspective towards a more distinctly occultist mindset in her metaphysical activities. Recall that Britten wrote in 1888 that the Orphic Society was the product of the organisation commenced by master adepts around 1830 of "true occultism" into secret associations in England, precisely those of a Kabbalistic nature derived in part from Hebrew doctrines we have been describing in preceding pages.

In 1865 Robert Wentworth Little in collaboration with fellow occultists established the Societas Rosicruciana in Anglia, an order consisting of nine degrees of initiation. The S.R.I.A.'s foundation documents were said to have appeared by chance discovery in the Freemasons' Hall. These were then embellished by Kenneth Mackenzie to endow them with the necessary "knowledge and authority" based on initiation procedures employed by Rosicrucian adepts from the then defunct Gold- und Rosenkreuz order in Germany. At a meeting of the S.R.I.A. in July 1870, Little, a future member of Warren's Quatuor Coronati Lodge, proposed that Lord Lytton of Knebworth be elected an Honorary Member and invited to serve as Grand Patron of the Order. Little's proposal was seconded by future Golden Dawn co-founder, William R. Woodman. Lytton evidently held the S.R.I.A in low regard for it appears that he was made its Grand Patron without his consent and he formally resigned in 1872, having not attended a single meeting.

Mackenzie was also not wedded to the S.R.I.A. He did not officially join it until 1872 and was more concerned with compiling his *pièce de résistance*, the *Royal Masonic Cyclopaedia* in which he announces the occult revival of the late nineteenth century. In this statement Mackenzie is referring to the objectives of Richard James Morrison's recently established Order. In his 1869 publication, *Almanac*, Morrison announced his intention to "resuscitate in England, and spread throughout Europe, India and America—the Most Ancient Order of the Suastica; or The Brotherhood of the Mystic Cross" in three degrees: Apprentice Brothers, Tao Sze (or Doctors of Reason) and Grand Master. Morrison said the original Order had been founded by the sage Foe in Tibet in about 1027 BCE. In 1870 the Order was duly established, meriting inclusion in Mackenzie's encyclopaedia with the remark that "this order was very little encouraged in England."

Orphic Society member ("Magian") Morrison grandiosely signed himself "Zadkiel the Seer," the cabalistic name for the Angel of Jupiter, "harbinger of wisdom, peace, freedom and reform." Morrison subsequently passed the "Zadkiel" mantle on to fellow Orphic Society member, Alfred J. Pearce.

Much more was to follow in the high-energy race by "master adepts" (for which read "Teuton elect") to establish multiple orders in Britain. We will briefly defer a critique of the deeply occult Hermetic Brotherhood of Luxor because although it began its work in 1870 it was not brought to public attention until 1884. Chronologically, therefore, the next Society to rear its head publicly was the brainchild of retired soldier, Lieutenant Francis George Irwin (1823-1898).

In 1873 Irwin reported contact with an entity calling itself "Count Cagliostro" (Count Alessandro di Cagliostro, pseudonym for eighteenth-century Italian magician Giuseppe Balsamo) and given, via the crystal used for their communications, the history and rituals of the Fratres Lucis. Other names used by the Order were Brotherhood of the Cross of Light and Order of the [swastika symbol].[45] Its objectives were the study and practice of "Natural Magic, Mesmerism, Science of Death and of Life, Immortality, Kabbalah, Alchemy, Necromancy, Astrology and Magic in all its branches."[46] Cagliostro told Irwin that Fratres Lucis had been established in fourteenth-century Florence and had counted among its subsequent members: Robert Fludd, Thomas Vaughan, Saint-Germain, Martines de Pasqually, Swedenborg, Eliphas Levi, Mesmer and Cagliostro himself. Mackenzie's *Cyclopaedia* provides more detail on the Florentine order. It was established in 1498 (since confirmed as 1499) and was linked to the publication of the *Hypnerotomachia Poliphili* or the *Dream of Poliphilo*, a masterpiece of early printing.

Emanuela Kretzulesco-Quaranta[47] has interpreted *Hypnerotomachia Poliphili* as the collective wisdom of a cadre of esoteric philosophers set out in the guise of a picturesque novel in order to preserve the doctrines when they were under persecution by the Roman Church. The Florentine society may well have been the "very different secret society" that Louis referred to grandiosely in *Ghost Land*:

> Its actual nature is only recognized, spoken or thought of as a dream, a memory of the past, evoked like a phantom from the realms of tradition or myth; yet as surely as there is a spirit in man, is there in the world a spiritual, though nameless and almost unknown

[45] Hamill, J., ed. *The Rosicrucian Seer. Magical Writings of Frederick Hockley*, Wellingborough: Aquarian. 1986.

[46] Howe, E., "Fringe Masonry in England, 1870-1885." *Ars Quatuor Coronatorum* 85 (1972), 242-295. [1972a].

[47] Kretzulesco-Quaranta, E., *Les jardin de songes: Poliphile et la mystique de la Renaissance*. Paris: Les Belles Lettres. 1986. (First ed., 1976).

association of men, drawn together by the bonds of soul, associated by those interior links which never fade or perish, belonging to all times, places and nations alike.

Few can attain to the inner light of these spiritually associated brethren, or apprehend the significance of their order; enough that it is, has been, and will be, until all men are spiritualized enough to partake of its exalted dispensations. Some members of this sublime Brotherhood were in session in England...

But have we not already encountered an order named Fratres Lucis? Yes, Ecker's Frankfurt Lodge later re-styled as the Asiatic Brethren, which had been active in Germany seventy years earlier and wielded enormous influence over subsequent occult developments in Europe. The only new feature of Irwin's Fratres Lucis was the reference to Cagliostro and one cannot rule out that the esoteric affiliations of the Frankfurt Lodge were similarly linked, if not actually spelled out.

It is as if Irwin's Florentine story was designed to relegate the Frankfurt Lodge to a relatively junior position in the rank and file of Masonic initiatives that were rolled out in the West in the nineteenth century. A cynic might say that the Teutonic influence was being heavily downplayed in an effort to shield it from serious scrutiny. In addition to Irwin, the Brotherhood of the Cross of Light's membership included Frederick Hockley, Kenneth Mackenzie and Benjamin Cox.

In 1883 the same quartet joined chemist, metallurgist and S.R.I.A. member Frederick Holland in founding an alchemical order, the Society of Eight. The remaining members were freemason John Yarker, London Coroner William Wynn Westcott and, possibly, clergyman and practising alchemist William Alexander Ayton. Both of the latter would play a part in instigating the Golden Dawn. It was Holland who in the course of his S.R.I.A. activities came across keen occult student Samuel Liddell MacGregor Mathers, who went on to join the Society of Eight (which perhaps should then have been renamed as Mathers' membership increased the roll to nine!).

The rush to establish new Orders went on unabated. In 1884 came the establishment of Anna Kingsford and Edward Maitland's mystical Christian Hermetic Society and the first public appearance of the H.B. of L. The two orders could not have been more different.

Virtually unknown to the wider public, Kingsford (née Bonus) was a leading figure in Victorian esoteric circles. She had always believed she was remarkable. Many children in their early years see out of a corner of an eye things that are invisible to grown ups: a light, a shape, movement, even a figure. Eventually, these heightened perceptions, reckoned by some to be the vestigial links to the world of spirit, fade.

By the age of seven they have usually disappeared except that in Anna's case they not only remained, they intensified. Kingsford could also see a person's aura which she believed was a secret window into one's innermost nature.

As she entered her teenage years Kingsford questioned all she had been taught. Blessed with precocious intellect, Anna published a novella, *Beatrice: a Tale of the Early Christian*, a tale written with astonishing maturity for a girl of thirteen. Gradually, Kingsford became convinced that traditional Christianity was a shroud behind which lie deeper and more beautiful truths. She came to believe that the Bible was wholly allegorical: at its heart a description of the destiny of the soul. She regarded the Crucifixion of Christ and of other solar saviours as a spiritual experience that one must undertake in a soul's evolutionary journey.

At twenty-one Anna married her cousin, Anglican priest Algernon Godfrey Kingsford. The marriage produced a daughter. However, when Anna was shown the newborn infant her only feeling was one of revulsion and asked that it should removed from her sight.

Algernon admired his wife's mystical character and was neither surprised nor put out when five years after their marriage Anna was accepted into the Catholic Church by Cardinal Manning and, inspired by visitations from a spirit she believed was the Magdalene, adopted the name Anna Mary Magdalen Johanna Kingsford. In the same year, Kingsford bought *The Lady's Own Paper*. Her role as editor brought her into contact with prominent women of the day, including the writer and feminist Frances Power Cobbe. It was an article by Cobbe on vivisection in *The Lady's Own Paper* that sparked Kingsford's lifelong interest in the subject. A few months later Kingsford wrote to Maitland,[48] a gentleman of straitened means who supplemented his meagre income by writing. Kingsford referred to the fact that they had both had articles published in the same magazine and that they evidently shared mutual interests. Should they meet, she asked?

Like Kingsford, Maitland claimed the gifts of a sensitive which, he said, enabled him to diagnose a person's spiritual health and to recall his self-professed past lives, which included Saint John the Divine, Daniel and Marcus Aurelius. Maitland was also a vegan and anti-vivisectionist who helped found and assume the vice-presidency of the Theosophical Society. The pair recognised in each other like-minded souls whose talents would advance the cause of anti-vivisectionism and the development of Blavatsky's new order.

---

[48] Maitland, E., *Anna Kingsford. Her Life, Letters, Diary and Work. By her Collaborator*. 2 vols. 3rd ed. Ed. S.H. Hart. London: Watkins, 1913. (First ed., 1896).

132

Alessandro Cagliostro, after Francesco Bartholozzi

Remarkably, Algernon Kingsford was all for the partnership, raising no objections to his wife working arm-in-arm with father figure Maitland. Algernon was confident that the relationship could not be anything other than platonic because he knew very well that intrinsically his wife was a cold, unemotional woman to whom sexual matters were an anathema. Kingsford told Henry Olcott in 1884 that she had never experienced human affection but did love her pet guinea pig, whose anniversary of passing she kept faithfully.

Together, Kingsford and Maitland travelled to Paris, one of the few cities in Europe whose medical schools admitted women. London was not among them. Kingsford enrolled at the Faculté de Médecine Paris Descartes to begin a career in medicine. Even in Paris's relatively progressive environment this was an extraordinary step for a woman but she was determined to succeed, driven by her desire to study vegetarianism and to promote her anti-vivisection beliefs.

Anna also wanted to prove that women are capable of rational thought and learning complex skills, traits almost universally ignored or belittled in Victorian patriarchal society. Much of the opposition to vivisection that had emerged in Victorian England was expressed in revulsion at the research being conducted in France. British anti-vivisectionists tricked their way into Paris teaching hospitals, gathered intelligence on what was happening and disrupted lectures. This was the toxic atmosphere in the city's medical establishments when the pair arrived. Anna wrote her husband that she had found her hell in the Faculté, a "Hell more real and awful than any I have yet met with elsewhere."

As well as being at the heart of the rapidly evolving European esoteric movement, Paris was also the centre of a revolution in the study of physiology. Much of this progress had been achieved as a result of experiments on animals, particularly dogs, and mostly conducted without anaesthetic.

Faculty researchers were enthusiastic participants in these abhorrent practices. Laboratory technicians would shout, "Tais-toi, pauvre bête!" as they cut deep into a shrieking canine. The sounds of animals' piteous screams and the dissectors' mocking cries would soak Kingsford in sweat from head to toe, prompting her to pray to God to remove her from the awful place.

Kingsford continued to receive visions and believed herself to be communicating with "genii," spirit entities that revealed truths about the afterlife and the correct way for humans to live. She and Maitland believed that "every human spirit-soul has attached to him a genius or daimon, as with Socrates; a ministering spirit, as with the apostles; or an angel, as with Jesus."

Anna Kingsford

Edward Maitland

Kingsford and Maitland's increasingly powerful psychic experiences convinced them that they were becoming the recipients of a new revelation. Seeking an esoteric basis with which to associate this revelation, they concluded that their work corresponded to an end-of-days scenario (there was much talk in esoteric circles that the end of the world would occur in 1881), and to the ensuing inauguration of the Age of Michael prophesised by Trithemius.

Anna's mediumistic communications accelerated rapidly. She claimed visitations from Swedenborg who told her: "Do not be too kind to the Christians." She had visions of the Greek gods who appeared to her as naked and shining like silver.[49] She even claimed a visitation from renowned 1st Century Greek philosopher Apollonius of Tyana, reported by his contemporaries to have achieved heavenly assumption.

The cumulative effect of these magical experiences was to formulate a cogent body of mystical Christian revelations. Before leaving Paris, Kingsford and Maitland came upon *Isis Unveiled* and learned of the existence of the Theosophical Society. Although not wholly impressed by Blavatsky's disorganised approach to writing, the pair were delighted that here was someone who appeared to be thinking along parallel lines. In London they joined the British Theosophical Society whose members were privileged to hear lectures during May and June 1881 from these new recruits on the "new gospel."

It was time to put these teachings together in a coherent form. Anna truly believed that she could make a very powerful contribution to the advancement of people's spiritual understanding. Thanks to financial support from Lady Caithness, *The Perfect Way, or the Finding of Christ* was published in 1882. Anna saw its teachings as a key to those seeking another way to find their inner spirit. She had sought inspiration for its foundations in the great family of mystery religions that spread around the Mediterranean in the early centuries before and after Jesus.

Nothing like it had been seen before. It sought to explain the misinterpretation and misuse of biblical texts over the centuries and described the potential for Christianity to become much more of a personal communication between believers and God and a lot less reliant on rigid tradition and the clergy.

The Perfect Way was also founded on a belief in the doctrine of reincarnation, an extremely divisive issue of the day. Orthodox spiritualists and theosophist Christians were aghast. Journalist S.C. Hall called it "a repulsive and unnatural doctrine [put about] by emissaries of Satan."

Very quickly this groundbreaking work came to the attention of the

---

[49] Ibid.

Blavatsky circle (although HPB herself was not an admirer), and in 1883 Anna was appointed president of the British Theosophical Society. However, controversy concerning her overarching focus on Christian text to the exclusion of a balanced consideration of Eastern philosophies led to bitter differences with leading Theosophist Alfred Sinnett and resulted in her parting company with the Society in 1884.

Seeking a way to defuse the mounting tensions, Olcott offered Anna a charter to found her own lodge, The Hermetic Lodge of the Theosophical Society. This move saved the day and prevented the breakup of the London Lodge of the Theosophical Society.

Kingsford immediately renamed her new group The Hermetic Society, which became instantly popular. Oscar Wilde was one of its first members. Hermeticism is a philosophical and religious belief system based primarily upon the writings of Egyptian sage, Hermes Trismegistus ("Thrice Great"). The movement can be traced to Alexandria in the first centuries of the Common Era, where it unified elements of Jewish and Christian mysticism with Hellenistic philosophy and Egyptian occultist beliefs.

The resulting composite tradition was attractive to Muslim scholars in the early Middle Ages and to European intellectuals at the dawn of the Renaissance period. In particular, the notion that the universe operated on orderly principles, represented as cosmic vibrations in the substance of the "All," was instrumental not only in the evolution of western occultism but also in the development of the modern scientific method. This connection can be seen most clearly in the hermetical and alchemical treatises written by some of the most influential thinkers of their respective eras, including Giordano Bruno, John Dee, Francis Bacon and Isaac Newton.

Despite Kingsford and Maitland's success in promulgating their new style of esoteric Christianity, Anna was going downhill mentally and physically. Nevertheless, she found the time and energy to establish the Paris Anti-Vivisection Society with Victor Hugo as Honorary President. Cruelty to animals incensed her to the extent that she sought ways to kill vivisectionists by occult means. She compared them to black magicians and their methods to blood sacrifice in ritual magic.

Kingsford believed she had developed a way to kill vivisectors by the occult power of dreaming, which she sought to enhance through sustained inhalation of chloroform. Anna's belief in her occult killing powers started with a horrifying dream aboard a runaway train at night. In her dream Anna was saved by Maitland who helped her to uncouple the engine (a dream that conjures up all sorts of Freudian images). Kingsford put a curse on Professor Claude Bernard who had subjected animals to heat tolerance experiments that involved baking them to death. She believed that his death in 1878 was a direct consequence of her astrally directed efforts.

To consolidate her powers so that she could kill more vivisectors, in 1886 Kingsford agreed to a proposal by Maitland to study practical magic. Her tutor was MacGregor Mathers, a man well versed in Hermetic and Kabbalistic science. Her first attempt in using her enhanced powers was directed against Louis Pasteur who lent credence to her efforts by falling dangerously ill. The mortality among Pasteur's patients also rose significantly. Buoyed by this apparent success, Kingsford tried her hand at killing Professor Paul Bert and claimed success for his death from dysentery.

Anna had little time remaining to further develop her occult faculties. Plagued by constant illness exacerbated by chloroform dependency, she died from pneumonia in February 1888. Maitland continued to evangelise Kingsford's teachings long after her death, founding the Esoteric Christian Union in 1891 to promote her beliefs.

The esoteric wing of Victorian English Christianity did not begin and end with Kingsford and Maitland. Among its number were two other leading female figures: Mary Ann South (1817-1910) and Anne Judith Penny (1825-1893).

Mary and her father Thomas collaborated on a book project[50] to reveal how ancient metaphysical teachings had been concealed over the centuries in alchemic, Hermetic and other sacred writings. Immediately after its publication the pair, worried about revealing the information they were putting into the public domain, got cold feet and burned all the books except for twenty-four copies retained for friends and confidants. It is not known just what it was they were so desperate to keep secret, although it is interesting to speculate if the Souths' work, published in 1850, was a source of metaphysical inspiration behind Westcott and Hort's decision to embark three years later on their *New Greek Testament* based on hitherto unseen Oriental textual material. After her marriage to Reverend Alban Thomas Atwood in 1859, Mary, like Kingswood and Penny, espoused the anti-vivisection cause. In 1886 Mary Atwood offered Alfred Sinnett her father's extensive library of esoteric and alchemical works.

Anne Judith Penny was a member of the Behemenist circle (followers of Jakob Böhme) who wrote in 1889 about age-old practices of ritual blood sacrifices. What she wrote was uneasy reading for those in her day who wanted to accept ancient and pagan religions as valid

[50] South, M., *Suggestive Inquiry into the Hermetic Mystery with a Dissertation on the More Celebrated Alchemical Philosophers,* London, Trelawney Saunders, 1850

and sacred. Penny believed that the sacrifice of animals in ancient times was necessary to demonstrate the efficacy of blood in attracting good invisible agents and repelling bad ones. Further, she posited that in episodes of sudden and violent death, a multitude of subordinate soul-entities are released from bondage and reinvigorated by higher spiritual influences, thus reflecting the spiritual outpouring conditional on the shedding of Christ's blood.

In other esoteric Christian groups, the influential Anglo-Catholic movement was agitating for the reinstatement of some older Christian traditions of faith and their inclusion into Anglican liturgy and theology. Its supporters regarded Anglicanism as a seamless expression of the "Attributes of the Church" of traditional Christian ecclesiology (One, Holy, Catholic and Apostolic), as expressed in the Nicene-Constantinopolitan Creed. The Anglo-Catholic movement was powered by a number of different factions, one such being the Order of Corporate Reunion led by eccentric, Dr. Rev. Frederick George Lee. Lee's Order counted among its membership four founders of the extremist Thames Legitimist Club, which sought to restore the Jacobeans to the British throne. Lee was also prominent in the Order of the White Rose, one of whose chief objectives according to the *Legitimist Kalendar* was to "oppose all that tends to democracy whether within these realms or beyond the sea." This wholly fascist ambition was revived fifty years later when General Lederowski formulated the objectives of the Jesuit branch established within the SS.

The Thames Valley Legitimists, whose members included Theosophist Annie Leadbeater and occultist MacGregor Matthers, received a letter from Cardinal Rampolla conveying the "choicest blessing of Heaven" from Pope Pius IX. The Club, which had campaigned against the Italian Government's breach of their promise to leave Rome a Papal city, was informed that: "such an act of homage is beyond measure pleasing and acceptable to the august Pontiff," a remarkable statement to make to a humble Anglican.

Dr Lee was subsequently re-baptised in 1877 and received into the episcopy by the Archbishops of Venice and Milan and by the wonderfully titled Byzantine Abbot-General of Ordo Mechitaristarum Venetiarum. Pius was persuaded to turn a blind eye. The Vatican's stated aim for proceeding with these extraordinary protocols was to establish a number of Anglican churchmen with orders valid in Rome. Quite why the Vatican bigwigs rolled out the red carpet for an English cleric with a relatively small congregation is unclear.

When Lee was not expending his energies on Anglo-Catholic

business, he exercised his esoteric interests by writing books on the supernatural: *Glimpses of the Supernatural* in1877, *More Glimpses of the World Unseen* in 1880, and *Lights and Shadows, being Examples of the Supernatural* in 1894.

Meanwhile, those disillusioned with Theosophy could find a home in the newly established Hermetic Brotherhood of Luxor. Whereas Kingsford's Hermetic Society promised a new perspective on Christian mysticism, the H.B. of L. offered practical occultism. Moreover, much of the H.B. of L.'s teachings was of a sexual nature in contrast to the relative puritanism of Blavatsky and her circle. Its first appearance was subtly phrased in the form of an advertisement in the back pages of the *Divine Pomander of Hermes Mercurius Trismegistus*, published in 1884 by Robert Fryar. It read:

TO WHOM IT MAY CONCERN

Students of the Occult Science, searchers after truth and Theosophists who may have been disappointed in their expectations of Sublime Wisdom being freely dispensed by HINDOO MAHATMAS, are cordially invited to send in their names to the Editor of this Work, when, if found suitable, can be admitted, after a short probationary term, as members of an Occult Brotherhood, who do not boast of their knowledge or attainments, but teach freely and without reserve all they find worthy to receive.

N.B. All communications should be addressed "Theosi" c/o Robt. H. Fryar, Bath.

CORRECTION

"Correspondents" will please read and address "Theosi" as "THEON."

Enquirers received a letter asking for a photograph and a horoscope. For a small fee a horoscope could be provided for those without one. The select few that gained admittance into the Brotherhood received mail order lessons and a mentor by way of a penpal. The name of the order printed on a slip of paper was burned after reading. By 1886 Fryar was thoroughly disillusioned, claiming that the leaders of the H.B. of L. had cheated him. The Theosophical Society's journal *Lucifer* published Fryar's complaint, even naming the H.B. of L.'s leaders:

For the purpose of correcting any prejudicial suspicion or erroneous misrepresentation of myself, arising from the insertion of the note at the end of the *Bath Occult Reprint Edition* of the *Divine Pomander* as associated with Society of the H.B. of L. known to me only through the names of Peter Davidson and T.H. Burgoyne, alias D'Alton, Dalton, etc, and the supposed adept to be a Hindu of questionable antecedents," I wish it be understood I have no confidence, sympathy or connection therewith, direct or indirect...

There are unresolved questions about the founding principals of the H.B. of L. The adept in question is Max Theon to whom we turn presently but we begin our review with the Brotherhood's "middle management": Scotsmen Peter Davidson (H.B. of L.'s "Provincial Grand Master for the North" until 1886) and Thomas Henry Burgoyne.

It is Davidson's signature that appears on an official document of the Order, which indicates that it began its work in 1870. As a violinmaker and occasional distillery worker, Davidson struggled to make a decent living for his wife and five children. At the same time he was an occultist to his fingertips, paying especial devotion to Rosicrucianism and its claims that music can play a profound role in developing one's esoteric insights. He joined the Theosophical Society in the early 1880s and made a notable contribution to *The Theosophist* on the consecration of magical mirrors by sex orgies, a theme that would become a key feature in the occult work of the H.B. of L. Davidson claimed that through his own work with magic mirrors he was in contact with a Tibetan adept.

Little is known about Thomas Henry Burgoyne's early life except that he once made a living as a grocer in Leeds. He claimed to have been passionate about occultism since childhood and he first put his head above the parapet when he began contacting well-known occult figures in 1882. One of these was

Max Theon

---

[51] Chanel, C., Deveney, J., Godwin, J., *The Hermetic Brotherhood of Luxor. Initiatic and Historical Documents of an Order of Practical Occultism*. York Beach: Weister, 1995.

Rev. William Alexander Ayton, vicar of Chacombe in Oxfordshire, who later said that Burgoyne had made to him a horrible confession concerning his use of black magic.

Burgoyne's occult ambitions were put on hold when in January 1883 he and an accomplice were sentenced to seven months' imprisonment for mail fraud. On his release Burgoyne rekindled his relationship with Davidson and took up the role of Secretary of the Order. In this capacity, Theon tasked Burgoyne with soliciting candidates for membership in the Order. Ayton was one such approached, becoming "Provincial Grand Master for the South." It was only later that Ayton learned that the Secretary was actually one Thomas Dalton who in 1882 served Max Theon as a seer. In this role Dalton was put in touch with "entities" which, it was suspected, were the real sources of occult power for the H.B. of L.

Theon tasked Davidson and Burgoyne / Dalton to guide the H.B. of L.'s development in America. The pair embarked on this task in 1886, Burgoyne using the pen name Zanoni, and Davidson, Mejnour. The H.B. of L. had planned to establish a colony in California but realising it lacked the funds to support such an expensive initiative the pair settled on Georgia.

Max Theon, the Brotherhood's "Chief Executive," is a true enigma. It is known that he was a son of a Polish rabbi, possibly a leader of the Frankist reformation among the Jews of Warsaw. Like the Khlysts, the Frankists gained notoriety for conducting orgiastic rites to evoke ecstasy for use as a sacrament. Theon's real name may have been Maximilian Louis Bimstein, possibly born in 1850.

Theon packed his suitcase and set off to learn from Arabic, Hindu and Jewish masters. It is believed that his first initiation may have been as a Zoharist, an erotically ecstatic sect of Chassidic Jews from whom he learned about the integration of sexuality and spirituality. It is speculated that in Cairo he came into contact with Blavatsky's old pal and Coptic occultist, Paolos Metamon. (It is even rumoured that Metamon was Max's father!) Theon's famous student, Mirra Alfassa ("The Mother"), co-creator of Integral Yoga, claimed that Blavatsky had been Max's student in Egypt, which begs the question as to whether she and Olcott were two of the very first members of the

William Alexander Ayton

142

H.B. of L. well before it became known publicly. In his book *Visions of the Eternal Present*, Max wrote:

> In 1870 (and not in 1884, as the Theosophists claimed), an adept of calm, of the ever-existing ancient Order of the H.B. of L., after having received the consent of his fellow-initiates, decided to choose in Great Britain a neophyte who would answer his designs. He landed in Great Britain in 1873. There he discovered a neophyte who satisfied his requirements and he gradually instructed him. Later, the actual neophyte received permission to establish the Exterior Circle of the H.B. of L.

Theon was the initiate and the neophyte was Peter Davidson, a student of Rosicrucian scholar, Hargrave Jennings. The Ancient and Noble Order of H.B. of L. had a charter signed: "M. Theon, Grand Master pro temp of the Exterior Circle." Deeply esoteric, the charter read:

> We recognize the eternal existence of the Great Cause of Light, the invisible center whose vibrating soul, gloriously radiant, is the living breath, the vital principle of all that exists and will ever exist. It is from this divine summit that goes forth the invisible Power which binds the vast universe in an harmonious whole.
>
> We teach that from this incomprehensible center of Divinity emanate sparks of the eternal Spirit, which, after accomplishing their orbit, the great cycle of Necessity, constitute the sole immortal element of the human soul. Accepting thus the universal brotherhood of humanity, we reject, nevertheless, the doctrine of universal quality.
>
> We have no personal preferences and no one makes progress in "the Order" without having accomplished his assigned task thereby indicating aptitude for more advanced initiation.
>
> Remember, we teach freely, without reservation, anyone worthy of instruction.
>
> The Order devotes its energies and resources to discover and apply the hidden laws and active forces in all fields of nature, and to subjugate them to the higher will of the human soul, whose power and attributes our Order strives to develop, in order to build up the immortal individuality so that the complete spirit can say I AM.
>
> The members engage themselves, to the best of their ability, in a life of moral purity and brotherly love, abstaining from the use of intoxicants except for medicinal purposes, working for the progress of all social reforms beneficial for humanity.

Finally, the members have full freedom of thought and judgment. By no means may one member be disrespectful towards members of other religious beliefs or impose his own convictions on others.

Each member of our ancient and noble Order has to maintain, human dignity by living as an example of purity, justice and goodwill. No matter what the circumstances may be, one can become a living center of goodness, radiating virtue, nobility and truth.

Although Grand Master of the Exterior Circle of the Order, Theon appeared to play a minor role in its day-to-day running, leaving matters in the hands of Davidson. With regard to the H.B. of L.'s esoteric curriculum it contained little of Theon's own occult teaching, which he later published under the name Aia Aziz as the *Cosmic Philosophy*. This work combined Kabbalistic philosophy with Vedic elements. Max undertook this new phase of initiatic teaching in collaboration with his wife, Irish poet Mary Chrystine Woodroffe Ware, an automatic writing medium whom Max married in 1885. Max called her Alma.

With Alma at his side as seer, Max appeared to lose interest in the H.B. of L. although after the demise of the lodges in America a branch in Paris, headed by Albert Faucheux ("F.-Ch.-Barlet"), flourished under his guidance. Subsequently, Max and Alma settled in Algeria. Alfassa describes Madame Theon in this period as an extraordinary woman with great powers. In her *Collected Works*[52] Alfassa refers to miraculous experiences at Tlemcen in Algeria where she stayed to learn occultism under the tutelage of the Theons.

Alma died in 1908 after twenty-three years of marriage. Max was devastated and fell into a deep depression. He suffered terrible injuries in a car accident but lived until 1927, reportedly known to his Algerian neighbours as a reclusive miracle worker.

We come once again to 1888, the year that heralded the arrival of the Hermetic Order of the Golden Dawn. On 12 February in the month that Anna Kingsford died, William Robert Woodman, William Wynn Westcott and Samuel Liddell MacGregor

Samuel MacGregor Mathers

---

[52] *Collected Works of The Mother*, Sri Aurobindo Ashram Trust, see: http://www.sriaurobindoashram.org/ashram/mother/writings.php

Mathers signed pledges of fidelity to and thereby founded the H.O.G.D. Recall that Woodman and Westcott were also busy stirring up trouble with Warren for submitting papers on undesirable occult themes connected with Frankfurt's Jewish Lodge.

The H.O.G.D would go on to become the most influential occult society of the nineteenth century. It peaked in popularity and influence in the 1890s before ostensibly running out of steam due to internal conflicts. Members, recruited through word of mouth and by notices published in the Theosophical journal *Lucifer*, were taught to use natural magic for the advancement of one's individual spirit. Influences included ancient Egyptian religion, the Kabbalah, Christianity, Freemasonry, theurgy, alchemy, paganism, early-modern grimoires and Enochian magic such as that employed by John Dee. Indeed, Godwin points out that the founders at first made out that the Order was a continuation of the Kabbalistic School of Dr. Samuel Jacob Chayyim Falk (1710-1782), a practising magician who attained the Kabbalistic degree of Ba'al Shem (Master of the Divine Name) and was spiritual mentor to both Swedenborg and Cagliostro.

Outwardly, though, the Order was founded on the principles of equality and inclusivity. Unlike the S.R.I.A. and the Masonic movement, for example, women were allowed to join and participate in the Order in "perfect equality" with men. A number of high-profile women were admitted. Actress Maud Gonne, artist and occultist Moina Mathers, theatre patron Annie Horniman and actress-composer Florence Farr exercised particular influence. These and other women welcomed a movement that in its early years, at least for newcomers entering the Order's initial grades, focused more on philosophical and classical metaphysical teaching than ritual magic. In such an environment women believed that they could express their femininity within the context of the individual quest for esoteric spirituality. Many believed that individual spiritual transformation would also lead to advancement in social conditions. It was only after the infamous occultist (and alleged lifelong British Intelligence operative) Aleister Crowley joined the Order in 1898 did the H.O.G.D. attract its less than salutary reputation.

The occult texts that underpin the foundation of the Order, sixty folios containing magical initiation rituals together known as the *Cipher Manuscripts*, are the subject of endless speculation regarding their true origin. Variously, they were found among the papers of Frederick Hockley, discovered in a second-hand bookshop, written by Lytton,

[53] Godwin, J., *The Theosophical Enlightenment*, State University of New York Press, 1994

passed on to Kenneth Mackenzie by a Hungarian named Count Apponyi, or simply forged by Mackenzie (although Mathers at one point declared that Westcott was the forger). The papers have been dated to somewhere between 1870 and 1880. Westcott claimed to have obtained the manuscripts from Rev. Woodford, who, he said, found them in a bookstore on Wellington Road in London and passed them to his friend Westcott for deciphering.

According to Westcott's account, the manuscripts contained the address of a woman in Nuremberg named Anna Sprengel. He contacted her and in reply Sprengel chartered the first Golden Dawn temple—the Isis-Urania Temple—for the development of the rituals noted in the *Cipher Manuscripts*. She also conferred honorary grades of Adeptus Exemptus on Westcott, Mathers and Woodman. At the same time, she gave Westcott permission to sign the official documents for the charter on her behalf. The Isis-Urania Temple in London was joined that same year by the Osiris temple in Weston-super-Mare and the Horus temple in Bradford.

During a later dispute, Mathers claimed that Westcott had forged the Anna Sprengel letters. This unequivocal statement from a fellow founder has led some scholars to conclude that the Golden Dawn had been based on a forgery from its very beginnings. More recent scholarship has indicated that the *Cipher Manuscripts* were actually obtained by Westcott from the widow of Kenneth Mackenzie, who had received the manuscripts from Hungarian Count Apponyi in 1850 together with Hermetic and Rosicrucian lineages with which to found the Hermetic Order of the Golden Dawn.

So why should have Westcott sought to conceal the truth about the manuscript's origins? It should be borne in mind that besides being a co-founder of the Golden Dawn, Westcott also held the position of Supreme Magus of the S.R.I.A. It has been suggested that it was therefore in Westcott's interest to appropriate the *Cipher Manuscripts* and their Rosicrucian pedigree for the S.R.I.A. and to concoct the Sprengel story as a blind to fool his Golden Dawn partners and members. It is claimed that in carrying out this subterfuge, Wescott forged the roll books of the S.R.I.A. to portray Mackenzie as a co-founder and moved his name from #114 to 0. Accordingly, in this theory Mrs Mackenzie was among the first members to be enrolled into the Golden Dawn and swore an oath of secrecy to safeguard the origin of the rituals. Mathers bought into the story that Count Apponyi was the source of the *Cipher Manuscripts* and claimed to have re-established contact with representatives of the Hungarian's continental Order of adepts in Paris in 1891.

Mathers referred to these adepts as the "Secret Chiefs," who, he said, gave him the rituals and curriculum for the Golden Dawn's Rosicrucian Second Order, the R.R. et A.C., which he founded in 1892. There is also an opinion among scholars that the documents originated in the Jewish Lodge. It has also been argued that both the *Cipher Manuscripts* and Sprengel are a piece of composite fiction invented by Westcott and are, in fact, based on the esoteric work of Anna Kingsford.[ʲ] Irrespective of their origins, the *Cipher Manuscripts* form the basis of the Golden Dawn's ceremonial and symbolic structure. They are written in English from right to left using a Trithemius cipher consisting of a poly-alphabetic code. In the mid-nineteenth century examples of the cipher were available for study at the British Museum and so a determined party could have forged them through access to these public records.

Members passed through various grades on their path to initiation, much of the hierarchical structure for the Golden Dawn coming from the S.R.I.A. (the paired numbers attached to the Grades relating to positions on the Kabbalah Tree of Life):

> First Order (pertaining to the invisible world of the Elementals and their stewardship of Earth, Fire, Air and Water)— Introduction-Neophyte 0=0, Zelator 1=10, Theoricus 2=9, Practicus 3=8, Philosophus 4=7, Intermediate-Portal Grade;

> Second Order—Adeptus Minor 5=6, Adeptus Major 6=5, Adeptus Exemptus 7=4;

> Third Order—Magister Templi 8=3, Magus 9=2, Ipsissimus 10=1.

Through the application of certain methodological practices initiates sought to bring about changes in consciousness and the material world in accordance with the universal will. For members of the Golden Dawn the concept of "will" was equated with the consciously focused intention of one's highest or God-like Self, energized by a desire free of egotistical influences, to bring an objective into existence by magical means.

With the arrival of the Hermetic Order of the Golden Dawn, the esoteric seeker's banqueting table was complete. One in quest of hidden truths in 1888 could choose from spiritualism, Theosophy, Hermeticism, the occult and a myriad of connecting tributaries to satisfy a hunger for arcane knowledge.

Instinctively, most people are pulled to esoteric movements for the purpose of progressing from an existing relative state of spiritual

---

[54] Cicero, C. and Tabitha, S., *The Essential Golden Dawn*, Llewellyn, 2003

ignorance to one of wisdom. Those drawn to explore orders such as the Golden Dawn, on the other hand, are lured by the promise of attaining supernatural power, more usually and specifically power over others.

But can a student new to occult learning ever be certain that their decision to embark on a pathway to initiation in a Frankfurt Lodge or a Golden Dawn is not a choice made by their suggestible, subconscious self to allow them to be controlled remotely by "Secret Chiefs"?

So many eminent thinkers and philosophers over the centuries have spoken, written and warned about the existence of these hidden forces that it would be unwise to dismiss them as the imaginings of deluded minds. Accepting for argument the existence of invisible entities that delight in directing the weak minded, the vain and the gullible then where is their "Olympus"? And who are their high-level human interlocutors through whom these inimical forces channel their efforts to subvert human affairs?

In these pages, the home of the dark gods has variously been located in the "Summer-Land" (Davis), in the subterranean world of Atlantis's Vril-powered survivors (Lytton), on Alpha Centauri (Maria Oršić), in the invisible Tibetan region of the Mahatmas (Blavatsky), in the angelic realms (Swedenborg, Vintras, et al.), in the astral dimension of Agartha (Saint-Yves), in "Ghost Land" ("Austria"), and in the nature-dimension of the Elementals (the Golden Dawn). In other words, if one chooses to believe in their existence they abide here, there and everywhere but, in reality, mostly in one's dreams, nightmares and subconscious imaginings. It may even be the case that their existence is purely a product of collective human thought.

As for the adepts through whom these invisible agencies control the masses, there has been repeated reference to masters from the Germanic regions whose magical powers have quietly but determinedly fed the rising flow of the occult underground in Europe for centuries.

Might the foregoing observations bring one any closer to a more complete understanding of the events in Whitechapel in 1888? Perhaps, but for now let us tell the story of Elizabeth Stride, Jack the Ripper's next victim.

148

Dr. William Wynn Westcott

Rev. A.F.A. Woodford

Chapter 9

"Long Liz"

Saturday, 29 September 1888, Whitechapel
Swedish born Elizabeth Stride devotes two hours during a windy and showery Sunday afternoon to the cleaning of two rooms in the common lodging house at 32 Flower and Dean Street. For these services lodging house deputy Elizabeth Tanner pays her tenant 6d.

Stride is 45-years old with pale complexion, light grey eyes and curly dark brown hair. She stands 5'5" tall and is missing all the teeth in her lower left jaw. After a three months absence from No. 32, Stride has been staying at the premises during these past four days after walking out on her man, Michael Kidney. She told fellow resident, charwoman Catherine Lane that she'd had words with the man she was living with. Later, Kidney will deny they had quarrelled, saying, "It was drink that made her go away. She always returned without me going after her. I think she liked me better than any other man."

Quite by coincidence, Dr. Thomas Barnardo, a doctor who had turned to street preaching before opening what would become a famous home for destitute boys, called into the lodging house some time after Stride's arrival. He was seeking opinions on his scheme "by which children at all events could be saved at least from the contamination of the common lodging houses and the street." He entered the kitchen where female residents, clearly frightened, were discussing the recent murders. One woman said, "We're all up to no good, no one cares what becomes of us! Perhaps some of us will be killed next!" Stride was among those in the kitchen group and Barnardo would subsequently identify the body of a murdered woman as hers.

In the late afternoon Stride leaves the premises and is seen by Tanner at 6:30 p.m. at the Queen's Head Public House. They drink together and return to the lodging house. Between 7:00 p.m. and 8:00 p.m. Stride asks resident Charles Preston, a barber by trade, for the use of his clothes brush. He tells her he has mislaid it. Before departing from No. 32 Stride gives Catherine Lane a large piece of green velvet and asks her to hold on to it until her return. Stride also shows Lane the sixpence that Tanner had paid her. On her way out, Stride passes by lodging house watchman Thomas Bates, who will later say that she looked quite cheerful.

At 11:00 p.m. two labourers, J. Best (sometimes referred to as John Best) and John Gardner, were entering the Bricklayer's Arms Public House in Settles Street, north of Commercial Road (200 yards from the murder site) when they saw a woman leaving with a man of short stature. The two men were interviewed by the *Evening News* for the 1 October edition. The woman, later identified as Elizabeth Stride, was with a man who was "hugging her and kissing her." Best remarked, "As he seemed a respectably dressed man, we were rather astonished at the way he was going on with the woman." He described the man as:

> …about 5'5" in height. He was well dressed in a black morning suit with a morning coat. He had rather weak eyes. I mean he had sore eyes without any eyelashes. I should know the man again amongst a hundred. He had a thick black moustache and no beard. He wore a black billycock hat, rather tall, and had on a collar. I don't know the colour of his tie…The man was no foreigner; he was an Englishman right enough.

Best and Gardner said that: "as he stood in the doorway he always threw sidelong glances into the bar but would look nobody in the face." They invited the man into the pub for a drink but Stride's clingy companion was having none of it and made no answer. Instead, Stride and her man carried on canoodling in the doorway. Rebuffed, Best called out to Stride, "That's Leather Apron getting 'round you," at which point the pair "went off like a shot soon after eleven" towards Commercial Road and Berner Street (modern day Henriques Street).

Gardner also mentioned that he noticed a flower pinned to the woman's dress. A flower would be found on or by Stride's body. Earlier witnesses had not mentioned a flower so it could have been given to Stride by the man in the black morning suit.

A quarter of an hour later labourer William Marshall, standing in the doorway of 64 Berner Street between Fairclough and Boyd Streets, saw Stride outside No. 63. She is kissing and carrying on with a man who, by Marshall's description, appears to be someone other than the man with whom she had earlier departed the pub. This man is wearing a short black cutaway coat and a sailor's hat. Marshall hears him remark: "You would say anything but your prayers."

Matthew Packer, who ran a fruit and sweets shop at 44 Berner Street, claimed that at around eleven he sold grapes to Stride and a male companion. (Senior) Assistant Commissioner Alexander Carmichael Bruce made a report of an interview held with Packer at Scotland Yard. Prefixing the report with the statement, "Matthew Packer keeps a shop in Berner St. has a few grapes in window, black & white," Bruce related what Packer had to say:

> On Sat night about 11pm a young man from 25-30 - about 5'7" with long black coat buttoned up - soft felt hat, kind of yankee hat rather broad shoulders - rather quick in speaking, rough voice. I sold him ½ pound black grapes 3d. A woman came up with him from Back Church end (the lower end of street) She was dressed in black frock & jacket, fur round bottom of jacket with black crape bonnet, she was playing with a flower like a geranium white outside and red inside. I identify the woman at the St.George's mortuary as the one I saw that night.
>
> They passed by as though they were going up Com- Road, but-instead of going up they crossed to the other side of the road to the Board School, & were there for about ½ an hour till I shd say 11.30, talking to one another. I then shut up my shutters.
>
> Before they passed over opposite to my shop, they wait[ed] near to the club for a few minutes apparently listening to the music.
>
> I saw no more of them after I shut up my shutters. I put the man down as a young clerk.
>
> He had a frock coat on - no gloves. He was about 1½ inch or 2 or 3 inches a little higher than she was.

Because of many inconsistencies in Packer's train of reporting (for example, his stated time of sale of 11.00 p.m., at which point Stride and her man were still standing outside the Bricklayer's Arms), his evidence has been generally regarded as dubious. Nevertheless, Packer's account of Stride and her companion cannot wholly be ruled out.

At 12:35 a.m. Police Constable William Smith saw Stride with a man on Berner Street opposite the International Working Men's Educational Club, a socialist and predominantly Jewish social club. He described the man as 28-years old, wearing a dark coat and hard deerstalker hat. He was carrying a parcel wrapped in newspaper approximately 6 inches high and 18 inches in length.

Approximately ten minutes later, dock labourer James Brown of 35 Fairclough Street saw Stride. He told *The Times* (published 6 October):

> I saw the deceased about a quarter to 1 on Sunday morning. At that time I was going from my house to get some supper from a chandler's shop at the corner of Berner-street and Fairclough-street.

As I was going across the road I saw a man and woman standing by the Board School in Fairclough-street. They were standing against the wall. As I passed them I heard the woman say, "No, not to-night, some other night." That made me turn round, and I looked at them. I am certain the woman was the deceased. I did not notice any flowers in her dress.

The man had his arm up against the wall, and the woman had her back to the wall facing him. I noticed the man had a long coat on, which came very nearly down to his heels. I believe it was an overcoat. I could not say what kind of cap he had on. The place where they were standing was rather dark. I saw nothing light in colour about either of them. I then went on and went indoors.

I had nearly finished my supper when I heard screams of "Police" and "Murder." That was about a quarter of an hour after I got in. I do not think it was raining at the time.

I should say the man was about 5'7" in height. He appeared to be stoutish built. Both the man and woman appeared to be sober. I did not notice any foreign accent about the woman's voice. When I heard screams of "Police" and "Murder" I opened the window, but could not see any one and the screams ceased. The cries were those of moving persons, and appeared to be going in the direction of Grove-street. Shortly afterwards I saw a policeman standing at the corner of Christian-street. I heard a man opposite call out to the constable that he was wanted. I then saw the policeman run along to Berner-street.

Around the time of Brown's sighting, Hungarian immigrant Israel Schwartz had an unnerving encounter. Chief Inspector Donald Swanson's statement, taken on the day of the murder, describes it:

12.45 a.m. 30th. Israel Schwartz of 22 Helen Street, Backchurch Lane, stated that at this hour, on turning into Berner Street from Commercial Street and having got as far as the gateway where the murder was committed, he saw a man stop and speak to a woman, who was standing in the gateway. The man tried to pull the woman into the street, but he turned her round and threw her down on the footway and the woman screamed three times, but not loudly. On crossing to the opposite side of the street, he saw a second man standing, lighting his pipe. The man who threw the woman down called out, apparently to the man on the opposite side of the road, "Lipski," and then Schwartz walked away, but finding that he was followed by the second man, he ran so far as the railway arch, but the man did not follow so far.

Schwartz cannot say whether the two men were together or

known to each other. Upon being taken to the Mortuary Schwartz identified the body as that of the woman he had seen. He thus describes the first man, who threw the woman down:- age, about 30; ht, 5'5"; comp., fair; hair, dark; small brown moustache, full face, broad shouldered; dress, dark jacket and trousers, black cap with peak, and nothing in his hands.

Second man: age, 35; ht., 5'11"; comp., fresh; hair, light brown; dress, dark overcoat, old black hard felt hat, wide brim; had a clay pipe in his hand.

If Schwartz is to be believed, and the police report of his statement casts no doubt on it, it follows…that the man Schwartz saw and described is the more probable of the two to be the murderer.

The authorities did not treat the term "Lipski" as an incidental remark unworthy of follow-up. Indeed, it was regarded as a highly significant clue in the pursuit to establish the identity of an extremely violent killer. The reason for crediting the term with such importance was that it had been used locally as an anti-semitic insult since the savage murder by Israel Lipski in 1887 of Miriam Angel at 22 Batty Street (parallel to Berner Street). At the end of a controversial case that generated considerable anti-Jewish sentiment in Whitechapel, Lipski was convicted and hanged for the murder.

The name Lipski is a relatively common surname, particularly among Jews from Poland (deriving from "lipa," meaning lime tree) and in the Ashkenazi (Diaspora) communities in other Eastern European regions. The police hoped that it was the name of the second man seen by Schwartz, with which knowledge they might establish the assailant's identity. In the event, the police drew a blank and concluded that the term was more probably an insult directed at Schwartz and his "Jewish appearance."

At 1:00 a.m. jewellery salesman and steward of the International Working Men's Educational Club, Louis Diemschutz who was driving a two-wheeled barrow harnessed to a pony, entered Dutfield's Yard in Berner Street. He had come to deposit that day's unsold stock before stabling his pony in George Yard, Cable Street. At the entrance the pony shied and refused to go further. Suspecting that something was in the way of the entrance of the pitchblack yard, Diemschutz probed with his whip and came into contact with a body, which he initially believed was someone drunk or asleep. He jumped down from his barrow and by the fleeting light of a match made out the shape of a figure and the dim outline of a dress.

Diemschutz entered the club to get some help in rousing the woman. On Saturday and Sunday evenings the two-storey wooden building with a capacity of over two hundred people hosted international gatherings of Russian, Jewish, British, French, Italian, Czech and Polish radicals. On this night, ninety to one hundred members had participated in a debate on "The Necessity of Socialism amongst Jews."

On returning to the yard with Isaac Kozebrodsky and Morris Eagle, the three discover that the figure is a dead woman with blood still flowing from a cut in her throat. It seems that Diemschutz's arrival interrupted the assailant who, unable to perform his mutilations, made his escape while the jewellery salesman sought help from club members. Diemschutz concurred with this supposition due to the warm temperature of the body and his pony's continuing skittish behaviour. Dr. Frederick Blackwell of 100 Commercial Road was called. He arrived at 1.16 a.m. and pronounced Stride dead at the scene.

Dave Yost   provides a useful point of reference for the years prior to Elizabeth Stride's arrival in England in 1866. She was born Elisabeth Gustafsdotter, 27 November 1843, to 32-year-old farm labourer Augustus Gustifson (the name she provided for her 1869 marriage certificate[55]) and 33-year-old Beata Carlsdotter on "Stora Tumlehed" farm in Torslanda parish, north of Gothenburg. She was baptized on December 5 and enjoyed a happy childhood in the island community of Hisingen in the company of her siblings: older sister, Anna Christina, and younger brothers, Carl Bernhard and Svante. It was an altogether pleasant place to live. The sea was a brief stroll to the west and delightful parks and gardens were dotted throughout the municipality.

Prior to her 16th birthday Elisabeth was confirmed at Torslanda Kyrka, the quaint Evangelical Lutheran parish church that exists today and which resembles a large cottage with its well-worn pathway and gated entrance set within a charming grove of trees.

Two months before her 17th birthday, following in the footsteps of Anna Christina who had relocated to the city three years earlier, Elisabeth quit the family home and travelled to Gothenburg. She soon found employment as a maid and nanny for *månadskarl*

Elisabeth Gustafsdotter

[55] Yost, D., *Elizabeth Stride and Jack the Ripper: The Life and Death of the Reputed Third Victim*, McFarland & Co. Inc., Jefferson N.C., 2008
[56] Begg, P., *Jack the Ripper: the Facts*, Pavilion Books, London, 2008

(journeyman) Lars Fredrik Olofsson, his wife, domestic servant Johanna Carlsdotter, and three young children, Carl-Otto, Johan Fredrik and Anders Gustaf, at their home in the Karl Johans Parish in the Majorna district. At the same time, Elisabeth applied for a certificate of altered residence, which was granted on 25 October 1860. The certificate noted her good behaviour and extensive religious knowledge.

In February 1864 Elisabeth walked out on the family, giving no reason. Her departure bore the signs of being a runaway. One can speculate on the possibility that something occurred in the household which forced her to make a quick exit. Elisabeth made her way to Domkyrko (Cathedral Parish) in Gothenburg city centre, claiming that she was a domestic servant by profession.

Tragedy ensued with the death in August of Elisabeth's 54-year-old mother from chest disease. More misfortune was to follow. By March 1865 Elisabeth was registered with the Gothenburg police, an act that many have interpreted as signifying that the authorities believed she was engaging in prostitution. This was almost certainly her mode of living at the time but it cannot be proven because the document does not state the reason for registration.

On 4 April, Elisabeth was treated for genital condyloma at Kurhuset infirmary, a hospital for treatment of venereal disease near the harbour at Lilla Bommen in Gothenburg's red light district. She registered under the name of Gustaffson, occupation domestic servant. In Kurhuset she went into labour eight weeks prematurely and gave birth to a stillborn girl, father unknown.

Might this explain why she felt compelled to leave the Olofsson household? Had someone, perhaps Lars-Fredrik forced himself upon her? One can speculate no further. Because the child was illegitimate it could not be baptised but Elisabeth did give her daughter the surname Gustafsson.

By 13 May Elisabeth was declared healthy but re-admitted to the infirmary 30 August for treatment of a venereal ulcer. On 17 October Elisabeth was officially recorded as a prostitute in the police records and was admitted for the third and final time to Kurhuset for treatment of chancre, a highly contagious ulcer that forms in the primary stage of syphilis. After a fifteen-day spell in the infirmary Elisabeth was discharged as healthy with the proviso that she report regularly to the police. She went to the police station twice within the first five days after leaving Kurhuset.

On a final visit to the police station three days later she was removed from the prostitutes' register. This remarkable and happy state of affairs was achieved because by 10 November Elisabeth had found honest work. Her new employers were married couple 39-year-old Carl

Wenzel Wejsner (formerly Wiesners) and his wife, 20-year-old Inga Maria (née Hansdotter), of 27-29 Husargatan Street in Gothenburg's upmarket Haga district. An immigrant from Bohemia (now part of the Czech Republic), Carl worked as a musician with the band of the West Götha Artillery Regiment. It is claimed that the Wejsners were Jewish and it was from them that Elisabeth learned to converse in Yiddish.

Around this time Elisabeth received an inheritance of sixty-five kroner from her late mother's estate. The money provided Elisabeth with the opportunity to apply for a new certificate of altered residence, her stated destination of choice being the Swedish parish in London's East End. On 2 February 1866 the certificate was approved. Five days later she said her goodbyes to the Wejsners and set sail across the North Sea for England, where she becomes Elizabeth.

Elizabeth did not register at the Swedish Church in Prince's Square in St. George's-in-the-East until the July of 1866. Her activities and movements in the preceding five months are undocumented. On registration she said she was single. Later, Elizabeth's man-friend, Michael Kidney, would inform police that she first told him she travelled to England to see the country before later telling him that "she came to England in a situation with a family." If this was true it is possible that Elizabeth was working for an unnamed employer as a domestic servant during the first few months of her time in England. Charles Preston told a different story at the the inquest, saying that Stride had come to England in the service of a foreign gentleman.

Another hypothetical explanation to account for the missing months is that Elizabeth came to London to fulfill a pre-agreed commitment to work with a brothel keeper. There is no evidential basis for this scenario but were it to be proven it would raise questions about any possible involvement by the Wejsners in setting up the liaison.

Elizabeth's first three years in London passed quietly until the day came when she met 42-year-old carpenter Thomas Stride of Sheerness, sixteen years Elizabeth's senior. At this time Elizabeth was also dating a policeman who may have lived near Hyde Park. But it was the relationship with Stride that endured. After a brief courtship the couple married 7 March 1869 at the St Giles-in-the-Fields Church in London's West End. Historically, St Giles was the last church on the route between Newgate Prison and the gallows at Tyburn. It was the tradition that the churchwardens paid for the condemned to have a drink (popularly named as a "St Giles Bowl") at the next-door pub, the Angel, before they proceeded onwards to be hanged.

The newly-weds moved to East India Dock Road in Poplar where they opened a coffee shop in Chrisp Street. That location was not a success and just before the autumn of 1870 the pair relocated the shop to Upper North Street. That, too, failed and by the spring of 1871 they moved the business for a final time to Poplar High Street.

After a slow start business picked up and did well for the next three years. Elizabeth ran the coffee shop while John brought in money from carpentry work. In late September 1873 John's father, William, died and by 1874 the coffee shop had been taken over by John Dale, two events which placed a great deal of pressure on John and Elizabeth's marriage. They continued to live together but money became increasingly scarce. Sven Ollson, clerk of the Swedish Church, observed Elizabeth's depressingly pitiful state and in March 1877 she was admitted to Poplar Workhouse.

Eighteen months later on the evening of 3 September the passenger steamer *Princess Alice* collided with the steam collier *Bywell Castle* in the River Thames by North Woolwich pier. More than 500 passengers and crew of the SS *Princess Alice* died that evening. Years later Elizabeth Stride sought to elicit sympathy by claiming that in the accident she had lost her husband and two of her nine children. She said she had been kicked in the mouth by another passenger as they swam to safety, which, she explained, was why she had stuttered ever since.

The obvious flaws in Stride's claim were the facts that John Stride had died of tuberculosis in Poplar and Stepney Sick Asylum on 24 October 1884, more than five years after the disaster, and that they had no children.

Elizabeth and her husband struggled on but towards the end of 1881 their 12-year marriage broke down and the pair separated. Elizabeth moved out of their East End home in Usher Road, Bow, and found lodgings in Brick Lane in Whitechapel. Within a few weeks she was admitted to Whitechapel Infirmary with bronchitis and after a week's recuperation was transferred to Whitechapel Workhouse.

After leaving the workhouse Elizabeth went not to Brick Lane but to the common lodging house at 32 Flower and Dean Street, a choice that dramatically illustrates just how far she had fallen since the better days of running a coffee shop with her skilled carpenter husband. There is no firm evidence which indicates that during her marriage Elizabeth had engaged in prostitution but in her new environment the pressure to succumb was all around her.

Somehow, Elizabeth, an immigrant with no family to turn to, got by on her own resources but the fact was that she was steadily sliding downhill. The month after her estranged husband's death Elizabeth was charged with being drunk and disorderly and for soliciting. She sought companionship to help alleviate the burdens of living a lonely, wretched existence and found solace in the company of Irish born dock labourer and army pensioner Michael Kidney, nine years Elizabeth's junior.

The sinking of the SS *Princess Alice* in 1878

Elizabeth moved in with her new man-friend at 33 Dorset Street and according to Sven Ollson and Elizabeth Tanner she did occasional sewing and cleaning work "among the Jews" in her community where her knowledge of Yiddish came in handy.

Nevertheless, despite little bits of money coming in now and again from such work, living with Michael was not improving Elizabeth's already parlous financial position and so she applied for and received cash support from the Swedish Church on 20th and 23rd May 1886. The Church's charity provided temporary financial respite but in March 1887 Elizabeth re-entered the Poplar Workhouse. From then until 1888 Elizabeth was convicted no less than eight times for drunkenness.

After Elizabeth and Michael made a move to new lodgings at 36 Devonshire Street their relationship deteriorated rapidly. Elizabeth brought a charge of assault against Michael in April 1887 but the case was dropped because she did not appear in court to offer evidence. Her episodic bouts of drunkenness continued, including an incident at the Ten Bells pub on Commercial Street, which led to a court appearance where she may have used the alias "Annie Fitzgerald."

Every so often Elizabeth would simply take off for a week or two; Kidney calculated that these disappearances totalled five months during their three years together. During these spells Elizabeth often returned to 32 Flower and Dean Street. The house deputy will tell the inquest: "She lodged in our house, on and off, for the last six years."

At the time of her death Elizabeth Stride was wearing a long black cloth jacket with fur trim around the bottom and pinned with a red rose and white maidenhair fern, black skirt, black crepe bonnet, checked neck scarf knotted on left side, dark brown velveteen bodice, two large serge petticoats, white chemise, white stockings and spring-sided boots.

On her person were two handkerchiefs, a piece of wool wound round a card, a thimble, a padlock key, a small piece of lead pencil, six large buttons and one small one, one whole and one broken comb, a metal spoon, a dress hook, a piece of

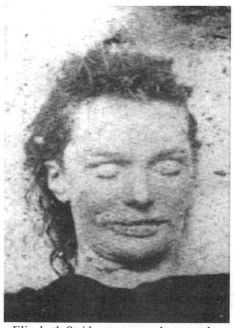

Elizabeth Stride mortuary photograph

160

muslin and one or two small pieces of paper. Clutched in her hand was a packet of cachous, commonly used by smokers to sweeten the breath.

(The mortuary photo of Elizabeth shows a distinctive swelling on her lip. One of her nicknames, seemingly bestowed by the American press, was "Hippie Lip Annie." Postings to the Casebook forum speak of Elizabeth suffering from a deformity of the lip caused by an untreated herpetic lesion brought on by a sexually transmitted disease. There does not appear to be mention of such in the inquest reports.)

Local doctor Frederick William Blackwell was roused from his bed. While he dressed, his assistant, Edward Johnston, attended the scene with a police constable. Johnston felt the body, which he "found all warm except the hands, which were quite cold." By this time, the slash to the throat had stopped bleeding. Dr Blackwell arrived at the scene at 1.16 a.m. shortly before Dr George Bagster Phillips. By the light of a police lantern, Blackwell made a meticulous investigation of the body. Two days later he reported to the inquest:

> The deceased was lying on her left side obliquely across the passage, her face looking towards the right wall. Her legs were drawn up, her feet close against the wall of the right side of the passage. Her head was resting beyond the carriage-wheel rut, the neck lying over the rut. Her feet were three yards from the gateway. Her dress was unfastened at the neck. The neck and chest were quite warm, as were also the legs, and the face was slightly warm. The hands were cold. The right hand was open and on the chest, and was smeared with blood. The left hand, lying on the ground, was partially closed, and contained a small packet of cachous wrapped in tissue paper.
>
> There were no rings, nor marks of rings, on her hands. The appearance of the face was quite placid. The mouth was slightly open. The deceased had round her neck a check silk scarf, the bow of which was turned to the left and pulled very tight. In the neck there was a long incision, which exactly corresponded with the lower border of the scarf. The border was slightly frayed, as if by a sharp knife. The incision in the neck commenced on the left side, 2½ inches below the angle of the jaw, and almost in a direct line with it, nearly severing the vessels on that side, cutting the windpipe completely in two, and terminating on the opposite side 1½ inches below the angle of the right jaw, but without severing the vessels on that side. I could not ascertain whether the bloody hand had been moved. The blood was running down the gutter into the drain in the opposite direction from the feet. There was about 1 lb. of clotted blood close by the body, and a stream all the way from there to the back door of the club.

On Dr Phillips' arrival the body was in the charge of Chief Inspector West and Inspector Charles Pinhorn. Phillips' report, dictated to Pinhorn at the scene and subsequently presented to the inquest on 3 October, stated:

> The body was lying on its left side, face turned toward the wall, head toward the yard, feet toward the street, left arm extended from elbow, which held a packet of cachous in her hand. Similar ones were in the gutter. I took them from her hand, and handed them to Dr Blackwell. The right arm was lying over the body, and the back of the hand and wrist had on them clotted blood. The legs were drawn up, the feet close to the wall, the body still warm, the face warm, the hands cold, the legs quite warm, a silk handkerchief round the throat, slightly torn (so is my note, but I since find it is cut)...This corresponded to the right angle of the jaw; the throat was deeply gashed, and an abrasion of the skin about an inch and a quarter diameter, apparently slightly stained with blood, was under the right clavicle.

Blackwell thought that Stride might have been pulled backwards on to the ground by her neckerchief before her throat was cut. Phillips concurred. Bruising on her chest suggested that she was pinned to the ground during the attack.

Meanwhile, police sought to ascertain the victim's identity. Detective Inspector Edmund Reid, already having assisted in the investigations into the deaths of Emma Smith, Martha Tabram and Annie Chapman, put effort into the task. At St George's Mortuary where the body had been taken at 4.30 a.m. Reid made careful notes of the woman's appearance and wired the particulars to all police stations.

Based on conclusive identifications from those familiar with the deceased, including Sven Ollson of the Swedish Church and PC Walter Stride (Stride's nephew by marriage), the investigation team swiftly concluded that the victim was Swede, Elisabeth Gustafsdotter.

However, the question of identity was almost immediately befuddled by the intervention of one Mrs Mary Malcolm of Red Lion Square, Holborn, who on being taken to the mortuary to view the body asserted that it was that of her sister, Mrs Elizabeth Watts. Her confident identification was made not so much on facial recognition but from a black mark on the leg, which, Malcolm said, was the result of her sister having been bitten by an adder when they were children.

Furthermore, at the inquest Malcolm was asked by Coroner Wynne Edwin Baxter if it was indeed the case that she had received "an occult warning of her sister's death." In reply, she said she had been lying awake in bed at "about twenty minutes past one on Sunday morning" when she felt a pressure on her breast. Suddenly, she heard "three distinct kisses" by her side. Since this was more or less the time when, according to the *East London Advertiser*, her "sister" was "giving up her life under the hands of the awful being in Berner Street, it [being] more than probable that Judas-like he first betrayed his victim with a kiss," the story went that what was happening to the woman at the hands of the murderer was being played out in the mind of her sister. Malcolm's bizarre claims were not completely dismissed until the genuine Elizabeth Watts appeared on 24 October, three weeks after the commencement of the inquest, as proof that she was very much alive and kicking.

Baxter opened the inquest on 1 October at the Vestry Hall, Cable Street, St George's in the East. Perhaps in acknowledgement of criticism concerning the post-mortem procedures in earlier murders, Doctors Blackwell and Phillips had made the examination of Stride's body jointly. Blackwell carried out the incisions while Phillips took notes. At the inquest Phillips gave their report on the autopsy findings:

At 3 p.m. on Monday at St. George's Mortuary, Dr Blackwell and I made a post-mortem examination. Rigor mortis was still thoroughly marked. There was mud on the left side of the face and it was matted in the head…The body was fairly nourished. Over both shoulders, especially the right, and under the collarbone and in front of the chest there was a blueish discolouration, which I have watched and have seen on two occasions since.

There was a clear-cut incision on the neck. It was six inches in length and commenced two and a half inches in a straight line below the angle of the jaw, three quarters of an inch over an undivided muscle, and then, becoming deeper, dividing the sheath. The cut was very clean and deviated a little downwards. The arteries and other vessels contained in the sheath were all cut through. The cut through the tissues on the right side was more superficial, and tailed off to about two inches below the right angle of the jaw. The deep vessels on that side were uninjured. From this it was evident that the haemorrhage was caused through the partial severance of the left carotid artery and a small bladed knife could have been used.

Decomposition had commenced in the skin. Dark brown spots were on the anterior surface of the left chin. There was a deformity in the bones of the right leg, which was not straight, but bowed forwards. There was no recent external injury save to the neck.

The body being washed more thoroughly, I could see some healing sores. The lobe of the left ear was torn as if from the removal or wearing through of an earring, but it was thoroughly healed. On removing the scalp there was no sign of bruising or extravasation of blood...The heart was small, the left ventricle firmly contracted, and the right slightly so. There was no clot in the pulmonary artery, but the right ventricle was full of dark clot. The left was firmly contracted as to be absolutely empty. The stomach was large and the mucous membrane only congested. It contained partly digested food, apparently consisting of cheese, potato, and farinaceous powder [flour or milled grain]. All the teeth on the lower left jaw were absent. [*Note that the stomach contents do not include grapes, although private detectives did discover a grape stalk in Dutfield's Yard.*]

On Saturday, 6 October, Elizabeth Stride was buried in the East London Cemetery, Plaistow, London, in grave #15509, square 37. The funeral was provided at the expense of the parish.

There is no absolutely agreed consensus among Ripperologists that Elizabeth Stride was killed by the Whitechapel murderer. The mode and time of despatch—use of a knife with a short rounded blade, no obvious signs of strangulation, the absence of abdominal mutilations, the evidence that Stride's attacker was right-handed (Tabram, Nichols and Chapman were killed by a left-handed assailant), and the fact that the attacker had to have travelled at near superhuman speed to reach the next murder site at Mitre Square—has thrown doubt on attaching to the Ripper the certain responsibility for her murder.

Yet it is a paradox that was offered a solution just prior to the murder of Stride. Israel Schwartz saw *two* men that night in Berner Street—one attacking at the murder scene a woman Schwartz later identified in the mortuary as Stride, and another lighting a pipe, possibly the killer's lookout.

I do not believe that sufficient consideration has been given to the probability that "Jack the Ripper" was a collaborative force involving more than one murderer. Perhaps the thought of teamwork, a notion suggesting that the murders were organised, more than they seemed, induces in some a nervous reluctance to consider the presence and implications of a bigger picture at play.

If Stride's murder, the first in that night's "double event," was carried out with an untypical "light touch," the same certainly cannot be said for the manner in which Catherine "Kate" Eddowes will be despatched between 1:35 a.m. and 1:45 a.m. in the City of London. The murderous energy abroad in London that night was not in the least dissipated.

The date of Elizabeth Stride's death, 1 October, is the feast day of Saint Thérèse of the Child Jesus and the Holy Face (Marie Françoise-Thérèse Martin, 1873-1897), popularly known as the "The Little Flower of Jesus" or, simply, "The Little Flower." Before reporting on Kate's brutal passing we turn to another Frenchwoman associated with flowers, not a saint like Thérèse but a nineteenth-century sorceress who during her mysterious life in England went by the name of Mary Heath.

Chapter 10

The Lady with the Lilacs

In 1862, Arthur Hughes, an artist and illustrator associated with the pre-Raphaelite Brotherhood, painted a stylised portrait of a woman, ostensibly as a working study for the younger figure featured in a subsequent work, *Silver and Gold*. Hughes titled the 1862 oil on panel work, *The Lady with the Lilacs*. It measures 17½ x 9 inches and was cut to its final arched shape after the wood was primed and painted. In *The Lady with the Lilacs* the redheaded subject is standing beneath a lilac tree. Around her neck is a five-point "Star of Isis" pendant suspended from a double chain. Pendant and chain appear to be fashioned from gold. Widely accepted opinion has it that Hughes's wife, Tryphena, modelled the subject just as it is believed that she similarly posed for her husband's *April Love* and *Home from the Sea* works.

Hughes expert, Canadian Leonard Roberts, compiler of catalogue raisonné *Arthur Hughes: his Life and Works* for the Antique Collector Club Ltd. in 1997, told me in correspondence in 2002 that Lewis Carroll saw the work while visiting the painter on 31 July 1863 and was immediately captivated. So much so, that Carroll asked Hughes to re-work it for his own collection, a task which he completed 8 October. Carroll's diary records that he took formal possession of the painting on the 12th.

Carroll is believed to have first become aware of Hughes' work in July 1862 when he saw and admired the illustrations the artist produced for George MacDonald's *The Light Princess*. Twelve months later Carroll accompanied pre-Raphaelite sculptor Alexander Munro to the Hughes household seeing, as noted in his diary, "some lovely pictures, and his four little children…He also is to come with his children to be photographed." "Uncle" Lewis Carroll, as the Hughes children dubbed him, was a very fine photographer in his own right. He conducted the sitting with the Hughes family 12 October 1863.

The story that Carroll became enamoured with *The Lady with the Lilacs* after seeing it in partly finished format while making his first visit to Hughes' studio is challenged by a remark in Leonard's catalogue raisonné, which describes the provenance as "Commissioned in 1863 by Lewis Carroll." The *Cambridge Dictionary* defines "commission" in this context as "to formally choose someone to do a special piece of work, or to formally ask for a special piece of work from someone." The use of the term therefore implies that the commissioner is the sole personality motivating the undertaking of an original artistic project to fulfill that person's unique requirements or specifications.

That Carroll saw a picture out of the blue, liked what he saw and asked the artist to finish it off does not, I suggest, meet the usual criteria of a commission. It does suggest, however, that Carroll had a special interest in the subject and instigated the sitter's representation in oils as *The Lady with the Lilacs*. The theory might seem a touch over-imaginative were it not for the consideration that, by all accounts, *The Lady with the Lilacs* was the only painting that Carroll ever owned.

Recent years have seen the emergence of a body of opinion that the subject in the *The Lady with the Lilacs* is a woman named Mary Heath. Interestingly, in Roberts' response to my letter of 2001 in which I made the case for Heath as *The Lady with the Lilacs* he first set out the popularly understood facts that support Tryphena Hughes as being the model before concluding, "Having said all this, I remain open-minded about the identity of the model..." In a subsequent email exchange, Roberts also noted Hughes' "odd" inclusion of the Star of Isis in *The Lady with the Lilacs*, as it had not been used in the artist's previous pictures. It was clear that Roberts was also beginning to entertain doubts about the sitter's identity. Had Carroll, a man who populated his library with books on occult and spirit phenomena, known of Mary Heath and desired to immortalise her in a work of art in a specially commissioned portrait that provided clues to a secret life in Victorian England? Just who was the enigmatic Mary Heath?

By means of ground research and psychic research, British investigator Andrew Collins and his colleagues have presented a fascinating account of her life. Mary is believed to have been born in France around 1840, the illegitimate daughter of wealthy and eminent printer and designer, Thomas de la Rue. She first came to London around 1855, possibly under the guardianship of the Dalziel brothers: engravers for Lewis Carroll's illustrator, John Tenniel, and illustrators for Madame Michelet's nature works. In this period Mary Heath was introduced to a number of individuals in pre-Raphaelite circles.

---

[57] Collins, A., *The Seventh Sword*, Arrow Books Ltd., London, 1991

The Lady with the Lilacs by Arthur Hughes

Collins speculates that Charles Dodgson was among those that were smitten by the fifteen-year old French girl. Such an encounter would have taken place seven years before the Oxford don on a boat trip down the Isis on a "golden afternoon" (a curious description as on that particular day, 4 July 1862, it was cool, cloudy and rainy) told a story at the request of his young passengers of a little girl's adventures underground. Dodgson's attentive listeners (his friend Reverend Robinson Duckworth and the three daughters of Oxford University Vice-Chancellor and Dean of Christ Church Henry Liddell: Lorina Charlotte, Alice Pleasance and Edith Mary) related that their storyteller told the tale in extempore fashion as if it were already largely thought out.

Any mystery of how Dodgson might have made up, on the spot, the complete story of Alice's adventures could be explained if he was narrating a work in which he had invested much time and energy beforehand. If, as some believe, the real source of creative and esoteric inspiration for the tales was Mary Heath, a powerful Christian mystic with a magical, spirited personality that sought adventure, then the question of timing and pre-preparedness is resolved.

Collins states that Mary returned to France. A few years later, prompted by the death of her mother, Mary's father revealed that the family was part of a clandestine mystical fraternity that linked their bloodline to the Guise-Lorraine family, which had championed Mary Queen of Scots. The Guise-Lorraine family is also a scion of the Merovingian line of kings, which, as many will know from numerous books and films on the subject, is reputed to have originated from a child born to Jesus and Mary Magdalene, mother and child brought to safety from Judea on a rudderless boat to the South of France after the crucifixion. It is believed that Julia Cameron (1815-1879), the leading photographer of her day, depicted Heath as Mary Magdalene in her *Angel at the Sepulchre*. Mary's family furnished her with the names of contacts and societies in England that shared similar beliefs and allegiances. The de la Rue family asked Mary to meet with them and establish, through their support, a new group of like-minded mystical Christians who accepted that the wisdom of Moses and King Solomon originated in ancient Egypt. This group became known as the Fire Phoenix.

Mary established the order at a ceremony held in the grounds of Biddulph Grange in Staffordshire, a few miles distant from a magical location known as the "Place of the Double Setting Sun." The area was also associated with a mysterious Gypsy tribe ("the golden red-haired folk") known as the "Azarkre," which, Collin's research indicates, was brought to Britain by the Knights Templar from the Holy Land.

In 1869, Biddulph Grange was sold by its owner, James Bateman, to Robert Heath, the wealthy owner of a number of coal mines, ironstone pits, blast furnaces and rolling mills. It appears that Mary lived at the Grange posing as Robert's sister or close relative, taking the surname as part of her cover.

Collins suggests that the Hermetic knowledge underpinning the Fire Phoenix was brought to Britain by an enlightened colony of Egyptians from the time of Pharaoh Akhenaten. These exiles, Mary's group understood, were the progenitors of the Celtic civilisation and the Druids. Akhenaten, born Amenhotep IV, is known in history as the Pharaoh who, uniquely, introduced into Egypt the worship of the one god, Aten the Sun-god. After a brief period (ruling seventeen years, circa 1352 BC to 1335 BC) Akhenaten, ousted by an all-powerful priesthood that yearned for the re-introduction of the traditional Egyptian pantheon, was forced into exile with his followers.

Historians (notably Ahmed Osman[58]) have argued that the Old Testament story of Moses and the Israelites' miraculous crossing of the Red Sea is an account of Akhenaten's enforced departure from Egypt. Mystical Christian groups go further, claiming that the exiles brought to Britain the hermetic teachings of Thoth, the Egyptian god of writing, knowledge and philosophy, which eventually became the basis of alchemic learning. Additionally, the Collins' group claims that the Moses-Akhenaten followers also brought to Britain an emerald-green stone which four hundred years later came to be worn as a symbol of magical authority by a Celtic priestess named Gwevaraugh. In the Middle Ages it became known as the Philosopher's Stone and in Mary Queen of Scots' time as the Meonia Stone. In common with other nineteenth-century esoteric groups, Mary's Fire Phoenix believed that the world would shortly be challenged by great changes which, once confronted and overcome, would open the way for a new golden age. Believing that Britain was the

A photograph said to be of Mary Heath

[58] Osman, A., *Moses and Akhenaten: The Secret History of Egypt at the Time of the Exodus,* Inner Traditions Bear and Company, 2002

epicentre of metaphysical progression in the Western world, the group anticipated that the revitalising energy of the new millennium would ripple outwards from these Isles into the rest of Europe to bring universal harmony.

Mary took into her confidence artist friend Arthur Hughes who, according to Collins' research, incorporated her image into a painting initially known as *A Mother's Grave*. It depicts a small boy who, tired after his long journey to visit his mother's resting place, is sleeping beneath a tree. In 1863, seven years after beginning the work, Hughes added the figure of a petite young woman clad in a dark shawl and dress sitting on the grass with her hands clasped. Art scholars commonly accept that the figure is that of Hughes' wife, Tryphena. Collins disagrees, arguing that the sitter was actually twenty-three year old Mary Heath whom Hughes added soon after her arrival from France. Hughes then gave the painting the alternative title, *Home from the Sea*.

Hughes also reportedly inserted in the section of the picture that depicts a wild tree rose festooned with spiders' webs a clue about a mysterious ceremony called the "Form of the Lamb," which the seven members of the inner order of the Fire Phoenix had carried out at a secret location called the "Heart of the Rose." The objective of the ritual was to open the gates to the coming golden age.

The arch adversary of the Fire Phoenix was the "Wheel," a European occult group established after the fall of the Templars in the early fourteenth century. The British arm of the Wheel was led by John Newton Langley who ran a school for boys in Wolverhampton. Langley is described as a tall man who wore a top hat, thick floor-length cape and white kid gloves (to my mind somewhat like a cross between Spring-heeled Jack and Alice's White Rabbit!). In his black magic rituals Langley used a large polished black stone referred to as the Running Stone.

Collins' investigations indicated that the Wheel's operations in England were funded and controlled by an organisation known as the People of Hexe, a name derived from the Germanic form of Hecate. The group comprised occult adepts of European origin whose mission was to take control of Britain's invisible energy matrix. To this end, the People of Hexe conducted ceremonies at power sites such as stone circles, long-barrows, holy hills and former pagan sites reconstituted as Christian shrines. The adepts regarded Britain as a giant labyrinth of all-powerful earth energies and invoked in their rituals the archetypes and symbols of the Cretan Minotaur and the spider-goddess Arachne.

At the time of Mary Heath's move to England one of her closest friends in France was Nina Chevret who was considerably older than Mary and married to artist, lithographer and occultist Édouard Chevret. In the early 1840s Nina was asked by her husband to infiltrate Eugène Vintras's L'Ouevre de la Miséricorde. Édouard had learned that Vintras and his movement were under the control of the "Saviours of Louis XVII," a political organisation dedicated to restoring the monarchy (the Bourbon Restoration) under Louis-Charles, Dauphin of France (son of the executed King Louis XVI and Queen Marie Antoinette).

In the course of her intelligence activities, Nina also discovered connections between L'Ouevre de la Miséricorde and the Johannite Church of Primitive Christians founded by Templar revivalist Bernard-Raymond Fabré-Palaprat, which, she understood, was an arm of the Wheel. Nina learned that in promoting these occult alliances Vintras made contact with Langley and appointed him British head of the Wheel in 1863.

Wheels within wheels within wheels—the story of Mary Heath, a visionary with precocious intellect and an impassioned sense of adventure, is a fantastical account of occult intrigue and spooky shenanigans in mid- to late-nineteenth century Victorian Britain. Despite its singularly eccentric British character, it is a story dominated by many of the principle features of Europe's occult scene that have been addressed in earlier pages: ancient Egyptian mysteries, a shadowy German magical sect, French occultists, Hermetic and Templar influences, Christian mysticism, the all-pervasive invisible presence of the Orphic Society and, not least, a bad guy in a top hat and cloak as if plucked for the occasion from the bloodied cobbles of Whitechapel's nighttime thoroughfares. It is also a story which connects seemingly straightlaced cleric, Reverend Charles Lutwidge Dodgson, to the underground activities of England's mystical Christian enterprise.

Collin's research indicates that Mary Heath died of natural causes in the mid-1890s. Some of her followers in the Fire Phoenix developed connections with the Hermetic Order of the Golden Dawn while others continued with Mary's work. The group survived in England until the outbreak of the Great War and then moved to Port Hueneme in California where its members fell in with Harvey Spencer Lewis, former member of de Guaïta and Péladan's Ordre Kabballistique de la Rose Croix and founder in 1915 of the Ancient and Mystical Order Rosae Crucis (AMORC).

In the summer of 1996, *Gnosis Magazine* printed an article by Donald Tyson titled *The Enochian Apocalypse*. Echoing the apocalyptic beliefs of Mary Heath's Fire Phoenix group, Tyson's theme was: "Were John Dee's Enochian Keys of magic intended to unleash violent occult forces that would hurl us into another age?"

Tyson recounted how between 1582 and 1589 Dee conducted a series of rituals with the intent of communicating with spirits he called the "Enochian angels." In these efforts, Dee was assisted by Edward Kelly who "did all his feats upon the Devil's looking glass, a (black obsidian) stone where, playing with him at bo-peep, he solv'd all problems ne'er so deep" (Sam Butler, *Hudibras*).

I was struck by the similarities between Dee's "new age" rituals and the work of Mary Heath's occult circle to facilitate the onset of a new golden age for mankind. I also noted the similarities between John Newton Langley's large polished black Running Stone and Edward Kelly's black obsidian scrying stone.

Above all, I was struck by Tyson's reference to Butler's "looking glass" analogy because it came at a time when I was researching Charles Dodgson and feeling that the children's writer had been slighted by the publication of a book by American child psychologist Richard Wallace, which names him as the Ripper. To me, the suggestion was as absurd in 1996 as it is today. There *was* more to Dodgson than was apparent on the surface but not, I feel, in the sense that he had the will and capacity to carry out multiple and psychopathically brutal murders. Dodgson was a highly complex character with a keen interest in the supernatural, the occult, fairy folk, other dimensions of existence and, it must be said, an unhealthy obsession with children. His personal library contained rare and valuable books on diverse esoteric topics including medium confesssions, demonic possession, systems of magick, the New England witch trials and the history of the black arts. Clearly a highly imaginative man, Dodgson truly believed that through meditation and transcendental prayer one can literally step into other worlds and experience unimaginable adventures.

Tyson's article provided me with the multi-synchronous connections that motivated my search for Abberline's apocryphal "Claston," a journey whose fruits I will share but not before we make a detour to Mitre Square. We arrive there around thirty-five minutes after Elizabeth Stride's murder in Dutfield's Yard.

---

[59] Wallace, R., *Jack the Ripper: Your Light-Hearted Friend,* Gemini Press, 1996
[60] Woolf, J., *The Mystery of Lewis Carroll*, Haus Books, London, 2010

Chapter 11

Kate

Friday, 28 September, 1888, Whitechapel

When Kate Eddowes and her man-friend, John Kelly, woke in the City of London Casual Ward in Shoe Lane they had just one thing occupying their thoughts—money. Despite a summer's hop picking in the fields at Hunton near Maidstone in Kent with their friend Emily Birrell (also reported as spelt "Burrell) the couple were stony broke.

"We didn't get along too well and started to hoof it home," Kelly said later. "We came along in company with another man and woman who had worked in the same fields, but who parted from us to go to Cheltenham when we turned off towards London. The woman [probably Birrell] said, 'I've got a pawn ticket for a flannel shirt. I wish you'd take it since you're going up to town. It is only for 2d, and it may fit your old man.' Kate took it and we trudged along...We did not have money enough to keep us going till we got to town, but we did get there, and came straight to this house [Cooney's Lodging House, 55 Flower and Dean Street]. Luck was dead against us...we were both done up for cash."

Cooney's was Kate and John's regular place of residence unless lack of money required that they lower their sights and seek meaner accommodation. Frederick Wilkinson, Cooney's deputy manager, described Kate as a "very jolly woman, always singing."

After the pair arrived in London on the 28th John earned 6d, keeping 4d for a bed at Cooney's while Kate took the remainder for a bed at the casual ward in Shoe Lane. The superintendent of the casual ward said that Kate was well known there but it had been some time since her last visit.

An uncorroborated story relates that Kate explained to the superintendent that she had been hopping in the country but "I have come back to earn the reward offered for the apprehension of the Whitechapel murderer. I think I know him." The superintendent warned her to be careful that he did not murder her. "Oh, no fear of that," she is said to have replied. Why Kate might have made this bold and enigmatic statement has never been satisfactorily explained.

Kate and John meet up at Cooney's on the following morning at 8:00 a.m. Kate says that she has been turned out of the Casual Ward for some unspecified trouble. Desperate for cash, John decides to pawn his boots. Kate takes the boots to a pawnbroker named Jones in Church Street and pledges them for two shillings and sixpence under the name of Jane Kelly. With the money the pair buys food, tea and sugar.

Between 10:00 a.m. and 11:00 a.m. they are seen by Frederick Wilkinson eating breakfast in the lodging house kitchen. By the afternoon they are again broke. Kate said she would walk to Bermondsey and cadge money from her daughter, Annie, who was married to gun-maker Louis Phillips. She parts with John at Houndsditch at 2:00 p.m., saying she will be back no later than 4:00 p.m.

John said at the inquest, "I never knew if she went to her daughter's at all. I only wish she had, for we had lived together for some time and never had a quarrel." In fact, Kate could not have seen her daughter who, fed up with her mother's scrounging, had moved to a new address and kept the details to herself. John had retained enough from the pawn money to pay for a bed at Cooney's. He arrived there just after 8:00 p.m and, according to the deputy keeper, remained there all night.

Thirty minutes after John entered the lodging-house, City Police Constable 931 Louis Robinson found Kate lying drunk outside 29 Aldgate High Street surrounded by a crowd of onlookers. Robinson asked those in the crowd if anyone knew her; no one replied. He got the woman to her feet and leaned her against the building's shutters but she slipped sideways.

At the inquest Robinson reported, "On the 29th at 8:30 I was on duty in Aldgate High Street, I saw a crowd of persons outside No. 29. I saw there a woman whom I have since recognised as the deceased lying on the footway drunk. I asked if there was one that knew her or knew where she lived but I got no answer." With the aid of City PC 959 George Simmons, Robinson brought the tiny middle-aged woman to Bishopsgate Police Station. She was no more than 5' tall with dark

Kate Eddowes

auburn hair, hazel eyes and a jolly smile. On her left forearm was a tattoo in blue ink, "TC."

At 8:45 p.m. Bishopsgate Police Station Sergeant James Byfield recorded Kate's arrival. Physically supported by Robinson and Simmons, the woman was asked her name to which she replies, "Nothing." Robinson looked in on her 8:50 p.m. in her cell; she was asleep and smelled of drink. At 9:45 p.m. the gaoler, City PC 968 George Hutt, took charge of the prisoners. On the directive of Sergeant Byfield, Hutt thereafter visited the cells every half hour.

Kate is heard singing softly to herself in the cell at quarter past midnight. At 12:30 a.m. she calls out asking when she shall be released. "When you are capable of taking care of yourself," Hutt replies. "I can do that now," is Kate's riposte. At 12:55 a.m. Byfield instructs Hutt to check if any prisoners are fit for release and Kate is judged to be sober. She gives her name as Mary Ann Kelly of 6 Fashion Street and is released. She asks Hutt the time.

"Too late for you to get anything to drink," he replies.

"I shall get a damn fine hiding when I get home," she tells him.

"And serve you right," says Hutt, pushing open the swinging door of that station, "You had no right to get drunk. This way missus, please pull it to."

"All right," Kate replies, "goodnight, old cock."

Kate then turned left out the doorway, which took her in the opposite direction of what would have been the quickest route to Cooney's in Flower and Dean Street. Her chosen route appears to be heading back toward Aldgate High Street where she had become drunk. On going down Houndsditch, she would have passed the entrance to Duke Street at the end of which was Church Passage leading into Mitre Square.

The last people apparently to see Kate alive were commercial traveller Joseph Lawende, butcher Joseph Hyam Levy and furniture dealer Harry Harris who had just left the Imperial Club at 16-17 Duke Street. At 1:35 a.m they observed a woman with a man at the entrance to Church Passage, which led southwest from Duke Street to Mitre Square along the south wall of the Great Synagogue of London. The woman is standing facing the man, with her hand on his chest but not in a manner to suggest that she is resisting him.

Lawende was the only one of the three who was able to provide any kind of description. He described the man as thirty years old, 5'7" tall, fair complexion and moustache, with a medium build. He is wearing a pepper and salt coloured loosely fitting jacket and a grey cloth cap with a peak of the same colour. He had a reddish handkerchief knotted around his neck. His overall appearance was that of a sailor. Lawende was later shown Eddowes' clothes at the police station and believed that they were the same as those worn by the woman he saw that night.

At 1:45 a.m. Kate's mutilated body was found in the southwest corner of Mitre Square by the square's beat policeman, PC Edward Watkins who had entered one minute earlier having previously been there at 1:30 a.m. With this murder the "double event" was complete. Watkins observed that the woman's head was about eighteen inches from the wall and railings around Heydemann's premises, her feet pointing towards the carriageway out of Mitre Street.

A coal plate to the left of the victim's head guarded the entrance to a coal chute. An arched grating to the left of her legs admitted light to the cellar of an empty house. In the beam of the lantern he carried on his belt, Watkins beheld one of the most gruesome sights he had witnessed in seventeen years of police work.

Mitre Square was about twenty-four yards square and largely accommodated respectable business premises. Although much used during business hours, at night the square was illumined by the mean light of just two sources: a lamppost in the northwestern part and a "lantern lamp" secured to the wall of Church Passage in the eastern corner. The square was not entirely given over to commerce. It had private dwellings but the only one that was occupied at the time of the murder was PC Richard Pearce's residence at 3 Mitre Square in the west part.

Watkins called for assistance at Kearley & Tonge's tea warehouse in the square. Night watchman George James Morris, a Metropolitan Police pensioner, recalled Watkins saying, "For God's sake, mate, come to my assistance." Morris asked what the matter was. "Oh, dear," replied Watkins, "there's another woman cut up to pieces!" Morris had noticed nothing unusual, neither had another watchman, George Clapp at 5 Mitre Square, nor off-duty PC Pearce 922. Watkins mounted guard over the body while Morris went for help.

Four days after the murder, Watkins described to the coroner's court what he had seen in the beam of his lantern:

> I next came in at 1.44. I turned to the right. I saw the body of a woman lying there on her back with her feet facing the square [and] her clothes up above her waist. I saw her throat was cut and her bowels protruding. The stomach was ripped up. She was laying in a pool of blood.

When Watkins spoke to *The Star* he said:

> She was ripped up like a pig in the market...I have been in the force a long while, but I never saw such a sight.

His account to *The Daily News* was more explicit:

> I came round [to Mitre Square] again at 1.45, and entering the square from Mitre Street, on the right-hand side, I turned sharp round to the right, and flashing my light, I saw the body in front of me. The clothes were pushed right up to her breast, and the stomach was laid bare, with a dreadful gash from the pit of the stomach to the breast. On examining the body I found the entrails cut out and laid round the throat, which had an awful gash in it, extending from ear to ear. In fact, the head was nearly severed from the body. Blood was everywhere to be seen. It was difficult to discern the injuries to the face for the quantity of blood which covered it...The murderer had inserted the knife just under the left eye, and, drawing it under the nose, cut the nose completely from the face, at the same time inflicting a dreadful gash down the right cheek to the angle of the jawbone. The nose was laid over on the cheek. A more dreadful sight I never saw; it quite knocked me over.

In Aldgate, Morris's frantic blows on his whistle brought the attention of PCs James Harvey and James Thomas Holland. At 1:55 a.m. the news reached Inspector Edward Collard at Bishopsgate Street Police Station. Before setting out for the crime scene, Collard telegraphed the news to H.Q. and sent a constable for Dr Frederick Gordon Brown, the City Police Surgeon, at Finsbury Circus. When Brown arrived at around 2:18 a.m. he found a doctor as well as several policemen already at the scene. The doctor, George William Sequeira, would tell the inquest that the woman had not been dead for more than fifteen minutes before he saw her, although Sequeira came to this conclusion without him or anyone else present having touched the body. This task was left to Dr. Brown who was confronted by

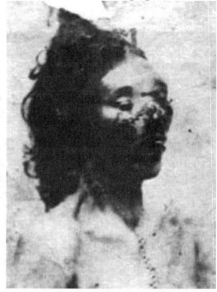

Kate Eddowes mortuary photo

the sight of a woman stretched out upon her back. Her throat had been cut and her abdomen ripped open. Her intestines had been lifted out and placed over her right shoulder. One detached portion of intestine around two feet long had been placed between her body and her left arm. Her face had been savagely mutilated. That afternoon Brown conducted a post-mortem at Golden Lane Mortuary. Four days later Brown made a report to the inquest:

> The body was on its back, the head turned to left shoulder...The abdomen was exposed...The throat cut across.
>
> The intestines were drawn out to a large extent and placed over the right shoulder, they were smeared over with some feculent matter. A piece of about two feet was quite detached from the body and placed between the body and the left arm, apparently by design...
>
> When the body arrived at Golden Lane...the clothes were taken off carefully from the body. A piece of deceased's ear dropped from the clothing.
>
> I made a post mortem examination at half past two on Sunday afternoon...The face was very much mutilated. There was a cut about a quarter of an inch through the lower left eyelid...The right eyelid was cut through to about half an inch.
>
> There was a deep cut over the bridge of the nose...This cut went into the bone and divided all the structures of the cheek except the mucous membrane of the mouth.
>
> The tip of the nose was quite detached by an oblique cut from the bottom of the nasal bone to where the wings of the nose join on to the face...There was a cut on the right angle of the mouth as if the cut of a point of a knife...There was on each side of cheek a cut which peeled up the skin, forming a triangular flap about an inch and a half.
>
> The throat was cut across to the extent of about six or seven inches...The big muscle across the throat was divided through on the left side. The large vessels on the left side of the neck were severed. The larynx was severed below the vocal chord. All the deep structures were severed to the bone....
>
> The carotid artery had a fine hole opening, the internal jugular vein was opened about an inch and a half...All these injuries were performed by a sharp instrument like a knife, and pointed.
>
> The cause of death was haemorrhage from the left common carotid artery. The death was immediate and the mutilations were inflicted after death.
>
> The front walls [of the abdomen] were laid open from the breastbones to the pubes...Behind this, the liver was stabbed as if by the point of a sharp instrument...The abdominal walls were divided in the middle line to within a quarter of an inch of the navel...Attached to

the navel was two and a half inches of the lower part of the rectus muscle on the left side of the abdomen...The incision went down the right side of the vagina and rectum for half an inch behind the rectum.

...An inch below the crease of the thigh was a cut extending from the anterior spine of the ilium obliquely down the inner side of the left thigh and separating the left labium, forming a flap of skin up to the groin...The skin was retracted through the whole of the cut through the abdomen...The cut was made by someone on the right side of the body, kneeling below the middle of the body.

...The intestines had been detached to a large extent from the mesentery. About two feet of the colon was cut away

Right kidney was pale, bloodless with slight congestion of the base of the pyramids.

...The pancreas was cut, but not through, on the left side of the spinal column. Three and a half inches of the lower border of the spleen by half an inch was attached only to the peritoneum.

The peritoneal lining was cut through on the left side and the left kidney carefully taken out and removed. The left renal artery was cut through. I would say that someone who knew the position of the kidney must have done it.

The lining membrane over the uterus was cut through. The womb was cut through horizontally, leaving a stump of three quarters of an inch. The rest of the womb had been taken away with some of the ligaments. The vagina and cervix of the womb was uninjured.

...The wounds on the face and abdomen prove that they were inflicted by a sharp, pointed knife, and that in the abdomen by one six inches or longer.

I believe the perpetrator of the act must have had considerable knowledge of the position of the organs in the abdominal cavity and the way of removing them. It required a great deal of medical knowledge to have removed the kidney and to know where it was placed.

The parts removed would be of no use for any professional purpose. I think the perpetrator of this act had sufficient time, or he would not have nicked the lower eyelids. It would take at least five minutes.

My attention was called to the apron, particularly the corner of the apron with a string attached. The blood spots were of recent origin. I have seen the portion of an apron produced by Dr. Phillips and stated to have been found in Goulston Street. It is impossible to say that it is human blood on the apron. I fitted the piece of apron, which had a new piece of material on it (which had evidently been sewn on to the piece I have), the seams of the borders of the two actually corresponding. Some blood and apparently faecal matter was found on the portion that was found in Goulston Street.

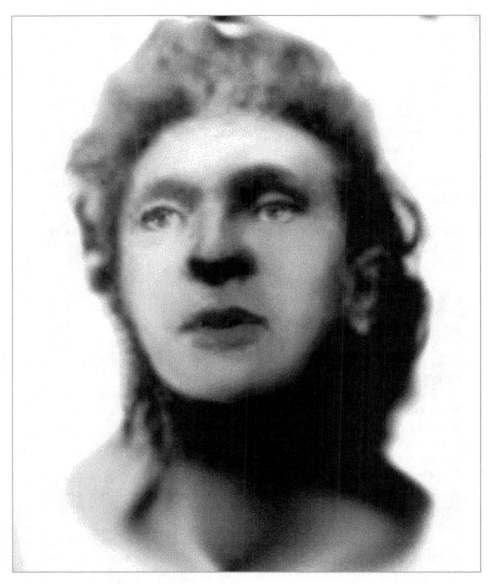

Artist Eric Stedman's facial reconstruction of Kate Eddowes

The portion of Eddowes' apron to which Brown referred, severed by a "clean cut" (Detective Sergeant Halse), had been found at 2:55 a.m., at least 70 minutes after the murder. It was lying in the passage of the doorway leading to Flats 108 and 119 of Model Dwellings in Whitechapel's Goulston Street, more than a quarter of a mile from Mitre Square. The *Daily Telegraph* reported: "...while throwing a light upon the movements of the murderer after he quitted Mitre Square, an important piece of evidence was obtained yesterday. When the body was examined there was a piece of white coarse apron still attached to it. The missing portion was discovered yesterday..."

Written in chalk on the brickwork above the doorway were these words, reportedly set out in this manner:

> *The Juwes are*
> *the men that*
> *Will not*
> *be Blamed*
> *for nothing.*

Sir Charles Warren agreed with Superintendent Thomas Arnold of H Division that the words should be wiped for fear of sparking anti-Jewish riots. Warren gave the order and before dawn the text was erased before a photographer could arrive to take a picture for the records. Neither the intended meaning of the words nor any connection with Eddowes' or, indeed, with other Ripper murders has ever been satisfactorily ascertained. If officialdom did know the true meaning behind the enigmatic sentence it kept quiet and continues to do so.

Police physician Thomas Bond disagreed with Brown's assertion that the killer must have possessed medical skill and knowledge to locate the kidney and then remove it. On 25 October, Robert Anderson sent a letter to Dr. Bond asking for his assistance with the Ripper investigation. He provided copies of the inquests evidence for Nichols, Chapman, Stride and Eddowes and asked Bond to deliver his "opinion on the matter." Bond examined the papers for a fortnight and wrote his response on 10 November. He had spent much of the 9th performing the post-mortem examination of Mary Kelly and was acutely aware of the urgency of arriving at an expert opinion to assist the investigation. Bond concluded that in each of the five cases:

> ...the mutilation was inflicted by a person who had no scientific nor anatomical knowledge. In my opinion he does not even possess

the technical knowledge of a butcher or horse slaughterer or any person accustomed to cut up dead animals.

George William Sequeira, the first doctor at the scene, also thought that the killer lacked anatomical skill (although how he came to this conclusion when he apparently made no physical contact with the body is puzzling). City medical officer William Sedgwick Saunders also believed that the murderer did not seek particular organs.

The identification of the Mitre Square victim was a relatively straightforward matter although at first it appeared that the investigating team had little to go on. The deceased was a thin woman aged around forty, dressed in dark and dirty clothes, a fact that marked her as a vagrant or, at best, a tenant of common lodging houses. She was 5' tall and had dark auburn hair and hazel eyes.

Her clothing consisted of a black straw bonnet trimmed with green and black velvet and black beads, a red gauze silk neckerchief, a black cloth jacket with imitation fur edging around the collar and fur edging around the sleeves, a dark-green chintz skirt patterned in Michaelmas daisies and golden lilies with three flounces, a man's white vest, a brown linsey dress bodice with a black velvet collar and brown metal buttons down the front, a pair of brown ribbed stockings mended at the feet in white, a pair of men's laced boots and a piece of old white apron.

She was dressed in numerous undergarments: a grey stiff petticoat, a very old dark-green alpaca skirt, a very old ragged blue skirt and a white calico chemise. She was carrying a number of items: a large white handkerchief, one blue striped pocket and two unbleached calico pockets, a white cotton pocket-handkerchief, twelve pieces of white rag, a piece of white coarse linen, a piece of blue and white shirting, two small blue bedticking bags, two short clay pipes, two tin boxes containing tea and sugar, one piece of flannel, six pieces of soap, a small tooth comb, a white-handled table-knife, a metal tea-spoon, a red leather cigarette case with white metal fittings, an empty tin match-box, a piece of red flannel containing pins and needles, and a ball of hemp.

The body did provide some clues. There was the tattoo "TC" on the left forearm and the mustard tin picked up by Sergeant Jones from beside the body, which contained two tickets from pawnbroker Joseph Jones of 31 Church Street, Spitalfields. One ticket was for a man's flannel shirt, pledged on 31 August for 9d in the name of Emily Burrell, 52 White's Row. The other was for a pair of men's boots, pledged on 28 September for 2s 6d in the name of Jane Kelly, 6 Dorset Street. On making enquiries, police found both addresses to be false.

Despite this setback, the leads soon led to John Kelly identifying the woman as his common-law wife, Catherine Eddowes, when he walked into Bishopsgate Police Station on 2 October after reading about the pawn tickets in the newspapers. Kelly's identification was also confirmed by Catherine Eddowes' sister, Eliza Gold.

Catherine Eddowes (a.k.a. "Kate Conway" and "Kate Kelly" after her common-law husbands) was born 14 April 1842 in Graisley Green, Wolverhampton, in the Black Country region of the industrial Midlands. Her parents were tinplate worker George Eddowes and Catherine (née Evans). They had ten other children. In the family Catherine was known as "Chick." The family moved to London a year after Kate's birth but she later returned to Wolverhampton to work as a tinplate stamper. Friends in her native town recalled Kate as an "intelligent, scholarly woman, but of fiery temperament."

Kate lost this job and subsequently took up with a Thomas Conway in Birmingham. Thomas drew an army pension from his service in the 18th Royal Irish Regiment in which he had enlisted as Thomas Quinn. After the pair moved to London they had a daughter and two sons. Together for nearly twenty years, Kate and Thomas never married. Eventually, Kate left her family in 1880, supposedly because of her drinking although her older sister, Emma, while agreeing that Kate's fondness for drink was the root cause of the parting said that John's habit of ill-treating and beating Kate was a contributory factor. By 1881, Kate was living with new partner, John Kelly, at Cooney's lodging house and was practising casual prostitution to help ends meet. To avoid contact with Kate, Thomas Conway drew his army pension under his name Quinn and kept their sons' addresses secret from her.

Catherine Eddowes was buried Monday, 8 October 1888 in an elm coffin in the City of London Cemetery, in an unmarked (public) grave 49336, square 318. Kelly and Eddowes' sister attended. In late 1996, the cemetery authorities decided to mark her grave with a plaque.

1 October saw the arrival at the offices of the Central News Agency of the "Saucy Jacky" postcard. It read:

I was not codding dear old Boss when I gave you the tip, you'll hear about Saucy Jacky's work tomorrow double event this time number one squealed a bit couldn't finish straight off. Had not got time to get ears off for police thanks for keeping last letter back till I got to work again.

Jack the Ripper

Some have argued that the card was sent prior to dissemination of the news of the Stride and Eddowes murders. In fact, it was postmarked 24-hours after the crimes were committed, long after news of the events became known to newspaper staff and to residents of the area. General opinion among the police was that the postcard was a hoax perpetrated by a journalist, a view shared by most Ripper historians.

During October 1888, George Lusk, Chairman of the Whitechapel Vigilance Committee, came to believe that his house at 1 Alderney Road, Mile End, was being surveilled by a sinister bearded man and requested police protection. On the 16th he received at his home a small package in the evening mail. It contained half a kidney and a note, which has become known as the "From Hell" letter.

It was written in a hand dissimilar to that which penned the "Saucy Jacky" postcard. Lusk thought he was the victim of a sick joke and placed the box and kidney into a desk drawer before showing them to Vigilance Committee colleagues, including four members who visited his home to inspect the items. Lusk wanted to discard them but his colleagues persuaded him to take them to Dr Frederick Wiles's nearby surgery in the Mile End Road. Wiles was out so his assistant, F.S. Reed, examined the contents of the box and took the kidney to Dr. Thomas Horrocks Openshaw at the London Hospital. Openshaw examined the kidney, which was then handed over to the City Police in whose jurisdiction Catherine Eddowes had been murdered.

Openshaw's professional opinion was that the organ was a human kidney from the left side, which had been preserved in spirit. *The Daily Telegraph* reported Openshaw as declaring that it was a "ginny kidney" from a 45-year-old (heavy-drinking) female, an assertion that Openshaw strongly denied on the same day (19 October) in *The Star* newspaper, averring that it was impossible to tell its age or gender or how long it had been preserved in spirits. Major Smith claimed in his memoirs that the kidney matched Eddowes' extracted organ because the length of renal artery attached to the kidney matched the missing length from the body, and that both the body and kidney showed signs of the Bright's disease with which Eddowes had been afflicted.

George Lusk

The infamous *From Hell* letter sent to George Lusk

Smith's recollections are not supported by medical reports submitted by the examining pathologists or the police records and have tended to be dismissed as over-dramatisation on his part to beef up his memoirs.

Dr Saunders who attended the post-mortem told the press, "the right kidney of the woman Eddowes was perfectly normal in its structure and healthy...my opinion is that it was a student's antic." The inquiry co-ordinator, Chief Inspector Donald Swanson, wrote, "Similar kidneys might and could be obtained from any dead person upon whom a post mortem had been made for any cause, by students or dissecting room porter."

Recall that PC Watkins said that he entered Mitre Square at 1:44 a.m. having been there last at 1:30 a.m. Kate was therefore killed between Watkins's earlier departure time and his next arrival in the Square. It is estimated that it would have taken less than ten minutes for Kate to reach Mitre Square after being released a little after 12:55 a.m. from Bishopsgate Police Station. These timings present the investigator with two issues.

Firstly, taking 1:30 a.m. as the earliest possible time for the commencement of an extensive murder process, this leaves approximately twenty-five minutes unaccounted for between Kate's departure from Bishopsgate and the time of her death in Mitre Square. The issue of time is put under even more pressure if one considers the possibility that it *was* Eddowes that Joseph Lawende and his friends saw with a man at the entrance to Church Passage at 1:35 a.m. However, there is a world of difference between positively identifying a corpse (it appears that Lawende was not actually shown the body) and offering an opinion that the deceased's clothing is a match for those on a person one saw. Nevertheless, the possibility that it was Eddowes cannot be ruled out.

Secondly, accepting that Kate was killed in Mitre Square, whoever had entered the square and carried out the assault in such a brief span (no more than fourteen minutes, including escape time, reducing to around eight minutes if the Lawende party did see Eddowes and allowing time for Kate and her killer subsequently to reach Mitre Square) came and went not just like a ghost but one with an Olympian turn of speed. When alerted by Watkins, George Morris, a former trained policeman, was working only about two yards inside Kearley & Tonge's front door, which itself had been ajar for only two minutes. Morris told *The Star* that he "had gone to the front door to look out into the square two moments before Watkins called to him." He neither saw nor heard anything untoward. Neither did George Clapp, the caretaker who slept on site at Heydemann's, which overlooked the murder site. How, then, does a ghost, albeit a spritely spectre remove and take away its victim's left kidney and womb so very quickly?

Let us for a moment put aside the generally agreed circumstances and timeline of Eddowes' murder and ruminate on some obvious questions. Kate's death is generally attributed to the Ripper. How does one entirely satisfy this attribution?

May there be other scenarios that require consideration in order to make better sense of the extremely brief window of opportunity available to the party that had murdered Elizabeth Stride? In order to square this seemingly irreconcilable circle, one must ask the question: did someone else kill her? Was Kate's murder the work of a joint enterprise, as suggested in Stride's case by Israel Schwartz's testimony of what he saw in Berner Street?

However, it is the case that both Schwartz's pipe man and attacker man would also have been hard pressed to get to Mitre Square on foot in time to kill Eddowes. Was a third confederate involved? If so, what new lines of thought might come to mind about the true nature, purpose, motive, planning and execution of the Whitechapel murders?

In the question concerning the place of death, let one reflect on the fact that no noise was heard of what was obviously a frenzied attack. Let one also not forget that the killer took the time, in very poorly lit conditions, to find and remove Eddowes' left kidney and womb. If he was not anatomically knowledgeable, as most medical authorities agreed, just how fortunate was he to have the Devil on his side to undertake, at speed, these difficult incisions and extractions more by luck than by judgement?

Bearing in mind the question of the missing twenty-five minutes, was Kate killed in Mitre Square at all? Could she have been killed perhaps in a well-lit curtained carriage with sound-deadened wheels during Kate's journey from Bishopsgate Police Station, her assailant(s) subsequently bringing her body to Mitre Square for reasons known only to them?

Of course, this scenario may only be considered if one assumes that Lawende was mistaken in his testimony about the clothing. If Kate Eddowes truly was in Church Passage at 1:35 a.m then logic appears to have little place in working out how the perpetrator conducted such complex actions in no more than eight minutes, even if equipped according to Dr. Brown's minority professional opinion with "considerable knowledge of the position of the organs in the abdominal cavity and the way of removing them [and] a great deal of medical knowledge."

Lastly, recalling Kate's remark to the superintendent at Shoe Lane Casual Ward might she have known her killer? Let us briefly follow this line of thought. Kate dismissed the superintendent's warning to be careful with a defiant, "Oh, no fear of that." Did she believe she had something on the murderer that she could use to her advantage? Believing that she had an opportunity to improve her lot did Kate Eddowes in the twenty minutes or so after leaving the police station do something very foolish and pay the ultimate price? Or was she under observation by those who knew of her interest in their business and, along the lines discussed above, grabbed Kate as quickly as possible after her release to silence her permanently?

Finally, why on two occasions—at the pawnbroker and in Bishopsgate Police Station—did Kate give the names Jane Kelly and Mary Ann Kelly, respectively? That she would call herself Kelly after her manfriend is obvious but why choose Jane and Mary Anne? Both creations appear too close to "Mary Jane" as in Mary Jane Kelly to be entirely coincidental. Did Kate's choices betray a connection with the Ripper's final victim that has not been sufficiently factored into the debate about any pre-existing links between the murdered women?

I do not have the answers to these vexing questions. They merely strike me as ones that should be posed and, if they are to be dismissed, to do so with good reason.

Kate Eddowes was murdered on the Saint Day of Jerome, one of the great figures in the Christian Church and a supremely gifted scholar. In iconography Jerome is often depicted with an owl to represent his deep wisdom in matters of Biblical study. It is now time to meet "Glen Claston," whose insights spurred me into my own studies of nineteenth-century Bible scholarship in the context of the socio-mystical environment under cover of which Jack the Ripper was at work in 1888.

Chapter 12

Claston

In the late 1990s when I made my Internet search for anyone named Claston living in the North American continent I frankly expected to draw a blank. It was a shot in the dark but I did it anyway because I'm pretty dogged about ticking things off my to-do list (in this instance, addressing the old chestnut: "Did Mary Kelly survive?") and because…well, one never knows.

My Internet trawl harvested twelve references to Claston, only one of which "seemed" to be of interest. This was a link to a Glen Claston who, when I went to his webpage, was listing references to the Elizabethan magus, Dr John Dee. This piqued my interest because I had recently become interested in Dee by virtue of certain aspects of his work that I felt were synchronous with elements of the Whitechapel story.

Claston's website did not list an email address and it took me two more years to find one. "Glen Claston," pseudonym for the late Tim Rayhel, codebreaker extraordinaire, was a very elusive fellow. We will come to our exchange but, firstly, just who was Tim Rayhel (1957-2014)? There is surprisingly little available information on Rayhel, described by contemporary cryptographers as a "super geek genius." According to the online obituary by his friend Nick Pelling,[61] Rayhel was a very private individual. He once told Pelling, "(Blogs) expose too much of the underbelly to the carnivores, and that I don't want to do."

Rayhel discovered what would become a lifelong interest in ciphers after joining the U.S. forces in the Army Security Agency. After completing military service he served in private armies in Nicaragua and other Central American regions. Rayhel described these private units as the forerunners of mercenary outfits such as Blackwater (today Academi), the American private military company founded in 1997 by

---

[61] http://ciphermysteries.com/2014/07/20/obituary-timothy-rayhel-glen-claston-1957-2014

former U.S. Navy SEAL officer Erik Prince.

Rayhel's superior during these activities was Oliver North, who many will recall was convicted in the notorious Iran-Contra affair of the late 1980s until all charges were dismissed in 1991. The scandal involved the illegal sale of weapons to Iran to encourage the release of U.S. hostages held in Lebanon. North's role was to devise a plan to divert proceeds from the arms sales to support the Contra rebel groups in Nicaragua. North was granted limited immunity from prosecution in exchange for testifying before Congress about the scheme. It appears that Rayhel was involved in some capacity in these politically scandalous activities, telling Pelling:

> My old boss Ollie North took a fall and I retired from that work, having seen a bit too much of what real American policy is all about. I suffered an attack of conscience, became a fundamentalist minister [in the Church of Christ], found that too extreme, and finally directed my efforts toward staying below the radar.

Having decided to lead the quiet life and dedicate his time and expertise to cryptography, Rayhel became interested in the cryptographic writings of Francis Bacon and their possible links to Shakespeare's works. Eventually, he concluded that a link between them was unlikely and that most Baconian researchers' claims were "false and misleading," a typically blunt remark from a man who, by all accounts, did not suffer fools gladly.

From 1986 onwards Rayhel put his cryptography skills to work on a study of the *Voynich Manuscript*, posting online under the pseudonym "Glen Claston." The MS has been called the "world's most mysterious manuscript," and is recognised as one of the main unsolved problems in the history of cryptography.

In 1639 Prague citizen Georgius Barschius wrote a letter to the Jesuit Athanasius Kircher in Rome, explaining that he owned a mysterious book that was written in an unknown script and profusely illustrated with pictures of plants, stars and chemical secrets. He could not read the text and hoped that Kircher would be able to translate it for him. It is not believed that Kircher succeeded in the task.

The MS is a 22.5cm x 16cm parchment with its leaves numbered up to 116, of which 14 are missing. Its parchment cover is blank, providing neither title nor author. The manuscript is written in an elegant but otherwise unknown script. The text, written from left to right, appears to be arranged in short paragraphs. In 2009 carbon dating of the parchment resulted in a date range of 1404-1438 with 95% confidence.

A page from the *Voynich Manuscript*

The MS is profusely illustrated, a study of which suggests that it is a scientific or medical work from the Middle Ages. Illustrations of similar type are mostly grouped together in the manuscript from which one may tentatively identify the following sections:

> A herbal section with drawings of herbs, some of which look realistic while others appear imaginary;
> An astronomical section with illustrations of the Sun, Moon, stars and zodiac symbols;
> A cosmological section with mostly circular drawings;
> A "biological" section, which contains some possibly anatomical drawings with small human (mostly feminine) figures populating systems of tubes transporting liquids;
> A pharmaceutical section, so called because it has drawings of containers next to which are aligned various small parts of herbs (leaves, roots);
> A recipes section, which contains over 300 short paragraphs, each accompanied by a star in the left margin.

The MS has been preserved in the Beinecke Rare Book and Manuscript Library of Yale University since 1969, where it is officially known as MS 408. It is far better known by its nickname, derived from Wilfrid Voynich, an antiquarian book dealer who brought the MS to light in 1912. Voynich described his acquisition of the work (purchased under conditions of absolute secrecy):

In 1912 I came across a most remarkable collection of preciously illuminated manuscripts. For many decades these volumes had lain buried in the chests in which I found them in an ancient castle in Southern Europe...While examining the manuscripts, with a view to the acquisition of at least a part of the collection, my attention was especially drawn by one volume. It was such an ugly duckling compared with the other manuscripts, with their rich decorations in gold and colors that my interest was aroused at once. I found that it was written entirely in cipher.

Even a necessarily brief examination of the vellum upon which it was written, the calligraphy, the drawings and the pigments suggested to me as the date of its origin the latter part of the thirteenth century. The drawings indicated it to be an encyclopedic work on natural philosophy...the fact that this was a thirteenth-century manuscript in cipher convinced me that it must be a work of exceptional importance, and to my knowledge the existence of a manuscript of such an early date written entirely in cipher was unknown, so I included it among the manuscripts which I purchased from this collection...two problems presented themselves - the text must be unravelled and the history of the manuscript must be traced...It was not until some time after the manuscript came into my hands that I read the document bearing the date 1665 (or 1666), which was attached to the front cover...This document, which is a letter from Joannes Marcus Marci to Athanasius Kircher making a gift of the manuscript to him, is of great significance.

Voynich took his "cipher MS," as he always called it, to London in 1912 and to the United States in January 1915, occasionally providing photographic copies of pages to experts in various disciplines. The MS has tasked the minds of first-rate code-breaking experts ever since 1917.

In the 1940s and 1960s the eminent cryptanalysts, William F. Friedman and Elizabeth Smith Friedman aided by groups of codebreaking experts, made serious attempts at deciphering its text to no avail. In 1961 the book was bought by antiquarian H.P. Kraus for the sum of $24,500.

Kraus tried to sell it for $160,000 but was unable to find a buyer. Finally, in 1969 he donated it to Yale. Despite the efforts of clever people such as Tim Rayhel, one can neither say what the MS is for and what it says, nor can one say what it is not. It is tempting to assume that the text relates to the illustrations, but this is not certain.

Variously, but not exclusively, it has been suggested that the MS comprises early discoveries and inventions by the 13th century friar Roger Bacon; a rare prayer book from the Cathars saved from the fourteenth-century Inquisition; nonsense written by a medieval quack to impress his clients; and meaningless strings of characters cleverly composed by John Dee and/or his associate Edward Kelley for monetary gain. The 2009 carbon-dating test rules out the first suggestion and makes the second very dubious. Experts are so far removed from cracking the code (supposing that there is actually a

Timothy Rayhel (Glen Claston)

code in the MS to be broken) that they are still not able to answer the most basic question as to whether the text is plain language, encrypted language, constructed language or simply meaningless gibberish. The MS continues to attract people from all over the world. Voynich stated that it would become more valuable as soon as it has been deciphered. But today everyone agrees—its mystery and its resistance to translation are what make it special.

Rayhel did not devote himself exclusively to the *Voynich Manuscript*. He was fascinated by the works of John Dee (particularly the *Monas Hieroglyphica*) and by numerous Renaissance books on cryptography. He also investigated the Beale ciphers, which allegedly state the U.S. location of a fabulous cache of gold, silver and jewels, before concluding in 2004 that they were a nineteenth-century hoax.

Rayhel was also well known for his research into the Zodiac Killer Ciphers. The Zodiac Killer was a serial murderer who operated in Northern California in the late 1960s. His identity has never been established. Although the Zodiac claimed 37 murders in letters to the newspapers, investigators agree on only seven that were targeted (four men and three women aged 16 to 29, two of whom survived). The name Zodiac Killer was coined in a series of taunting letters sent to the press until 1974, correspondence that included four cryptograms, three of which have yet to be solved. Despite his penname, the Zodiac Killer had not shown any interest in astrology and it is speculated that he drew inspiration from previous killers, in particular Jack the Ripper and his alleged taunts to the police. Compare for style, for example, this Zodiac message (the "Bus Bomb" letter of 9 November 1969): "I gave the cops som bussy work to do to keep them happy. I enjoy needling the blue pigs. Hey blue pig I was in the park -- you were useing fire trucks to mask the sound of your cruzeing prowl cars."

Rayhel battled with various health issues, including a heart attack. Crippling back pain in 2012 was later diagnosed as "peripheral neuropathy that may be related to MS." He died in Albuquerque in 2014, cause of death unknown.

In 2001 I finally found an email address for "Glen Claston" and sent off my message. I went for broke, figuring I had nothing to lose if I laid out all the points I wanted to cover. He replied as Claston and I refer to him as that for the remainder of this work. I explained that I was looking for genealogical links with Mary Kelly, mentioning that I had been struck by the concluding scene in that year's cinematic release of *From Hell* starring Johnny Depp as Abberline and Heather Graham as Kelly which shows her alive and well in the West of Ireland.

Elizabethan magus, Dr. John Dee

I outlined my points of interest concerning Lewis Carroll and John Dee, beginning with Edward Kelley's use of the "Devil's looking glass." I went on to say that it was my hunch that Dee's work was also connected with the motive force behind the Ripper murders, having arrived at this conclusion after finding Charlotte Fell-Smith's work on Dee[62] and noting some curious coincidences.

The first chapter has a header quotation from a "George Chapman": "O, Incredulities, the wit of fooles that slovenly will spit on all things faire, the Coward's castle and the sluggard's cradle, How easy 'tis to be an infidel!" As is well known, George Chapman, Polish serial killer Seweryn Antonowicz Kłosowski, also known as the Borough Poisoner, is a Ripper suspect. And, with a bit of imagination and loose interpretation, "Whitechapel" can be translated as "coward's castle."

Additionally, Fell-Smith's work describes how when Dee returned to England from his travels in Europe one of his travelling companions was a Mary Nicholls, daughter of his friend Francis Nicholls whom Dee taught astrology and the art of skrying.

More in hope than in expectation, I said that if he was able to throw any light on these correspondences I would be very pleased to hear in return, otherwise to consign my message to the trash and to accept my sincere apologies for the intrusion. Frankly, I expected my approach to be a wild goose chase and that Claston, if he took the time to reply, would say he knew nothing of the topic and couldn't help me. In contacting a complete stranger several thousand miles away out of the blue, why should I expect anything different? But that was not the outcome, not by a country mile. He replied almost as if he had been expecting my message and had pre-considered his response with much thought and deliberation. This is Glen Claston's reply:

> I've studied your message very carefully, and have come to the conclusion that there is no information I now possess that would be of interest to you, other than to point out that I too hold some uncommon views of historical characters.
>
> John Dee was above all a mathematician, a man who consorted with the likes of Gerard Mercator and Henry Billingsley. He was indeed an astrologer in a time when astrology was inextricably linked to health and medicine, but he was also an inventor of navigational instruments and a dabbler in the science of optics. He was also an intelligence agent for Elizabeth and Walsingham, serving England with his every effort. I share Robert Hook's opinion that Dee's books on "angelic magic" are nothing more than very complex cipher.

---

[62] Fell-Smith, C., *John Dee*, Constable & Co. Ltd, London, 1909

Hook gave a private demonstration of his claim to the Royal Society in 1705, but nothing survives of that demonstration other than the fact it took place.

If Dee's books are indeed cipher as an increasing number of researchers believe, their contents are mathematically and scientifically oriented, and all the "cover text" of scrying and spirits is a ruse in the fine tradition of Johannes Trithemius and Cornelius Agrippa, both of whom were well studied by John Dee.

Lewis Carroll was also a mathematician and logician. "Through the Looking Glass" was, in his words, "a diversion for my students." It was a logic puzzle that contained a summary and statement of current political events, and not intended to be a bestselling fiction big enough to be a Disney production. If one chooses to ferret out the truth behind the "looking glass," one has to backtrack to the state of logic as taught in those times, while familiarizing oneself with the intricacies of contemporary current events.

I did indeed see *From Hell* with Johnny Depp, one of my favorite off-color actors. Your e-mail prompted me to visit some information about Mary Kelly, specifically the report of her autopsy conducted hours after her death. From this report I gain two very keen insights - first, that Mary Kelly died, the body being identified by numerous witnesses as that of Mary Kelly. Second, that the method of execution bore no singular mark of a surgeon, as is the current mythology. People look for things that are familiar to them, and when their scope of search is limited, they return only items discovered within the range of their limited search.

If it were me, I would begin my search in scripture, as this was most probably the work of a twisted religious mind. There were several "puritan" groups in London at the time, and not all of them used the *King James Bible*. Contemporary biblical translation would be my first area of study, with emphasis on spelling, not entirely standardized by this time. This would narrow the field.

Bear in mind that the author of these words was both a former Church minister with insights into Christian fundamentalist extremism and a highly skilled codebreaker from the shadowy world of military intelligence and analysis. In these respects, one should be prepared more for suggestion than for outright clarity in seeking the identity of the putative "twisted religious mind" behind the Whitehapel murders. And so it follows that in Claston's remark about the truth behind the "looking glass," I sensed he was indicating that he possessed more insights about the broader context of the Ripper affair than he was prepared to share initially. By this, I felt that Claston was saying that the key to a complete understanding of events in Whitechapel is to be found through adopting a Gilbert and Sullivanesque perspective   upon the wider esoteric and geopolitical imperatives confronting Britain and its European neighbours in 1888.

I wondered what Claston meant by: "there is no information I now possess that would be of interest to you"? Was this just an irrelevant syntax issue or was he indicating that he did once have information but possessed it no longer? If he did have it once why could he not provide some detail from memory? What was he not saying or, rather, what *was* he saying that I needed to decipher?

Consider firstly Claston's seemingly unequivocal remark: "Mary Kelly died, the body being identified by numerous witnesses as that of Mary Kelly." It is a clear instance of "looking glass" logic. The body on the bed was hacked to pieces such that it was unrecognisable (see images on pages 219 and 225). Claston, of course, knew this very well and in sardonic manner exposed the absurdity of accepting facts in a murder case based on faith instead of empirically based evidence. In Claston's words: "People look for things that are familiar to them [in this case, a body on a bed in a room known to be Mary Kelly's residence], and when their scope of search is limited [there is only one body in the room], they return only items discovered within the range of their limited search [*ipso facto*, the body on the bed in No. 13, Kelly's room, must therefore be Kelly's]". Our fear of the unfamiliar trumps logic and reason, a fact about which former U.S. Intelligence operative Claston was well aware.

Following on, Claston's remark about Biblical translation blew me away because I had been advancing my research along similar lines believing that, to my knowledge, no one had previously interpreted the facts surrounding the Ripper murders in the context of scriptural study. That former Church of Christ minister Claston was suggesting codes and ciphers were at the heart of the mystery is evidenced by his emphasis on scriptural spelling as a key entry point for investigation. Government papers   state that by 13 October Sir Charles Warren was voicing an opinion that the murders could have been carried out by a secret society. Such bodies throughout history have routinely employed codes and ciphers to hide sensitive information from the profane and the uninitiated. The papers quote Warren as saying:

---

[63] "Things are seldom what they seem; Skim milk masquerades as cream." H.M.S. Pinafore, 1878

[64] No.A49301D/1, Date 12 Oct 88, Foreign Office, References & c, Whitechapel Murders

As Mr. Matthews is aware I have for some time past inclined to the idea that the murders may possibly be done by a secret society, as the logical solution of the question, but I would not understand this being done by a Socialist because the last murders were obviously done by someone desiring to bring discredit on the Jews and Socialists or Jewish Socialists.

To illustrate the point, we have seen that Warren himself was the leading figure behind the founding of the Quatuor Coronati Lodge in London. Similarly, there were many others connected with the Ripper case that concerned themselves with Masonic affairs. Detective Sergeant Eugene Charles Bradshaw, for example, who was involved in the arrest of one-time Ripper suspect William Wallace Brodie in 1889, was a member of Prince Leopold Lodge, which met at Three Nuns Hotel, Aldgate High Street. George Lusk was a member of the Doric Lodge (meeting place, The Duke's Head, 79 Whitechapel Road). Inspector Charles Digby who was in charge of police reports for H Division was also a member of Doric and was present at Lusk's initiation in April 1882. Similarly, cart and van builder Arthur Duttfield was a Doric member. (It was his old yard in Berner Street where Elizabeth Stride was found.) Incidentally, the Doric Lodge met on the nights of both the Nichols and Chapman murders.

I do not make these points to suggest that Masons were connected with the murders but to illustrate that if one is going to pursue a line of Ripper research concerning these societies then be prepared for a mountain of work and likely failure. But Claston was referring to something quite different: a Bible translation group dedicated to contemporary study. There were a number of small-scale efforts concerned with Bible revision in the late 19th century, among them:

- Francis Patrick Kenrick's *Holy Bible* in 7 volumes, 1849;
- Forshall and Madden's *New Testament*, 1850;
- Ambrose Leicester Sawyer's *Holy Bible*, 1860;
- Robert Young's *Holy Bible*, 1863;
- Otis Clapp's *The Word of the Lord: the Old and New Testaments*, 1869;
- Thomas Newberry's *The Englishman's Bible*, published in various stages, 1870-1884;
- Frederick Charles Cook's *Holy Bible*, 1871;
- T.K Cheyne and Others' *The Holy Bible Variorum Edition*, 1876;
- Julia Smith's *The Holy Bible*, 1876

Nevertheless, these initiatives were dwarfed by one major scholarly enterprise. In 1870 the Convocation of Canterbury commissioned the New Testament revision company "to adapt King James' version (published in 1611 and usually referred to as the KJV) to the present state of the English language without changing the idiom and vocabulary…and to adapt it to the present standard of Biblical scholarship." The result was the *Revised Version* (RV), alternatively called the *English Revised Version* (ERV). The work was entrusted to more than fifty scholars from various denominations in Britain. American scholars were invited to co-operate by correspondence.

The New Testament was published in 1881, the Old Testament in 1885, and the Apocrypha in 1894. The best known members of the translation committee members were Brooke Foss Westcott and Fenton John Anthony Hort. The early sixteenth-century *King James Version* translators had fewer than twelve manuscripts of the New Testament in Greek to work with. In fact, they had no Greek at all for part of the book of Revelation so they had to "conjecturally amend" (guess) what the section actually said.

It is known today that the original Greek of the New Testament was "common" or koine Greek, which was the marketplace Greek of Alexander the Great. The KJV translators did not know this and sometimes mistranslated words because of this lack of understanding. This knowledge also indicates that the New Testament was written generally in a sort of "popular tabloid" style of language. Modern translation, therefore, that uses literary or grand language is not generally reflecting the text and style of the Greek manuscripts of the New Testament.

Recognising this, expert Bible scholars Westcott and Hort worked for twenty-eight years from 1853 in compiling Greek language manuscripts, taking note of the earliest and best of them to produce in 1881 *The New Testament in the Original Greek*, also known as the Westcott and Hort text. This was followed by an Introduction and Appendix by Hort in a second volume in 1882.

Westcott and Hort's acclaimed achievement in critical textual analysis was to summarise the best information available to produce the most accurate Biblical text. Their *New Testament in the Original Greek*, based on cutting edge increased knowledge, became the basis of the RV of 1881. As a result, the RV kept the KJV-style language but was generally considered to be a much more accurate translation.

Nineteenth-century biblical study and translation is a large and complex topic. Before seeking "to ferret out the truth behind the "looking glass" let us turn its lens upon Jack the Ripper's final and most enigmatic victim.

Chapter 13

From Lilacs to Violets—Mary Kelly

Thursday 8 November, 13 Miller's Court, Whitechapel
Fish porter Joseph Barnett paid a visit to his lover, Mary Jane Kelly, arriving at 7:00 p.m. and leaving, he later said, at 8:00 p.m. with laundress Maria Harvey who had been visiting Kelly. Harvey's own subsequent testimony casts doubt on Barnett's timing, stating that she left No. 13 at 6:55 p.m. Maria left behind two men's shirts, a boy's shirt, a black overcoat, a black bonnet, a pawn ticket and a girl's white petticoat.

Joseph returned to his lodgings at Buller's Boarding House where he played whist until retiring at 12:30 a.m. Earlier on Thursday another friend, Lizzie Albrook, a resident of Miller's Court, had visited Kelly. As Lizzie was leaving, Mary said to her without elaborating, "Whatever you do, don't you do wrong and turn out as I have."

There are no extant authenticated photographs of Mary Kelly. Contemporary descriptions differ. To Barnett, Mary was fair with a fresh coloured complexion. Mrs Elizabeth Phoenix, Mary's landlord's sister-in-law, described her as "5'7" in height, and of rather stout build with blue eyes and a very fine head of hair which reached nearly to her waist." Mary's upstairs neighbour, Elizabeth Prater, said Mary was "tall, pretty, fair as a lily, and on good terms with everybody." Caroline Maxwell, wife of a local lodging-house deputy, described her as "a pleasant little woman, rather stout, fair complexion, and rather pale...spoke with a kind of impediment." From these meager scraps one must formulate one's own impression of Mary Kelly's fair features.

Inspector Dew knew Mary by sight and said she paraded around Whitechapel, usually with two or three friends. She never wore a hat, always wore a spotless clean white apron, and had a reputation for violence and a quick temper. Her reputed nicknames were "Black Mary," "Fair Emma" and "Ginger," although Kelly's actual hair colour is unknown and generally described as "blond."

On 10 November, American newspapers quoted Kelly's neighbour, Mrs Hewitt, as referring to Mary as Mary Jane Lawrence.

Joseph Barnett met Mary in April 1887. Something must have clicked because when they met the next day they agreed to live together. A few months later, in early 1888, the pair moved into 13 Miller's Court, a furnished single room, 10 feet x 12 feet, actually the partitioned ground floor back room of the main house, No. 26 Dorset Street, Spitalfields.

One approached Miller's Court from Dorset Street through a flag-stoned passage that ran under the arch, which was a yard wide and about twenty feet long. The only door to No. 13 was the last on the right in the arched passage before it opened out into a yard about fifteen-feet square. The houses in the court were all whitewashed at ground floor level. The yard contained a water tap and a communal dustbin. Light was provided by a wall-mounted gaslamp. The Miller's Court dwellings, known as "McCarthy's Rents," were owned by John McCarthy who ran a chandler's shop at 27 Dorset Street.

13 Miller's Court, Dorset Street

Dorset Street, situated within H Division of the Metropolitan Police and a part of what Rev. Barnett dubbed the "wicked quarter mile," was renowned for its poverty and crime, its fearsome reputation being such that the police double-patrolled the court. Early sociologist Charles Booth produced his colour-coded poverty map of London in 1887. Dorset Street had the woeful distinction of being shaded black, the lowest ranking, marking it out as vicious and semi-criminal.

The contents of No. 13 were a bed and two tables, one by the bed and a larger one for eating, two chairs, a washstand and a fireplace. Above the fireplace was hung a print of *The Fisherman's Widow*. There was also a kettle, a chipped china plate with patterned border, a candlestick, a bowl and spoon, an empty glass jar and kindling for the fire. On her tiny bedside table Mary kept a small hand mirror and a heart-shaped trinkets dish.

Mary said she had lost the doorkey, so she bolted and unbolted it from outside by putting a hand through a broken window. Julia Venturney, Mary's German neighbour, claimed that Kelly had broken the window when drunk. In fact, it was broken 30 October during a row with Joseph, a bust-up provoked by Mary's decision to share her room with a prostitute known as "Julia," perhaps Julia Venturney.

In July 1888 Joseph lost his license as a fish porter, apparently for theft. The loss of income prompted Mary to return to prostitution to make ends meet. After their quarrel Joseph moved to accommodation in Bishopsgate. However, the pair remained on good terms and saw each other frequently, Joseph giving Mary money.

There are no confirmed sightings of Mary Kelly between 8:00 p.m. and 11:45 p.m. although there is an unconfirmed story that she was seen drinking with a woman named Elizabeth Forster in the Ten Bells situated on the corner of Commercial Street and Fournier Street in Spitalfields, a short walk from Miller's Court. At sometime in the evening Mary ate a meal of fish and potatoes. Prostitute Mary Ann Cox of 5 Miller's Court, describing herself as "a widow and unfortunate," reported seeing Kelly returning to No. 13 drunk at about 11:45 p.m. with a man in his thirties. She described him as short, stout and blotchy faced. Carrying a quart pail of beer, he had a short carroty moustache, small side whiskers, wore a billycock hat and a

Mary Cox, *Pictorial News*

longish dark shabby coat.

Kelly was wearing a linsey frock and a red knitted crossover shawl around her shoulders. She and the man stood ahead of Cox as they went up the court. Cox said, "Good night, Mary Jane." Mary replied drunkenly, "Good night. I'm going to have a song." Kelly started singing and Cox knew she was drunk. The man made no noise but closed the door at No. 13 behind them as they went into Mary's room. There was a light from the window but the shade was drawn. Cox heard Mary singing *A Violet I Plucked from Mother's Grave When a Boy*, a popular song of the day composed in 1881 by American, Will H. Fox. Mary was still singing when Cox went out at midnight.

At 12:30 a.m. flower seller Catherine Pickett who lived above Mary is disturbed by her neighbour's singing. Pickett's husband persuades his wife not to go downstairs and complain, telling her: "You leave the poor woman alone." Mary was still singing when Cox returned home at 1:00 a.m. Also at 1:00 a.m. Elizabeth Prater who occupied room 20 situated almost directly over No. 13 stations herself at the entrance to Miller's Court waiting for a man (presumably in the hope of attracting a client). She stands there for about thirty minutes, hearing no singing nor seeing anyone coming in or out of the court during this period. Eventually, she goes into McCarthy's at No. 27 to chat. After a few minutes Prater goes back to her room, places two chairs in front of her door and, very intoxicated, goes to sleep without undressing.

When Prater was interviewed in 1891 by Kathleen ("Kit") Blake Watkins, a journalist from the *Toronto Mail*, she mentioned how she had heard Mary Kelly "crooning to herself through the night," a fact at variance with her statements in 1888 but seemingly corroborated by another Miller's Court neighbour. Prater took Watkins across the court to meet "Lottie," then-occupant of the still bloodstained room in No. 13. Lottie told Watkins:

> I was her friend. I was living further up the court then. She (Kelly) says "I'm afraid to go out alone at night because of a dream I had that a man was murdering me. Maybe I'll be next. They say Jack's been busy in this quarter." She said it with such a laugh, ma'am, that it just made me creep. And been sure enough, ma'am, she was the next to go. I heard her through the night singin' - she had a nice voice – "The violets grow on your mother's grave," but that's all we 'eard.

Joe Barnett said at the inquest, "she had on several occasions asked me to read about the murders [in the newspapers]; she seemed afraid of someone." (This also suggests that Mary may have been illiterate.) Sometime after 1:00 a.m. Mary went out again. This is known because labourer George Hutchinson who knew Kelly said that he met her in the street at about 2:00 a.m. and that she asked him for a loan of sixpence. He pleaded poverty and Mary went on her way. Hutchinson said later:

About 2:00 a.m. on the 9th I was coming by Thrawl Street, Commercial Street and just before I got to Flower and Dean Street I met the murdered woman Kelly and she said to me: "Hutchinson, will you lend me sixpence?" I said: "I can't. I have spent all my money going down to Romford." She said: "Good morning, I must go and find some money."

She went away to Thrawl Street. A man coming in the opposite direction to Kelly tapped her on the shoulder and said something to her. They both burst out laughing. I heard her say: "All right" to him and the man said: "You will be alright for what I have told you." He then placed his right hand around her shoulder. He also had a kind of small parcel in his left hand with a kind of strap around it.

I stood against the lamp of the Queen's Head Public House and watched him. They both came past me and the man hung his head down with his hat over his eyes. I stooped down and looked him in the face. He looked at me stern. They both went into Dorset Street. I followed them. They both stood on the corner of the court for about three minutes. He said something to her. She said: "All right, my dear. Come along. You will be comfortable." He then placed his arm on her shoulder and she gave him a kiss. She said she had lost her handkerchief. He then pulled out his handkerchief, a red one, and gave it to her. They both went up the court together. I went to the court to see if I could see them, but I could not. I stood there for about three quarters of an hour to see if they came out. They did not, so I went away.

Despite the very late hour and poor lighting conditions, Hutchinson was able to provide the police with an extremely detailed description of the man:

Age about thirty four or thirty five; height 5'6"; complexion pale; dark eyes and eyelashes; slight moustache curled up at each end and hair dark; very surly looking; dress – long dark coat; collar and cuffs trimmed with astrakhan and a dark jacket underneath; light waistcoat; dark trousers; dark felt hat turned down in the middle; button boots and gaiters with white buttons: wore a very thick gold chain with linen collar; black tie with horseshoe pin; respectable appearance; walked very sharp; Jewish appearance.

Hutchinson's statement is at least partly corroborated by laundress Sarah Lewis who reported seeing a man watching the entrance to Miller's Court as she passed into it at about 2:30 a.m. to spend the night with her friends, the Keylers.

Hutchinson said that he maintained his long vigil because he was suspicious of the man whose opulent appearance made him stand out. He said that Kelly appeared to know him. Note that Hutchinson only reported these particulars to the police after the inquest on Kelly had been hastily concluded.

When Cox returned home at 3:00 a.m. she neither heard music nor saw light coming from Kelly's room. Between 3:30 a.m. and 4:00 a.m. Prater who was woken by her kitten "Diddles" walking over her neck heard two or three cries of "Murder!" in a female voice, while Lewis reported hearing just one at around 4:00 a.m. They did not react because such cries were commonplace in the East End.

At 5:30 a.m Prater left Miller's Court to visit the Ten Bells for some rum. She reported seeing nobody except two or three carmen harnessing horses in Dorset Street. She returned to her lodgings and slept until 11:00 a.m.

Fifteen minutes before Prater awoke, John McCarthy sent his assistant, ex-soldier Thomas Bowyer, to collect the rent. Mary was six weeks behind on her payments, owing 29 shillings. Bowyer later said that on the night of Wednesday, the 7th, he saw Kelly talking to a man in Miller's Court. The man was 27-28 years of age with a dark moustache and "very peculiar" eyes. He had a very smart appearance and was noticeable because of his very white cuffs and somewhat long white collar, the ends of which came down over his coat.

Shortly after 10:45 a.m. Bowyer knocked on her door but received no response. He reached through the crack in the window, pushed aside a coat being used as a curtain and, peering inside, saw a dreadfully mutilated figure lying on the bed. Bowyer informed McCarthy who after seeing the remains ran to Commercial Street Police Station where he spoke with Inspector Walter Beck who returned to Miller's Court with McCarthy.

The Manchester Guardian of 10 November 1888 reported that Sergeant Edward Badham had accompanied Beck to the murder site. The Inspector told the inquest that he was the first police officer at the scene and that Badham *may* have accompanied him. However, there are no official records to confirm Badham being with him. One must ask why a professional police officer did not have a clear recollection of who was with him at a major crime scene just three days earlier.

A LOST WOMAN
MARY KELLY
IN MILLER'S COURT

A contemporary impression of Mary Kelly

The scene was also attended by Superintendent Thomas Arnold and Inspector Edmund Reid from Whitechapel's H Division, as well as Frederick Abberline and Robert Anderson from Scotland Yard. While a proposal to use bloodhounds to track the killer's scent was under consideration, police officers at the scene kicked their heels. Eventually, the idea was dismissed as impractical.

Another reason for delay was Charles Warren's standing instruction that if there was another murder (after the "double event") nobody was to enter the scene of the crime until he arrived to take charge of the investigation. Warren, however, had tendered (for the second time) his resignation as Commissioner to Home Secretary Henry Matthews the previous night. On this occasion Matthews had accepted it so when Kelly was murdered Warren was no longer in the employ of the Metropolitan Police. Many have wondered why Warren referred to entering "the scene of the crime" as if he knew or expected that a future murder would be carried out indoors, unlike those previously.

At 1:30 p.m. Arnold ordered McCarthy to force open the door, which struck a small table standing on the left of the bed. A search was made and photographs were taken. Dr. Phillips examined the body and Abberline made an inventory of the room's contents.

The room was spartanly furnished. The body, clad in a thin chemise, was situated in the middle of the bed. Opposite the door was a fireplace; to the left was the broken window and, to the right, the table and bed. A cupboard was in the corner. A pair of boots was placed in front of the fireplace. At the foot of the bed was a chair upon which lay folded clothes.

13 Miller's Court, *Reynolds Newspaper*, 18 November 1888

By far, the mutilation of the corpse in No. 13 was the worst inflicted on the Ripper's victims, possibly because the killer was in a private room, and also had much more time to wreak unspeakable damage. The body was taken to the mortuary in Shoreditch. Dr. Thomas Bond, a distinguished police surgeon from A Division, and Dr. George Bagster Phillips examined the body, timing death to about twelve hours before examination. Bond, noting that rigor mortis set in during the examination, calculated that death occurred between 2:00 a.m. and 8:00 a.m.

Phillips believed that the victim was killed by a slash to the throat before the mutilations were made, suggesting that it would have taken two hours for them to be carried out.

Bond stated in a report that the knife used was about one inch wide and at least six inches long. As noted earlier in the chapter on Eddowes, Bond did not believe that the murderer had any medical training or knowledge.

Because the body had been taken to the Shoreditch mortuary the inquest was opened by the coroner for North East Middlesex, Dr. Roderick Macdonald, MP, instead of Wynne Edwin Baxter who handled many of the other Whitechapel murders.

The speed of the inquest, opened and concluded in almost unseemly haste in just one day on the 12th at Shoreditch Town Hall, was criticised in the press. Joseph identified the victim as Mary Kelly by "the ear and the eyes." John McCarthy was also certain that the body was Kelly's. Her death was registered in the name "Marie Jeanette Kelly," age 25. Dr. Bond presented the inquest with his report on the murder:

> The body was lying naked in the middle of the bed, the shoulders flat but the axis of the body inclined to the left side of the bed. The head was turned on the left cheek. The left arm was close to the body with the forearm flexed at a right angle and lying across the abdomen.
>
> The right arm was slightly abducted from the body and rested on the mattress. The elbow was bent, the forearm supine with the fingers clenched. The legs were wide apart, the left thigh at right angles to the trunk and the right forming an obtuse angle with the pubes.
>
> The whole of the surface of the abdomen and thighs was removed and the abdominal cavity emptied of its viscera. The breasts were cut off, the arms mutilated by several jagged wounds and the face hacked beyond recognition of the features. The tissues of the neck were severed all round down to the bone.

The viscera were found in various parts viz: the uterus and kidneys with one breast under the head, the other breast by the right foot, the liver between the feet, the intestines by the right side and the spleen by the left side of the body. The flaps removed from the abdomen and thighs were on a table.

The bed clothing at the right corner was saturated with blood, and on the floor beneath was a pool of blood covering about two feet square. The wall by the right side of the bed and in a line with the neck was marked by blood which had struck it in a number of separate splashes.

The face was gashed in all directions, the nose, cheeks, eyebrows, and ears being partly removed. The lips were blanched and cut by several incisions running obliquely down to the chin. There were also numerous cuts extending irregularly across all the features. The neck was cut through the skin and other tissues right down to the vertebrae, the fifth and sixth being deeply notched.

The skin cuts in the front of the neck showed distinct ecchymosis. The air passage was cut at the lower part of the larynx through the cricoid cartilage.

Both breasts were more or less removed by circular incisions, the muscle down to the ribs being attached to the breasts. The intercostals between the fourth, fifth, and sixth ribs were cut through and the contents of the thorax visible through the openings.

The skin and tissues of the abdomen from the costal arch to the pubes were removed in three large flaps. The right thigh was denuded in front to the bone, the flap of skin, including the external organs of generation, and part of the right buttock. The left thigh was stripped of skin fascia, and muscles as far as the knee.

The left calf showed a long gash through skin and tissues to the deep muscles and reaching from the knee to five inches above the ankle. Both arms and forearms had extensive jagged wounds.

The right thumb showed a small superficial incision about one inch long, with extravasation of blood in the skin, and there were several abrasions on the back of the hand moreover showing the same condition.

On opening the thorax it was found that the right lung was minimally adherent by old firm adhesions. The lower part of the lung was broken and torn away. The left lung was intact. It was adherent at the apex and there were a few adhesions over the side. In the substances of the lung there were several nodules of consolidation.

The pericardium was open below and the heart absent. In the abdominal cavity there was some partly digested food of fish and potatoes, and similar food was found in the remains of the stomach attached to the intestines.

Dr. George Bagster Phillips reported:

> The mutilated remains of a female were lying two-thirds over towards the edge of the bedstead nearest the door. She had only her chemise on, or some underlinen garment. I am sure that the body had been removed subsequent to the injury which caused her death from that side of the bedstead that was nearest the wooden partition, because of the large quantity of blood under the bedstead and the saturated condition of the sheet and the palliasse at the corner nearest the partition.
>
> The blood was produced by the severance of the carotid artery, which was the cause of death. The injury was inflicted while the deceased was lying at the right side of the bedstead.

The inquest returned a verdict of "Willful murder by person or persons unknown." Mary died on the birthday of Prince Albert Edward ("Bertie"), the eldest son of Queen Elizabeth and Prince Albert of Saxe-Coburg and Gotha. Interestingly, on 10 November Queen Victoria, staying at Balmoral, wrote to her ministers on the subject of Kelly's death, saying: "…you promised, when the first murder took place, to consult with your colleagues about it." Unless the Queen instructed the Prime Minister to take personal action over every murder in England, which, of course, she did not, her statement appears to indicate that she believed Polly Nicholl's death was to be the first in a series.

Inconveniently, Caroline Maxwell claimed to have seen Kelly alive at about 8:30 a.m. on the day of the murder. They spoke:

"What brings you up so early?" asked Maxwell.

"I have the horrors of drink upon me, as I have been drinking for some days past."

"Why don't you go to the Ringers [the Britannia pub] and have a half pint of beer?"

"I have been there and had it, but I have brought it all up again," said Mary, pointing to a pool of vomit.

"I pity the feeling."

The coroner was clearly not impressed with Maxwell's testimony, saying to her: "You must be very careful about your evidence, because it is different to other people." Yes, indeed it was, but did that necessarily make it wrong?

Maxwell further claimed to have seen Kelly at about 8.45 a.m. outside the Ringers talking to a man who looked like a market porter. He was "a short man, dressed in dark clothes, and wearing a sort of plaid coat." (An article in the *Herts and Cambs* of 16 November 1888 named the man as Joe Barnett.)

Maxwell had met Kelly only once or twice before and her description did not match that of those who knew Mary more closely. Tailor Maurice Lewis swore he saw Kelly returning home with milk at 9:00 a.m. on the morning of the 10th and subsequently, like Maxwell, saw her at about 10:00 a.m. outside the Britannia pub. Lewis also said that he had seen Kelly the previous evening in the company of "Julia" in the Horn of Plenty pub on the corner of Crispin Street and Dorset Street.

"Julia" was not identified but may have been charwoman Julia Venturney (or Van Teurny / Van Turney) who lived with Harry Owen at 1 Millers Court just across from Kelly. Julia later said that she had last seen Kelly having breakfast with a woman in her room at around 10:00 a.m. on the morning of the 8th. Police dismissed both statements because they did not fit the accepted time of death. Might they have been too hasty in ditching these sightings?

Hutchinson's eyewitness account was of immediate importance to the police. Curiously, although he furnished a detailed description of the man in Commercial Street Hutchinson did not provide a similarly detailed description of Kelly. Nor, it appears, did the police ask him for one, an astonishing omission in the circumstances seeing that the remains on the bed were unrecognisable. But it appears that Hutchinson's statement gave the police all they needed to pursue their investigation. They proceeded with vigour to find the man of "Jewish appearance." Abberline ordered that Hutchinson be sent out with officers in an effort to spot the man again but to no avail. Oddly, Hutchinson's name does not appear again in the existing police records and so it cannot be ascertained whether his testimony was ultimately dismissed, disproven or corroborated.

When one drills into it, Hutchinson's statement is full of holes. Why did the police gave it such credence? He said that he stood by the lamp of the Queen's Head "at the corner of Flower and Dean Street" to watch the man with Mary near Thrawl Street. There was no public house of any name at this location. The nearest Queen's Head pub was located at the corner intersection of Commercial Street and Fashion Street. To reach it, Hutchinson would have had to turn his back on the couple and walk 120 yards further up Commercial Street. How also, in relative darkness, did he observe such a small detail as what he described as a strap around the parcel he saw in the man's left hand? (It has been suggested that "Hutchinson" was, in fact, a policeman working under cover to dissemble the true nature of events in Miller's Court.)

On Monday 19 November, Mary Kelly was buried in a public grave at St Patrick's Roman Catholic Cemetery, Langthorne Road, Leytonstone. Her grave was no. 66, in row 66, Plot 10. No family member could be found to attend the funeral. As a mark of sympathy for the poor people of the neighbourhood, Kelly's funeral expenses were paid by Henry Wilton, fifty years Clerk of St Leonards Church, Shoreditch, from his own pocket.

Question: Who was Mary Kelly? Answer: No one knows for certain. These are the various "facts" attributed to Kelly or said of her.

According to Joseph Barnett, Mary had told him she was born in Limerick, Ireland, around 1863, although she did not stipulate if she was referring to the city or the county.

She said that her family moved to Wales when she was young. She claimed to speak fluent Welsh. Her father, John, was a ganger at an ironworks in what listeners' ears heard and construed as "Caernarvonshire" or "Carmarthenshire."

She had six or seven brothers and one sister, who travelled from market place to market place with materials. One of her brothers was nicknamed "Johnto" who, she said, served in the 2nd Battalion Scots Guards. Another brother was named Henry.

Lizzie Albrook said she had a relative on the London stage.

At sixteen, around 1879, she married a man named Davies who died two or three years later in a colliery explosion. There was a possible child from this marriage.

She moved to Cardiff where she plied as a prostitute. Her nickname was "Black Mary." She became ill and spent eight months in Cardiff Infirmary. Afterwards she went to live with a cousin who may have been Ellen Kelly, aged twenty-five, who was jailed for four months in February 1882 for "keeping a house of ill-repute" at 21 Ruby Street in the Roath district of Cardiff.

Around 1884 she moved to London and worked in a West End gay house. She went to Paris for two weeks with a gentleman but returned, not liking France although she enjoyed reminiscing about her visits to the Folies Bergère cabaret music hall. It is believed that it was on her return from France that Mary decided to adopt the French name "Marie Jeanette."

Sometime in the period 1884-1886 she moved in with Mr Morganstone (possibly Morgan Stone) near Stepney Gas Works and, later, also lived for a time with Joseph Flemming, a mason's plasterer from Bethnal Green Road of whom she was very fond.

The Press Association discovered that Kelly made an acquaintance with a well-to-do French woman in Knightsbridge who, Kelly claimed, led her into a degraded life of prostitution. They rode about together in a carriage and made several visits to Paris. She then lived with and possibly worked for a Mrs Buki in St George's Street. Buki accompanied Kelly on a visit to Knightsbridge and demanded from the Frenchwoman the return of a large box full of Kelly's expensive clothes.

She went on to live with a Mrs Carthy at Breezer Hill, Ratcliff Highway. Carthy is said to have remarked that Kelly's family were well-to do-people, and that Kelly herself was: "an excellent scholar and an artist of no mean degree." After leaving Breezer Hill she moved to Colley's lodging house in Thrawl Street.

She meets Joseph Barnett in 1887; they agree to live together and move to 13 Miller's Court in early 1888.

She may have been the Mary Kelly who was fined two shillings and sixpence on 19 September 1888 at Thames Magistrate Court for drunk and disorderly conduct.

John McCarthy claimed that Kelly received infrequent correspondence from Ireland.

None of these biographical snippets has led to a formal consensus on Mary Kelly's origins. In acknowledgement of excellent work carried out a number of years ago, at my suggestion, by staff in the reference section of Merthyr Tydfil Public Library, I offer this possibility for Mary Kelly:

St. Iltyd's Roman Catholic Church in Dowlais, Merthyr Tydfil, records the birth of a girl on 13 November 1861. She was baptised on the same day and given the name Mary Kelly.

Her father was William Kelly and her mother Honora (née Sullivan).

Mary's Godparents were Cornelius Healy and Julianna Conway.

William Kelly was born around 1802 in Ireland. He married Honora Sullivan 19 January 1856. Honora was born around 1820 in Ireland.

Mary's elder sister, Honora, was born in Dowlais 31 March 1858.

In the 1861 census William is described as a labourer, aged 59, residing at 54 North Street, Dowlais.

The 1871 census lists William as labourer at Iron Works, aged

69. It records William, Mary and sister Honora as living at 6 Bethania Court in Upper Merthyr Tydfil with 6 other people (the Coffey family). Mary's mother, Honora, had died 12 May 1866.

William died 2 April 1872. Mary was therefore 10 years and 4 months of age when she was orphaned.

Honora married John Carthy (son of Jeremiah) 18 October 1873, aged 15.

The 1881 census describes Mary Kelly as a servant, occupation Nurse, living in a household in St. Mary, Cardiff. The Head of the house was John George Todd, Bank Accountant. In total, 11 people living at the address, including Benjamin R. Huntley, ship owner.

The same census names Honora as Honora McCarthy, 22 years of age, married, lodging in the home of John Bullen in Baker's Row, St Mary, Cardiff. There is no mention in the census of Honora's husband living at the premises.

The question as to the identity of the "Caernarfon" or "Carmarthen" ironworks at which Mary Kelly's father is reported to have worked is resolved in the context of this impressive Merthyr Library research. In their heyday the Dowlais ironworks and sister Works at nearby Cyfarthfa (which, when pronounced, can sound much like Caernarfon or Carmarthen to a non-Welsh ear) were enormous enterprises, said to be the most productive in the world.

In 1844, a truly memorable export year, 50,000 tons of iron were shipped from Dowlais to enable expansion of railways across Russia to Siberia. William would have been one of 7,000 employees who operated eighteen blast furnaces and the world's most powerful rolling mill. Bustling, noisy Dowlais was a suburb of Merthyr Tydfil shrouded in a constant haze of industrial smoke from tall factory chimneys.

Such was the predominance of Irish workers in the ironworks many children living in Merthyr and surrounding villages reached school age before realising that they were not actually living in Ireland. Perhaps William's daughter, Mary, similarly lived under this misconception until she learned better.

If by the faintest chance the Mary Kelly born in Dowlais in November 1861 should turn out to be the resident of 13 Miller's Court one must solve the riddle of the absence of "Johns" in her family. Her father was William (although it is possible he had a middle name John) and she is listed as having just one sibling, an older sister.

Consider, though, that her older sister, Honora, married a John in

1873: John Carthy, who, it appears, is referenced in the 1881 census as John McCarthy but who is not listed as living with his wife at that time in the Bullen household in Baker's Row, St Mary, Cardiff.

May Mary have concocted the name "John"? In her use of the name, may she have been alluding to a relationship or an acquaintance concerning a "John" that was of significance to her? Was Mary by her sister's marriage related to Mrs Carthy of Breezer Hill or even to John "Jack" McCarthy who, reportedly a bit of a hard case (fined in 1882 for his involvement with others in organising illegal prize fights), allowed Mary out of the kindness of his heart to run up six weeks' rent arrears?

The Jamaican newspaper, *Daily Gleaner*, published a story on 17 November taking its source from *The Herald's* London Bureau in the Strand. It reported an interview with Dr. John Rees Gabe of Mecklenburgh Square who had turned up at the scene of Kelly's death on the day of the murder.

It is a fact that in total seven doctors were summoned to 13 Miller's Court after the murder—Dr. George Bagster Phillips, Mr. Anderson (Dr. Phillips' Assistant), Dr. Thomas Bond, Dr. Charles Alfred Hibbert, Dr. Frederick Gordon Brown, Dr. Duke and Dr. J.R. Gabe. Gabe, however, differed from the other medics in that he appeared to possess intimate details of the victim.

After telling the journalist that the furniture in No. 13 included an oil stove, two rickety chairs, a Tumble Down bed quilt and, at the head of the bed, a piece of looking glass such as one buys in Petticoat Lane for half a penny, Gabe also said that Kelly went by the aliases of Fisher and Ginger. Intriguingly, Dr. Gabe, who was surgeon to the Society for the Protection of Cruelty to Young Children (*The Times*, 29 March 1888), went on to say that Mary had a son ten years of age and that her murder was the *seventh* in the series. Who was this all-knowing Dr. Gabe? How had he come by this information?

Caroline, "my" dogged researcher in Merthyr Reference Library, found in 2002 a reference in the 1881 Census records to a Dr. John Bernard Gabe, cousin of Dr. John Rees Gabe, viz:

John Bernard Gabe
Head, Aged 27
Born: Merthyr Tydfil, Glamorgan, Wales
Occupation: General Practitioner, LSA Etc
Annie Gabe
Wife, Aged 22
Born: Aberavon, Glamorgan, Wales

Margaret Rosser
Widowed, Mother In Law, Aged 59
Born: Cowbridge, Glamorgan, Wales
Retired Publican

Jenny Rosser
Unmarried Daughter, Aged 19
Born: Aberavon, Glamorgan, Wales
John S. Rosser
Unmarried Son, Aged 15
Born: Aberavan, Glamorgan, Wales
Occupation: Scholar

Margaret Davies
Unmarried Servant, Aged 17
Born: Llansamlet, Glamorgan, Wales
Occupation: General Servant

Dwelling: Llangefelach Road
Census Place: Clase, Glamorgan, Wales
Family History Library Film: 1342290
Public Records Office Reference: RG11
Piece/Folio: 5353 / 26
Page Number: 9

Clase or, more accurately, Clas-Lower, was a hamlet in the parish of Llangyfelach, which, in 1881, was situated partly within the limits of the borough of Swansea and partly in the hundred of Llangyfelach, county of Glamorgan, South Wales. Today, Llangyfelach Road is in the small Swansea village of Brynhyfryd, which mostly falls within the Cwmbwrla ward. I regard it as little more than coincidence that the census records a Margaret Davies residing in the Gabe household. However, it spurred me to look again at mine disasters in the South Wales region and I came across a very useful website,[65] which includes entries worthy of investigation.

In particular, I noted that on 16 July 1880 William Davies (age not supplied), occupation Stower, was one of 120 men killed at the Risca New Mine Colliery at Waunfawr. Other fatalities named Davies are recorded but, bearing in mind Kelly's alleged remark that she married at 16 around 1879 and that her husband died 2-3 years later, the dates may be too wide of the mark. For the record, the site reports: Edward Davies, one of 77 that died at Dinas Colliery in the Rhondda, 13

[65] http://www.welshcoalmines.co.uk/DisastersList.htm

January 1879; and Thomas Davies (49), Isaac Davies (33), Evan Davies (28), William Davies (25) and Lewis Davies (32) killed in an explosion at Maerdy Colliery, 23 December 1885.

Caroline's research showed that both John Bernard Gabe and John Rees Gabe were members of a very influential Merthyr family, their forebears having mostly been builders and pub owners. Her browse through parish records indicated that the family influence extended to the honour of residential areas named after them (Gabe's Court and Gabe's Steps). That Dr. John Rees Gabe seemed so knowledgeable about Mary Kelly may be explained by his connections to this esteemed South Wales family. The influential Gabes, highly respected in the Merthyr area, may well have known William and Honora Kelly's family, to the extent that when Mary came to London she kept in touch with the family pal from Merthyr who was only seven years her senior.

It is possible that in Welshman Dr Gabe, she saw a trusted friend in whom she could confide when times were difficult or, more pointedly, dangerous seeing that there was a violent murderer abroad in Whitechapel. Mary made remarks that indicated she believed she was a target. Why might she have believed this? Had Mary taken some action that she feared had brought upon her an inevitable death sentence?

In 2012 the late Chris Scott posted on the Casebook forum a photo of "Kelly" purportedly taken in 1885. He had received it from a woman who requested anonymity. Scott's source claimed that Kelly was one of six children: four brothers (a fifth dying young) and two sisters. One sister was named Bridget and the eldest brother was Henry John Joseph. Her parents were John Joseph and Bridget. (Recall that Joseph Barnett said that Mary had one sister and six or seven brothers, including one named Johnto.)

The source said that at an unspecified date after Mary's murder the family moved to the U.S.A. Scott understood that the family resided there still. Scott was dubious about the photo's provenance. I share his doubts but include it here as image 3 of 3 in the following two pages because it does appear to bear a passing resemblance to Eric Stedman's 2005 final reconstruction of Kelly's features. I invite readers to judge for themselves. If Scott's source's photo can be authenticated and Stedman's reconstruction is judged a comparative likeness, then my Kelly survival theory is challenged (unless Stedman subconsciously created an image of a woman who evaded murder). With this unlikely thought in mind and recalling Claston's cryptic remarks about the human need for the comfort of the familiar, may it have been in someone's interests to produce the photo to perpetuate a myth?

Removal of skin flaps & smoothing reveals
face shape and location of main features

Clues in existing curves of features are followed
& reveal general shape of features

Completion of shapes reveals additional details;
addition of eyelids, lashes, lips, highlights in eyes gives
more realistic appearance

Eric Stedman's reconstruction by stages of Mary Kelly's face

220

Stedman's reconstruction and the photo of "Mary Kelly" sent to Chris Scott

Joseph Barnett told *The Star* (reported 10 November 1888) that Mary had a boy aged 6-7 years living with her in Miller's Court. *The Times* reported the same story but added that the child was removed to a neighbour's house on 9 November. *The Herts and Cambs* story covering the events of 8-9 November supplied more detail:

> She [Kelly] had a little boy, aged about six or seven years, living with her, and latterly her circumstances had been so reduced that she is reported to have stated to a companion that she would make away with herself, as she could not bear to see her boy starving...a man who is described as respectably dressed, came up and spoke to the murdered woman Kelly and offered her some money.
>
> The man accompanied the woman to her lodgings, which are on the second floor, the little boy being sent to a neighbour's house. Nothing more was seen of the woman. On Friday morning, it is stated, the little boy was sent back into the house, and the report goes that he was sent out subsequently on an errand by the man who was in the house with his mother. Confirmation of this statement is, it is true, difficult to obtain, and it remains in doubt whether anyone really saw the unfortunate woman on the morning of the discovery.

As *The Herts and Cambs* admitted, confirmation of the facts was difficult to obtain but consider the report's implications and, of course, its many paradoxes. Mary has a child, one that she is struggling to feed. Seeing no way out of her fix, she is contemplating suicide. (A young woman named "Margaret," an alleged friend of Mary's, possibly from Elephant and Castle area, told the Press Association, "I saw Kelly on Thursday night in Dorset Street She told me she had no money, and intended to make away with herself. Shortly after that a man of shabby appearance came up, and Kelly walked away.") A respectably dressed man then turns up and offers Mary money. He then accompanies the woman (presumably Kelly) to her lodgings *on the second floor* and the boy is sent to a neighbour's house. Nothing more is seen of the woman but on *Friday morning* the little boy is sent back *into the house,* and subsequently sent on an errand by the gentleman who was *in the house with his mother.* There are some obvious questions:

i.   Whose were the 2nd floor lodgings referred to (Mary lived in a ground floor room at No. 13 Miller's Court)?

ii.   Who was the gentleman? Was he possibly the man named "Lawrence" mentioned in the 10 November article by *The Herts. Advertiser & St. Albans Times*? The article describes

Kelly's son as around 10-11 years of age. Drawing on local opinion, it said: *"The story of the crime current among the neighbours is that this morning - what time cannot at present be ascertained, but at any rate after daylight - she took a man home to her own room, presumably for an immoral purpose."* The article goes to quote a Mrs Hewitt of 25 Dorset Street who *"stated that a man - a drover - called on her* [Kelly] *some time ago. He asked her if a summons came in the name of Lawrence to accept it. This man Lawrence, she says, she believes lived with the dead woman. He was off and on in London, sometimes being absent for five or six weeks"*;

iii. How could the boy have been sent back into the house (where the man was with the lad's mother) on Friday morning unless it was before 6:00 a.m., (the latest estimated time of death being 8:00 a.m., according to Dr Bond, with the murderer needing a minimum of two hours to inflict the mutilations)? However, the article then states that after the boy's return the gentleman, in the presence of his mother, sent him out on an errand. One can only interpret this to mean that Kelly was alive both at the time the boy went back into the house on Friday morning and also when the gentleman later sent him back out on an errand. If between his arrival and being sent out again, his mother had been butchered in his presence the boy would certainly have suffered complete emotional collapse, unable to do anything let alone run an errand;

iv. Last, but not least, who was the boy's father?

Questions i, ii and iii are only resolved if one considers that the lodgings referred to are somewhere other than No. 13 Miller's Court; and that if the gentleman, boy and mother are together on the Friday morning in the unidentified 2nd floor residence then it has to have been a body other than Kelly's that was found (or placed?) in No. 13.

All these deviations from the popularly accepted version of Kelly's death also throw up another question. Did Mary have some insight, even prior knowledge of coming events? May she have been in some way complicit, either by omission or, shocking to contemplate, by design in their undertaking? I seem to recall reading that an elderly nun from the Providence Row Night Refuge in Crispin Street once said: "If it were not for the Kelly woman none of these murders would have happened." What might the nun have meant by this remark? Did Kelly harbour a secret that she let slip when she thought she was perhaps speaking in confidence? Why did James Munro, appointed to the post of Commissioner of Metropolitan Police after Warren's resignation, call the Whitechapel affair a "political hot potato"? He would not have said that if he believed that the murders were the work of a single deranged killer. The more I reflect on the case, it is not so much that I regard Mary Kelly as the key to the Ripper murders as the boy. The issue of paternity is the $64,000 question and for this I have no answer, except to suggest that Dad was no ordinary "Joe."

Mary Kelly was not what she seemed. And, for sure, Mary's room at No. 13 Miller's Court was not what it seemed. According to researcher Simon D. Wood, the scene was staged. In his excellent 2005 paper[66] Wood concludes that the events in Miller's Court were part of something that was very different to the preceding murders, a phenomenon that "almost 120 years later, we are only just beginning to unravel and understand." (For the record, Wood believes that Elizabeth Stride's death was "a domestic look-alike murder.") Wood argues convincingly that high-level jiggery pokery was at play in the immediate aftermath of Mary Kelly's murder.

In 1988 the photograph known as MJK3, together with photographs of Nichols, Chapman, Stride and Eddowes, was found in an album sent to Scotland Yard. Stewart Evans and Donald Rumbelow disclosed[67] that the album was returned by the family of the late Deputy Commissioner, Ernest Millen. It is believed that MJK3 used to form part of Millen's lecture material. MJK3 shows the Kelly murder scene from the opposite side of the bed as shown in photograph MJK1, an image which has been in the public domain since the time of the murder and whose provenance has hitherto been accepted absolutely.

MJK3

[66] Wood, S., *The Enigmas of Miller's Court,* Ripperologist, December 2005

[67] Evans, S. & Rumbelow, D., *Scotland Yard Investigates*, The History Press, Stroud, 2006

Wood's analysis of MJK3 suggests that between 11:00 a.m. and 1:30 p.m. on Friday the 9th, the police or another party ignored Warren's order, entered Kelly's room, took photographs, moved the bed, removed items of evidence, re-arranged the scene and, subsequently, brought in Hutchinson after the inquest to provide frankly fatuous testimony that was designed to demolish reports that Kelly was seen on the morning of the murder. Wood also suggests that Dr. Philips examined Kelly's body knowing that the the scene had been rearranged.

Bear in mind also that the murder was carried out within yards of a temporary police station in Dorset Street from which officers made hourly patrols. Its presence might explain why Kelly's death certificate states the scene of the murder as 1 Miller's Court. It also might explain why Dr. Macdonald asked Mary Ann Cox if the person she heard walking outside Miller's Court at 6.30 a.m. on the morning of the 9th November might have been a policeman. It has been speculated that what Cox heard was Abberline removing documentation that had supposedly been left in Miller's Court, an act which would prove that the police were already aware of the murder.

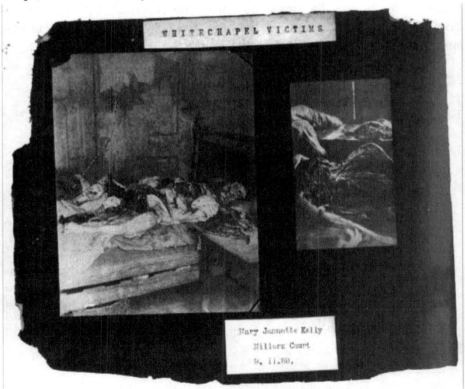

MJK1 and MJK3 in the Ernest Millen album

What, Wood asks, happened in No. 13 to make Abberline undertake such an elaborate cover-up? What was so gruesome or politically sensitive that it had to be cleaned up and passed off as the final Ripper murder? Wood returns to MJK3 in an effort to answer these questions. In the area below the raised left knee Wood finds concentric circles containing the letters HO, possibly standing for Home Office. Inside the circles Wood identifies the phrase, "SIB8FGA." He interprets this as: "Secret Irish Branch [Department?] 8 Frederick George Abberline."

Abberline had formerly been on "special service" many times, most notably on 24 January 1885 when he arrested Cunningham, an Irishman, for his part in the bombing of the Tower of London. Two other policemen who worked alongside Abberline on the Tower bombing also assisted on the Ripper murders: Superintendent Thomas Arnold and Sergeant Stephen White. It is a fact of record that on 12 November two MPs, a high-ranking Post Office official and two members of the Royal Irish Constabulary visited 13 Miller's Court. No official reason for their visit has ever been made known.

Wood's theory about a connection between the murder in Miller's Court and the Irish troubles may not be far off the mark. The members of the 19th century Fenian movement were predominantly from the powerful Anglo-Irish community during the time of the Protestant Ascendancy.

The "Ascendancy" was the political, economic and social domination of Ireland between the 17th and early 20th century by a minority of landowners, Protestant clergy and members of the professions, all members of the Church of Ireland or the Church of England. The Ascendancy excluded other groups (primarily Roman Catholics but also Presbyterian and other Protestant denominations, and non-Christians such as Jews). Significantly, many from the Anglo-Irish community were drawn to occult movements including the H.O.G.D. Wood's pixel-by-pixel examination of MJK3 reveals objects of interest:

> [Between] the victim's thighs [lies] a flat circular object [which] is a china plate with a patterned border, behind which stands a bowl partially obscured by a smaller, lipped, bowl and a bottle laying on its side. Behind this large bowl are three smaller shallow vessels. Atop these, sloping from left to right, a spoon rests in a heart-shaped dish, behind which sits what might be a plume of feathers or a bunch of leaves. And to the right of the photograph, half out of shot, is a round short-necked glass or porcelain container which is possibly for wine, beer or spirits. Also on the china plate is a small lump of unidentifiable matter.

Wood does not try to discern any possible symbolism in this tableau of items, inviting those interested to find any meaning. It may be a fanciful idea but it occurs to me that these accoutrements are suggestive of objects required for a ceremonial undertaking. Dwelling on this notion conjures a highly disturbing image, one that explains why the bed had to be pushed into the middle of the room. With little effort, I can picture a scene in which two or more people are gathered around the bed enacting sacrificial murder upon a young woman. It is an act too gruesome to contemplate, one that goes against all that human decency holds sacred but that does not make the act impossible.

The murder in No. 13 was committed on the feast day of Ireland's Saint Benignus of Armagh who together with a pagan druid was tied inside a burning timber building. The druid was reduced to ash while Benignus was untouched. I cannot prove it but my hunch is that if one transposes this story to Miller's Court then the roles are reversed: "the (unknown) druid" in No. 13 is butchered while the "Benignus" figure, Mary Kelly who sang of violets plucked from a mother's grave, is miraculously left unscarred by Jack the Ripper's volcanic rage.

Benignus made a valuable contribution to Christian literature. If he had been alive in the nineteenth century he may well have been invited to contribute his knowledge and skills to the massive task of making the first universally accepted revision to the Bible in nearly three hundred years. But was this highly ambitious programme more than it seemed?

Home from the Sea by Arthur Hughes

Chapter 14

Baconalia

King James VI of Scotland and James I of England (usually referred to as King James the First and Sixth) was in a jovial mood and for good reason. He held in his hands a beautifully presented leather-bound book bearing the imperious title: *THE HOLY BIBLE, Containing the Old Testament, AND THE NEW: Newly Translated out of the Original tongues: & with the former Translations diligently compared and revised, by his Majesties special Commandment.*

In 1604 James, the "wisest fool in Christendom" as described by contemporaries, convened the Hampton Court Conference. After acceding to the English throne in 1603 James quickly became unpopular because of his homosexual nature and unsavoury character. He pretended to be a scholar in theology and philosophy but his learning was regarded as shallow and superficial. He was said to wallow in moral and physical filth but was grudgingly attributed with a streak of cunning that his associates called a "kind of crooked wisdom."

The main item of business for Conference was to debate the production of a new English version of the Bible in response to problems of earlier translations that had been highlighted by the Puritans, a powerful faction within the Church of England. Conference delegates were swayed as a body by the King's reasoned and impassioned arguments. The conclusion was never in doubt. Delegates unanimously agreed that the work should proceed without delay.

James issued a set of personal "Rules" that the translators were to follow, which were intended to limit the Puritan influence on the new translation. The Bishop of London added a qualification that the translators would add no marginal notes. The extensive use of such notes in the popular *Geneva Bible* of 1539, the primary scripture of 16th-century English Protestantism used by leading figures such as Shakespeare, Cromwell and John Donne (and also one of the Bibles taken to America on the *Mayflower*), was regarded by the King as offensive to the principles of divinely ordained royal supremacy.

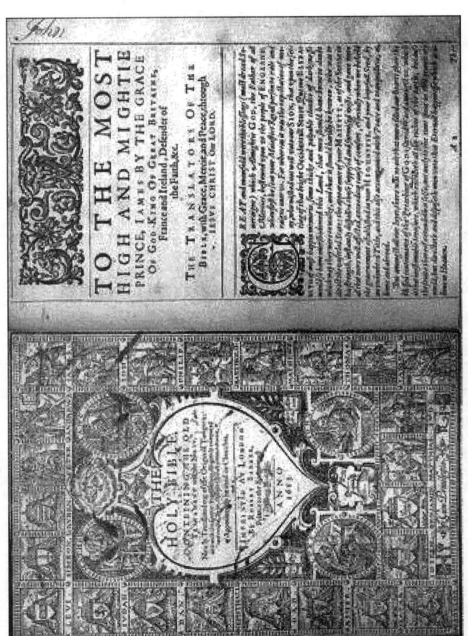

The King James Bible of 1611

Instead, James decreed that in order that the new translation should be familiar to its listeners and readers the text of the *Bishops' Bible*, an English translation produced under the authority of the Church of England in 1568, would serve as the primary guide for the translators and that the familiar proper names of the biblical characters would all be retained.

James did allow translators the leeway to refer to other source material in cases where the *Bishops' Bible* proved problematic. The pre-approved list of permitted translations included the *Tyndale Bible*, the *Coverdale Bible*, *Matthew's Bible*, the *Great Bible*, and James's unloved *Geneva Bible*. The King's "Rules," ostensibly prepared by Richard Bancroft, Bishop of London and high-church Anglican, were these:

1. The ordinary Bible, read in the church, commonly called the *Bishop's Bible*, to be followed, and as little altered as the original will permit.

2. The names of the prophets and the holy writers, with the other names in the text, to be retained, as near as may be, according as they are vulgarly used.

3. The old ecclesiastical words to be kept; as the word church, not to be translated congregation, &c.

4. When any word hath divers significations, that to be kept which has been most commonly used by the most eminent fathers, being agreeable to the propriety of the place, and the analogy of the faith.

5. The division of the chapters to be altered, either not at all, or as little as may be, if necessity so require.

6. No marginal notes at all to be affixed, but only for the explanation of the Hebrew or Greek words, which cannot, without some circumlocution, so briefly and fitly be expressed in the text.

7. Such quotations of places to be marginally set down, as shall serve for the fit references of one scripture to another.

8. Every particular man of each company to take the same chapter or chapters; and having translated or amended them severally by himself, where he thinks good, all to meet together, to confer what they have done, and agree for their part what shall stand.

9. As any one company hath dispatched any one book in this manner, they shall send it to the rest to be considered of seriously and judiciously: for his Majesty is very careful in this point.

10. If any company, upon the review of the book so sent, shall doubt or differ upon any places, and therewithal to send their reasons; to which if they consent not, the difference to be compounded at the general meeting, which is to be the chief persons of each company, at the end of the work.

11. When any place of special obscurity is doubted of, letters to be directly by authority to send to any learned in the land for his judgment in such a place.

12. Letters to be sent from every bishop to the rest of the clergy, admonishing them of this translation in hand, and to move and charge as many as being skillful in the tongues, have taken pains in that kind, to send their particular observations to the company, either at Westminster, Cambridge, or Oxford, according as it was directed before the king's letter to the archbishop.

13. The directors in each company to be deans of Westminster and Chester, and the king's professors in Hebrew and Greek in the two universities.

14. These translations to be used when they agree better with the text than the *Bishop's Bible*, viz. *Tyndale's, Coverdale's, Matthew's, Wilchurch's, Geneva*.

King James ordered revisions to proceed. The translators' role was actually more of a refining task than wholesale translations because the *Tyndale* and the *Geneva Bibles* were already in print in English. James sent a letter to Archbishop Bancroft asking him to contact all English churchmen requesting that they make donations to his project. The King never contributed as much as a farthing to its cost.

The task of translation was undertaken by between 46-54 scholars, the exact number compensated for their work is cited in contemporary records as unknown. All, however, were members of the Church of England, and all except Sir Henry Savile were clergy.

The scholars worked in six committees, two based in each of the University of Oxford, the University of Cambridge and Westminster. The committees included scholars with Puritan sympathies as well as High Churchmen.

King James the First and Sixth, Daniel Mytens

The overseeing of the translators fell on two men: Thomas Bilson and Miles Smith, neither of whom was ever known to write elaborate literal documents or to possess the linguistic flair to write with such style.

The committees started work towards the end of 1604. Each man received thirty shillings per week for his contribution. They had all completed their sections by 1608, the Apocrypha committee finishing first. From January 1609 a General Committee of Review met at Stationers' Hall, London to review the completed marked texts from each of the six committees. Robert Barker, the King's Printer, published the completed and approved *King James Bible* in 1611.

Stop and rewind. The foregoing is the official story of why and how the *King James Bible* came into being. However, all was not as it appeared. The revised translation of the Bible was undertaken as a national work under the personal supervision of the King but every record of the proceedings has disappeared, despite centuries of searching by scholars. The British Museum does not possess a manuscript connected with the committees' proceedings. On the whole, the Public Record Office preserves original documentation concerning important proceedings of that period but a request for any records connected with the *Authorised Version of the Bible* is met with: "We have none."

The revision project was a hugely important work carried out under royal command for the benefit of all English-speaking Christians. As such it is unthinkable that its manuscripts and documents would not be preserved for posterity and future theological scholarship. Where are they to be found?

It was American artist and illustrator, William T. Smedley, who first theorised that Sir Francis Bacon rewrote the translators' manuscripts to produce the literary masterpiece that is the *King James Authorised Version*.

> There was a conference held at Hampton Court Palace before King James in January 1603...(Puritan) John Rainoldes urged the necessity of providing for his people a uniform translation of the Bible...The King approved the suggestion and commissioned for that purpose 54 of the most learned men in the universities and other places.
>
> A set of rules was drawn up for their guidance, almost the only record that remains of this great undertaking. These concise rules

---

[68] Smedley, W., *The Mystery of Francis Bacon*, Robert Banks & Son, London, 1912

have a homogeneity, breadth and vigour which point to Bacon as their author.

Subsequent scholarly research has reiterated Smedley's conclusions and greatly enlarged them to acknowledge, for example, the KJV's distinctive Masonic and Rosicrucian *leitmotif.*

> The first edition of the *King James Bible*, which was edited by Francis Bacon and prepared under Masonic supervision, bears more Mason's marks than the Cathedral of Strasburg.
>
> —Manly P. Hall, from a lecture, *Rosicrucian and Masonic Origins*, 1929.

> Bacon edited the *Authorised Version* of the Bible printed in 1611. Dr. Lancelot Andrewes, Bishop of Winchester, one of the chief translators, was Bacon's close friend. The MSS are missing. That Bacon revised the manuscripts before publication is certain. Neither Bilston nor Miles, to whom the MSS were entrusted for final revision, could have given the world such a literary masterpiece. We have their writings. They are mediocre, barren of style, lacking the creative touch.
>
> —Alfred Dodd, *Francis Bacon's Life Story*, 1986.

Upon completion of the committees' work in 1609 the translators handed over their manuscripts to King James for his final personal approval. James was not competent to check and edit their work so he passed the manuscripts to Bacon, who at the King's request six years earlier had drafted the Rules. It was now Bacon's task to shape the manuscripts into the literary masterpiece that is the KJV. The secrecy behind this undertaking has necessarily denied Bacon the credit and acknowledgment for such a monumental achievement.

Sir Francis Bacon (1561–1626) was called the genius of his age, the man against whom the combined brainpower of all the learned men of England was no match. He mastered every subject he undertook: mathematics, geometry, music, poetry, painting, law, languages, astronomy, classical drama, philosophy, history, theology and architecture. He was the father of modern science, remodeller of modern law and patron of modern democracy.

It has long been speculated that Bacon was the illegitimate son of Queen Elizabeth 1 and the Earl of Leicester, Robert Dudley, and was lovingly adopted by Lord and Lady Bacon, parents of great wealth, education and social influence.

Bacon embarked on his studies at Trinity College Cambridge at the age of twelve. At Queen Elizabeth's request he went to Paris at sixteen to study Egyptian, Arabian, Indian and Greek philosophy, with particular emphasis upon the Ancient Mysteries and their Ritual Rites.

In Paris Bacon created a secret cipher system that could be inserted into a document without arousing suspicion. He travelled on to a number of European centres where he was initiated into an Order of the Knights Templar and, according to his diary, "learnt a very special secret."

He returned to England and at eighteen entered law chambers at Grey's Inn. One year later this extraordinary young man founded at Grey's Inn the secret Rosicrosse Literary Society and the Lodge of Free and Accepted or Speculative Masons. He became a Member of Parliament at twenty. By then Francis Bacon had already crammed more into his growing years than most men and women do in a lifetime. And it was only just the beginning of a unique span of unparalleled learning, statesmanship and international subterfuge.

Corridor whispers said he was a court spy, a heretic, a necromancer, a magician, a metaphysician and a charlatan. He was all of these and so very much more. Bacon the brain box and the polymath was the outward persona. Students of the Western mystical tradition speak of Bacon as a Merlinesque figure who served as guardian and teacher of ancient wisdoms. In June 1607 Bacon was appointed Solicitor-General and Chief Advisor to the Crown. He had presented new ideas to the Government for the Reformation of the church and was instructed to commence restructuring the Bible. Research undertaken in the Records Office of the British Museum reveal that original documents still exist that refer to important proceedings associated with Sir Francis Bacon's involvement with the editing of the Old and New Testaments. They reveal that he personally selected and paid the revisers of the New Testament who completed their task under the instructions of Bacon's close friend, Dr Andrewes.

Francis Bacon

Having been handed the translators' work by the King, Bacon set to work and wasted no time in capitalising on this unparalleled opportunity to add some very special touches to the *King James's Bible*. In the space of one year Bacon hammered the various styles of the translators into the unity, rhythm and music of Shakespearean prose, wrote the Prefaces and created the whole scheme of the *Authorised Version*. Employing prodigious skill and drawing on his vast learning, Bacon inserted signs, symbols and patterns that could be perceived at an unconscious level of understanding by the most casual or poorly educated reader. In particular, Bacon is believed to have hidden encoded information into both the Old and New Testament on the true history of early Christianity as imparted to the Knights Templar by Theocletes, the Grand-Pontiff of the Order of the Temple of the Nazarene sect.

The scope and breadth of Bacon's work went way beyond monumental. In addition to his reputed founding of the Rosicrucian Order, Bacon is also said to have been the true author of Shakespeare's works. It is outside the scope of this book to present the pros and cons of the argument, except to say that the evidence in support of the theory appears compelling. Those who consider that the final print-ready version of the KJV is to all intents and purposes Bacon's own work also tend to believe in his sole authorship of the Shakespeare canon. There are many books on the topic but for those interested in the debate my own favourite is John Michell's excellent work.[69]

> The 1611 *King James Bible* is ornamented with Bacon's symbols…Rosicrucianly marked to call the attention of the initiated to tell them that the 1611 Bible is without possibility of doubt, one of Bacon's books…When Bacon was born, English as a literary language did not exist but once he died he had succeeded in making the English language the noblest vehicle of thought ever possessed by mankind. This he accomplished merely by his Bible and his Shakespeare.
>
> —Edwin D. Lawrence, author of *Bacon is Shakespeare and The Shakespeare Myth* from a lecture, October 9, 1912.

> The Bible which all of us read and admire from a literary point of view because of its peculiar and beautiful English was written in that form by Bacon who invented and perfected that style of English expression. The first editions of this Bible were printed under the same guidance and in the same manner as were the Shakespeare

---

[69] Michell, J., *Who Wrote Shakespeare?*, Thames and Hudson, 1996

plays, and the ornaments for the various pages were drawn in pen and ink and on wood by artists engaged by Bacon who worked under his supervision. Every one of the ornaments concealed some Rosicrucian emblem and occasionally a Masonic emblem or some initials that would reveal Bacon's name or the name of the Rosicrucians. Such ornaments were put not only in the Christian Bible that Bacon had rewritten but in the Shakespeare plays, and in some of Bacon's own books, and a few other books that were typically Rosicrucian in spirit.

—Dr. H Spencer Lewis, Imperator of the Rosicrucian Order during the 1920-30s, from the *Rosicrucian Digest,* April 1937

If in accordance with growing opinion the nineteenth-century programme of Bible revision was commenced in a quest to find scriptural secrets, including Bacon's KJV ciphers, what were scholars really looking for? The true history of early Christianity is an interesting subject to theologians but would its discovery have truly been worth all the time and money invested in the project? Perhaps not but there are those who believe that their investigations have identified a legendary candidate for the much sought after treasure.

Peggy Parker's decipherment of the clues inserted by Bacon into the KJV has identified a recurrent theme related to "Mercy," which is reflected in references to a treasure in "darkenesse" and the hidden riches of secret places. Parker points out that in the first degree of Freemasonry rituals the initiate is said to be "coming out of darkness," which she interprets as a reference to "d-ARK-enesse." She believes that ARK is a literal reference to the Ark of the Covenant, the "Weapon of Mass Destruction" wielded in ancient times by Israeli sorcerers against their Aryan enemies.

The recurrent theme of MERCY relates to the Ark's Mercy Seat, the gold lid with two cherubim beaten out of its ends to cover and create the space where God would appear. Parker supports Norwegian freemason Petter Amundsen's theory that the Ark is a part of a treasure cached on Oak Island in Nova Scotia. Amundsen's research follows in the footsteps of earlier investigators, notably Penn Leary who claimed that Francis Bacon used the pit to hide documents proving him to be the author of Shakespeare's plays. Mark Finnan elaborated on these ideas.

---

[70] https://www.fbrt.org.uk/pages/essays/1611_KJV_research_paper_Peggy-Parker.pdf
[71] Leary, P., *The Oak Island Enigma: A History and Inquiry Into the Origin of the Money Pit,* 1953
[72] Finnan, M., *Oak Island Secrets,* 2002

Amundsen's decipherment of the *First Folio* of the Shakespeare plays led him to travel to Oak Island where he found a stone cross and also further stones that reveal a Kabbalistic Tree of Life.

According to Jewish Kabbalist, Ellie Crystal, the Old Testament Ark of the Covenant was an inferior artefact constructed in the fashion of an earlier model from the Atlantean period. This original Ark represented a covenant between the fallen angels and mankind. Crystal describes the Atlantean Ark as an instrument or storehouse that contained a crystal with the power to generate the cosmic forces capable of transforming matter into pure energy-force and energy-force into matter.

The imputed limitless power of the Ark is exemplified in the final island scene of Spielberg and Lucas's *Raiders of the Lost Ark* when archaeologist René Belloq (an ill-deserved synonym for Grail historian Otto Rahn) and his Nazi cohorts are incendiarised by the Light of God released from the Ark.

What possible connection is there between these sensational ideas and the signs and symbols that it is claimed Francis Bacon concealed in the KJV? He was a principled man to whom man's base desires for earthly powers and dominion over fellow man would have been of no interest.

If he impregnated the KJV with secrets steering truthseekers along a pathway towards spiritual enrichment, where does one look for the substantive insights into what Bacon was truly trying to achieve? One must turn, I submit, to the philosophic ideal of Rosicrucianism for answers.

> ...the tongues of Flame are in-folded
> Into the crowned knot of Fire,
> And the Fire and the Rose are One!
> —T .S. Eliot, *The Rosy Cross*

Danish-American Christian occultist, astrologer and mystic, Max Heindel (1865-1919), once described the Rosicrucian temple as an etheric structure that was formerly located in and around the home of a European country gentleman. He said that it was later moved to the American continent.

On first consideration this a very curious statement but one that nevertheless chimes with a communication received in 1997 by Arfst Wagner, anthroposophist, co-producer of the *Flensburger* journals, and in 2012-2013 a member of the German Bundestag. Back in the nineties Wagner, like me, was taking an interest in the extraordinary life of

German Grail historian, Otto Wilhelm Rahn (1904-1939).

One day Wagner received an anonymous email that read: "*I have reason to believe that many artefacts, including some found by Otto Rahn were shipped to the U.S. in 1938...I think the Grail you may be looking for is a superconducting stone that Hitler shipped to the L.A. area.*"

The correspondences between the bizarre message in Wagner's inbox and the storyline of *Raiders of the Lost Ark* are startling. Recall the film's final scene where the wooden crate containing the Ark of the Covenant, heroically captured from the Nazis by Indiana Jones and brought to the U.S.A. in a submarine, is wheeled into a vast anonymous military depository. It has been suggested that movies of this kind are made at the suggestion of U.S. Government security services as a means of imparting official truths on alternative topics in a universally acceptable manner.

The word Rosicrucian is said to derive from Christian Rosenkreutz (the allegorical co-founder of the Order), possibly from Ros and Crux— alchemical terms connoting dew as a solvent of gold and crux as the equivalent of Light. Rosicrucianism as a movement is a spiritual and cultural skein of philosophy that arose in Europe in the early seventeenth century after the publication of three anonymous manifestos, firstly in Germany and later throughout Europe, which declared the existence of an esoteric order and made seeking its knowledge attractive to many. They were the *Fama Fraternitatis Rosae Crucis* (1614), the *Confessio Fraternitatis* (1615), and the *Chymical Wedding of Christian Rosicross* (1617).

German theologian Johannes Valentinus Andreä claimed to be the author of the latter text and therefore was regarded as one of the founders of the Order. However, this was thrown into doubt as early as 1621 by "Democritus Junior," pseudonym for Robert Burton, an intimate of Francis Bacon who in his *The Anatomy of Melancholy* wrote the footnote: "*Joh. Valent. Andreas, Lord Verulam,*" indicating Burton's belief that Andreas and Bacon (made Baron Verulam in 1618) were one and the same person. The doctrine of the order drew upon esoteric truths of the ancient past, which provide insight into nature, the physical universe and the spiritual realm. The manifestos, which according to an Italian edition of the *Fama Fraternitatis Rosae Crucis* heralded a "universal reformation of mankind," combine references to the Kabbalah, Hermeticism, alchemy and mystical Christianity.

---

[73] See my book, "*Otto Rahn and the Quest for the Holy Grail: The Amazing Life of the Real 'Indiana Jones'.*" Adventures Unlimited Press, Illinois, 2008

The Temple of the Rose Cross
Teophilus Schweighardt Constantiens

The hero of the manifestos is Father C.R.C. or Christian Rosenkreutz who now invites others to join the Order. The preface to the Fama suggests that the manifesto was setting forth an alternative to the Jesuit Order. Controversies rage on the validity of the manifestos, whether the Order of the Rosy Cross existed as described in them, or whether the whole thing was a metaphor disguising a movement that did exist but in a different form. The overall theme of the *Fama* is the discovery or, rather, the re-discovery of an ancient philosophy that is primarily alchemical but which is also related to the healing arts.

The story emphasises the importance of the miraculous discovery in 1604 of the vault housing the body of Brother Rosenkreutz who died in 1484. The allegory of the vault and its everlasting light is a central feature of the Roscicrucian legend. The sun never shines in the vault, which is eternally lit by an inner sun. Geometrical figures adorn the walls. Treasures lie all around, including the works of Paracelsus, magical bells, lamps and "artificial songs."

The *Confessio Fraternitatis* states that God had sent a sign that the Great Council of the Elect was to be convened to usher in the Reformation, an act reminiscent of Johannes Trithemius's coming of the "New Age" proclamation one hundred and fifty years earlier. To indicate that the Fraternity was to play a leading role in the instigation of the Reformation, God would create new stars in Serpentarius and Cygnus: snake and swan, thus demonstrating that the Maker reveals in visible nature signs and symbols for all events coming to pass.

In *Secret Teachings of All Ages* (1928) Manly P. Hall discussed several theories as to the true beginnings of the Rosicrucian Order before eventually identifying with the belief that the philosophy was born from a real movement of a transcendental nature. In this model of thinking it is held that the true Brethren of the Rosy Cross are at home in both the outer world and in the inner planes of Nature, which can be reached only by those who can transcend the limitations of the material world. These adepts, possessed of supernatural powers, were literally citizens of two worlds able to function fully consciously in both a physical and an etheric body, the latter not subject to the laws of time. To substantiate this view, the mystic quotes the *Confessio Fraternitatis*: "…wherefore now no longer are we beheld by human eyes, unless they have received strength borrowed from the eagle." In mysticism the eagle is a symbol of initiation (the spinal Spirit Fire), and by this is explained the inability of the unregenerated world to understand the Secret Order of the Rosy Cross.

John Heydon, prominent Rosicrucian thinker, wrote that the

---

[74] Heydon, J., *The Rosie Cross Uncovered*, A. Reader, London, 1891

mysterious brethren possessed polymorphous powers, able to appear in any desired form at will and, if necessary, in more than one place simultaneously. Thomas Vaughan corroborated Heydon's claims of the brethren's powers of invisibility, saying that they "can move in this white mist. Whosoever would communicate with us must be able to see in this light..." [75]

Brethren were buried in a womb or glass casket, sometimes called the Philosophical Egg, out of which from time to time they emerge to function before returning to their shell of glass. These descriptions are mindful of the Arthurian legend which describes a crystal cave as being both the eternal resting place of Merlin, imprisoned there by Nimue the sorceress, and the home of Arthur, the Once and Future King, in Avalon.

The early Rosicrucian adepts were conversant with those mysteries that concerned the quest to regenerate through a process of transmutation the "base elements" of man's lower nature into the "gold" of intellectual and spiritual realisation. Initiates taught that spiritual nature was attached to the physical form at certain points, symbolised by the three nails of the crucifixion. One is then able to draw these nails and permit the divine nature of Man to come down from its cross through the undertaking of three alchemical processes— "The Casting of the Molten Sea," "The Making of the Rose Diamond" and "The Achieving of the Philosopher's Stone."

By following these processes one can fashion a unique personal key, in Otto Rahn's terminology a *dietrich*, whose function is to allow the removal of the "rose from the cross," which in alchemic context opens the doors to the invisible and allows one's etheric or Nature Self to travel freely and safely in the inner worlds. Dr. Franz Hartmann[76] believed that the brethren were also able to command the Elemental spirits and nature folk that reside in these higher realms.

Otto Rahn wrote[77] that in the Middle Ages there were those who believed that the Philosopher's Stone and the mythical Golden Fleece were one and the same. Professor Antoine Faivre argues that the Fleece is actually a book of alchemy.[78] He describes the ceremonial collar worn by members of the Order of the Golden Fleece. It consists of eight golden links joined by flintstones in which the spark of the "Holy Spirit

[75] Waite, A., *The Real History of the Rosicrucians*, London 1887

[76] Hartmann, F., *Secret Symbols of the Rosicrucians*, Boston Occult Publishing Co., 1888

[77] Rahn. O., *Luzifers Hofgesind: Eine Reise zu den guten Gelstern Europas,* Schwarzhaupter Verlag, Leipzig, 1937

[78] Faivre, A., *The Golden Fleece and Alchemy*, State University N.Y. Press, 1993

Fire" lies latent. We see here correspondences with the three nails that attach the spirit to the cross of the physical body.

Henry Corbin, Faivre's predecessor at the Sorbonne, associated the Golden Fleece with the Avestian concept of the *xvarnah* (depicted in Christian literature as the halo around saintly figures). The sacred oak of Dodoni on which the Golden Fleece was hung is symbolic of the human body. Draped around it is the immortal *xvarnah* held in place by twig and branch, once again representations of the three nails of the Rosicrucians. Written upon the Fleece in words of fire is ultimate wisdom—the pearl of illumination which Dr. Henry Jones declared to his son in *Indiana Jones and the Last Crusade* was the cherished prize he had finally found in his lifelong quest to attain the Holy Grail.

In general terms, Rosicrucianism stood for the individual's quest to undertake private and personal religious experiences by which his total being—body, mind and spirit—was refined and strengthened. Initially, it was an inclusive movement that welcomed all religious attitudes. However, in Germany especially it rapidly encouraged anti-Catholic sentiments as it evolved into a broad evangelical system of belief attractive to all denominations of Protestants.

In 1604 a very curious work dedicated to the Duke of Wurttemberg was published in Stuttgart. It was a book of huge length by Simon Studion titled *Naometri*. Its theme focused upon apocalyptic prophecy, which involved a system of numerology based on Biblical descriptions of the Temple of Solomon that Studion claimed led to prophecies about future events. Studion's discoveries bring us to our next step in *Jack the Ripper's New Testament*.

No one knows with certainty what prompted the nineteenth-century revision of the Bible but the Bacon-KJV story offers every possible prize for the esoteric adventurer—the secrets of the Templars and what they found beneath Solomon's stables, the Ark of the Covenant, the Holy Grail, alchemic riches, the Philosopher's Stone, the Golden Fleece, power over Nature and the Elementals, the gift of prophecy, direct access to the higher worlds and, above all, the ability to arrogate to oneself the limitless power of the gods—in short, immortality.

Evidently, Bible revisers and their deep-pocketed backers believed that concealed in the KJV and other scriptural source documents were the key, lock and door to these fabulous riches. They set to work on the long task of mining the material, in a spirit of industriousness, objectivity and anticipation that was truly not what it seemed.

Chapter 15

"Rothschild's" Bible

The commonly accepted account of English Bible revision begins in 1853 when Brooke Foss Westcott and Fenton John Anthony Hort set out to produce a New Greek Text. Their plan was to put aside the *Textus Receptus*, the name given to the succession of traditionally accepted printed Greek texts of the New Testament, as their primary source material and to restore the most ancient reading current in manuscripts of the Alexandrian text-type. Present day fundamentalist Christians claim that Westcott and Hort chose corrupt manuscripts.

However, revision of the English Bible actually began in 1816 as a joint project of the Church of England and American Baptists. Bible scholars Barbara Aho and the late Janet Moser go a step further and make the bold claim[79] that the programme was sponsored and substantially financed through front organisations by the House of Rothschild whose agenda, they submit, was to transform the Christian Bible into an instrument of Zionism.

The facts which establish the early date of English Bible revision are available in *A History of the Baptists: Traced by their Vital Principles and Practices, from the Time of Our Lord and Saviour Jesus Christ to the Year 1886* by Thomas Armitage who was a member of the revisionist American Bible Union.

On 11 May 1816 thirty-five local scriptural societies from diverse parts of the U.S.A. sent delegates to a Bible Convention hosted in New York by wealthy Christian philanthropists. The purpose of the gathering was to found the American Bible Society whose objective was "the dissemination of the Scriptures in the received versions where they exist, and in the most faithful where they may be required." Delegates agreed that the new Society's remit was to include translation as well as circulation of the Bible. Financial support for the Society's

---

[79] https://watch.pairsite.com/revision.html, accessed 31/7/2018

244

establishment was received from the British and Foreign Bible Society of London.

One of the American Bible Society's founding Vice-Presidents was Dewitt Clinton, a U.S. Senator and Grand Master of the Masonic Lodge in New York. Clinton introduced the 12th Amendment to the Constitution, which relates to procedures for electing the President and Vice President. A work published in 1818 in New York by Salem Town (*System of Speculative Freemasonry*) urged American Freemasons to be bold in publicising that "the foundation (of Freemasonry) is laid in evangelical truth." Clinton wote the publication's endorsing preface.

Conference resolve did not equate with speedy action and by 1827 the American Baptist University of Rochester was repeating the mantra that the Bible should be thoroughly revised. Three years later the American Bible Society funded Adoniram Judson's *Burman Bible*, which changed "baptism" to "immersion," a change designed to polarise the Baptists.

In 1838 Dr. Spencer H. Cone, President of the American and Foreign Bible Society, sought immediate action to revise the English Scriptures but his fellow members voted against it. Pressure for revision maintained its momentum and in 1842 Reverends David Bernard and Samuel Aaron issued a treatise on the need of "Revising and Amending *King James Version* of the Holy Scriptures."

Later that year Bernard and Aaron procured and published a revised version of the Old and New Testaments, "carefully revised and amended by several Biblical scholars…in accordance with the advice of many distinguished brethren, the services of a number of professors, some of whom rank among the first in our country for their knowledge of the original languages and Biblical interpretation and criticism…"

Evidently, this revised version did not garner support because in 1849 the American and Foreign Bible Society at its annual meeting resolved "that the restriction laid by the Society upon the Board of Managers in 1838 to use only the commonly received version in the distribution of the Scriptures in the English language" should be removed. The passing of this resolution allowed the Society's board to refer the question of revision to a committee of five. After long consideration the committee presented its majority report:

> "Resolved, that, in the opinion of this board, the sacred Scriptures of the Old and New Testament ought to be faithfully and accurately translated into every living language.
> "Resolved, that wherever, in versions now in use, known and obvious errors exist, and wherever the meaning of the original is

concealed or obscured, suitable measures ought to be prosecuted to correct those versions, so as to render the truth clear and intelligible to the ordinary reader.

"Resolved, that in regard to the expediency of this board undertaking the correction of the English version, a decided difference of opinion exists, and, therefore, that it be judged most prudent to await the instruction of the Society.

Despite the resolution, the Society voted on 22 May 1850 against revision of the English Scriptures (the KJV). Consequently, Dr. Cone resigned as president and gathered together twenty-four revisionists to plan a new Bible revision society. Among the revisionists were three men from Britain who did more to promote the revision of the English Bible than any others: Drs. Archibald Maclay, William H. Wyckoff, and Deacon William Colgate.

On 10 June the American Bible Union was established for the purpose of revising the English Bible. Dr. Cone was elected as President. The project quickly got underway with revisers in America and in Europe assigned respective tasks. Dr. Cone began with the Old Testament and was aided in the Hebrew text by Dr. Rodiger of Halle, Germany. The revisers of New Testament were to use *Bagsters' Greek New Testament* of 1851.

Meanwhile in England, Trinity College fellows Brooke Foss Westcott and Edward White Benson, future archbishop of Canterbury, established The Cambridge Association for Spiritual Inquiry (informally, the Cambridge Ghost Society or "Ghostly Guild"), one of the pioneer bodies of modern Spiritualist inquiry and the precursor to the Society for Psychical Research. The Society was formed to "conduct a serious and earnest inquiry into the nature of the phenomena vaguely called supernatural and a number of distinguished persons became members."[80] Westcott became very active in the Guild's paranormal investigations and worked as its Secretary until 1860. William Gladstone, British Prime Minister 1865-1874, called psychical research, "The most important work which is being done in the world, by far the most important work." The

Brooke Foss Westcott

---

[80] Gauld, A., *The Founders of Psychical Research*, New York, Schocken Books, 1968

founding of the Ghost Society, which was revived in 1862 as The Ghost Club, laid the groundwork for the establishment in 1884 of the socialist Fabian Society, an outgrowth of the Fellowship of New life founded by Scottish intellectual Thomas Davidson and eight colleagues a year earlier.

Also in this period Hort joined the Cambridge Conversazione Society, better known as the Cambridge Apostles, a secret intellectual fraternity with a more or less open homosexual spectrum of membership that was founded in 1820. The Apostles have long been suspected of wielding undue influence over Britain's social, religious and political affairs. Becoming an Apostle involves taking an oath of secrecy and listening to the reading of a curse, originally written by Hort in 1851. The Apostles received unwelcome publicity in 1951 after it was established that MI6 officer Guy Burgess, one of the three participants in the infamous Cambridge spy ring that passed British secrets to the KGB, was a former Apostles member. The Society came under the spotlight once again in 1964 when member Anthony Blunt, Surveyor of the Queen's Pictures, was similarly identified as a traitor.

Notably, records of the Society's affairs and debating topics are stored in a cedar chest that members refer to as the "Ark." This tradition may not be just an instance of nineteenth-century whimsy but actually one connected to a practice with far older provenance. Christopher McIntosh has discovered that in sixteenth-century Germany there existed an Orden der Unzertrennlichen (the Order of the Lovebirds), a mystico-religious system in five degrees that can be dated back to 1577.

Fenton John Anthony Hort

The Order's members studied alchemy, the results of successful experiments placed in an "Archa," a secret chest whose contents were continually added to. The implication was that like Mary Poppins's carpetbag, no matter how much one added to it the magical chest never filled up. The resemblance is too striking to be coincidence and indicates that the founding principles of the Apostles actually pre-date its recorded inauguration by nearly 250 years. Once again we see an instance in which occult affairs in Germany in the Middle Ages

---

[81] McIntosh, C. *The Rosicrucians: The History, Mythology, and Rituals of an Esoteric Order,* Red Wheel Weiser, 1998

continued to exert control over the activities of secret societies in Britain centuries later.

In 1853 Westcott and Hort began their production of the *New Greek Testament* using Alexandrian manuscripts. In a letter to Reverend John Ellerton dated 19 April, Hort revealed that he and Westcott were proceeding with the editing of a Greek text of the New Testament. Lachmann and Tischendorf would supply some of the required textual materials, which would be supplemented with "Oriental versions." Their object was to supply clergymen and schools and the like with a portable Greek text that should not be disfigured with Byzantine corruptions brought into Bible research in preceding centuries by the Eastern Orthodox Church.

Lobegott Friedrich Constantin von Tischendorf was a world-leading Bible scholar. He discovered the world's oldest and most complete disputed Bible, dating from 325 A.D. with, for the first time, a complete New Testament. Tischendorf's Bible is called Codex Sinaiticus after the Saint Catherine's Monastery at Mount Sinai where he discovered it. Karl Konrad Friedrich Wilhelm Lachmann was a German philologist and critic, noted particularly for his contributions to the field of textual criticism. In his own work undertaken between 1831 and 1846 on the New Testament, Lachmann became the first major editor to break from the *Textus Receptus*, an act that made him an obvious choice to partner with Westcott and Hort's endeavour.

It is clear from Hort's letter to Ellerton that the proposed program of work would require the procurement and analysis of scriptural texts—"Oriental versions"—not previously investigated by Western scholars. It would be a striking coincidence if, very soon after committing to the work of two controversial societies, one dedicated to paranormal research and the other a secret intellectual elite at the apex of British society, Westcott and Hort suddenly decided to embark on a twenty-eight year Bible odyssey, one moreover that required reference to ancient scriptural documents not hitherto seen in the West.

By 1858, Dean of Westminster and poet, Dr. Richard Chevenix Trench, was calling for a "better" revision (than that being undertaken by the American Bible Union under Dr. Cone), which would "set aside the so-called Baptists" as revisers because they "interpret" rather than translate. He complained in an article in the Edinburgh Review that the instalments being received from American revisers were not very encouraging and he was persuaded that a "revision ought to come, I am convinced that it will come" but clearly, Trench believed, from a new team and not from the unsatisfactory revisers in America.

Thus, in the last part of his article Trench submitted a plan of revision in which he proposed to invite the Biblical scholars of "the land to assist with their suggestions here, even though they might not belong to the church...setting aside, then, the so-called Baptists, who, of course, could not be invited, seeing that they demand not a translation of the Scripture but an interpretation, and that in their own sense." One suspects also that the real reason for Trench's position was that American Baptists were limited to translating from the *Textus Receptus* and the Dean wanted to use the Westcott-Hort New Greek Testament based on their never-before-seen "Oriental" source documents.

Seven years later, the American Bible Union's version was completed and printed. It is estimated that about 750,000 copies of the newly translated version were circulated by the Union. Contrary to the Union's expectations their new work did not generate universal acclaim, despite the editors' proud boast that no expense had been spared to obtain both the oldest translations of the Bible and copies of the ancient manuscripts in order to make a perfect translation. In fact, the faithful were so unimpressed that no sooner had the Union's translation been printed than Christians in both America and in England were calling for a fresh effort, a movement that culminated in the Convocation of Canterbury in 1870.

In the meantime the British Monarchy was spearheading the formation of a new institution dedicated to the "rediscovery" of the Holy Land. In 1865 under the patronage of Queen Victoria all of the elite institutions of Britain, including the Anglican Church, the Grand Lodge of England and the Universities of Oxford and Cambridge gathered to fund the new institution, naming it the Palestine Exploration Fund. Sir Charles Warren replaced the PEF's first Chairman, freemason Walter Besant, in 1886, the same year that Warren became the first Grand Master and, later, Treasurer (succeeding Besant) of the Quatuor Coronati lodge, which was established to promote the cause of Masonic archaeology, the first such lodge in the history of freemasonry. Together with James Rice, Besant wrote the novel *Monks of Thelema*, which describes a "church of Thelema" similar to the Abbey of Thélème in Rabelais's *Gargantua*. Aleister Crowley later founded an occult order by this name with its notorious

Sir Charles Warren

---

[82] Besant, W., and Rice, J., *Monks of Thelema*, Chatto & Windus, London, 1878

maxim: "Do what thou wilt shall be the whole of the Law. Love is the law, love under will."

In 1867, when the Ottoman Turks were administering the Holy City, Warren was commissioned by the PEF to make excavations in the Temple Mount. Stories circulated that the excavation team was searching for the citadel at Silwan, a reputed location of the Ark of the Covenant, the holiest of holy Jewish artefacts. According to the second Book of Samuel, King David captured the walled city through an entrance in a water shaft. It is rumoured that the excavation team found the fortress near Gibon Spring, an ancient underground watercourse that runs beneath the city. It is claimed that in it they identified a narrow shaft similar to the one described in Samuel.

Researchers Tom Slemen and Keith Andrews claimed in their 2010 collaboration[83] that the Ripper was a British agent, Lieutenant Claude Reignier Conder. I do not share this view but what is noteworthy is that Conder worked alongside his good friend Charles Warren in the Jerusalem excavations. Conder was renowned in Britain as the highest authority on Biblical archaeology. He and Warren are said to have made "discoveries." Warren had a thorough knowledge of ancient languages and was able to decipher many inscriptions including the Meshe Stele (also known as the Moabite Stone). Although Anglican missionary Frederick Augustus Klein discovered the Mesha Stele intact at the site of ancient Dibon in August 1868, George Grove of the PEF announced the find in a letter to *The Times* of 8 February 1870 and attributed the discovery to Charles Warren.

Members of the Palestine Exploration Fund

---

[83] Andrews, K., and Slemen, T., *Jack the Ripper: British Intelligence Agent*, The Bluecoat Press, Liverpool, 2010

According to Slemen, the markings cut into the face of the Ripper's penultimate victim, Kate Eddowes, closely resemble Moabite hieroglyphics. Architect and City of London surveyor Frederick William Foster presented plans and maps to the inquest relating to the Eddowes murder, as well as sketches of her injuries. The latter comprise one full-length depiction of Eddowes *in situ* in Mitre Square, one in the mortuary and one concentrating on the facial injuries. In April 1889 Foster would be asked by the police to document a manslaughter case that occurred in a public house but his account was nowhere near as detailed as that for Eddowes. This suggests that Warren may have specially commissioned Foster to survey Eddowes' particulars in precise detail. If so, why might Warren have done this?

Warren and Conder were also well versed in the Altaic languages from which Manchu derives. We have seen that Warren ordered the removal of the lines chalked on the brick wall in Goulstone Street: "*The Juwes are the Men that will not be Blamed for Nothing.*" In Manchu, juwe means "two," equating in English with duo. During a lecture in London presided over by Warren, Conder chalked the word Juwe on the blackboard and paired it with "two" in English and "deux" in French. Slemen and Andrews ponder the significance of this action, asking if it gives a clue that there were two people acting together in committing the murders, perhaps with a French or continental connection.

In 1887 the Chairman of the Executive Committee of the Palestine Exploration Fund wrote to the editor of *The Times* praising Conder, who, the Chairman said, was an expert in the decipherment of Hittite hieroglyphics. He said that Conder had placed his results in the hands of Sir Charles Wilson and Sir Charles Warren and that the findings threw great light on the early chapters of Genesis. The chairman added that:

> There are reasons why the language in which the inscriptions are written, and the manner in which the discovery was arrived at should be kept back until (Conder's) memoir is completed and the whole story can be told at length.

One is bound to ask: What were these reasons for keeping back the information? What was the precise nature of the "discovery"? Was it what Warren and Conder had been seeking? Or, having found it were they still following the scent of additional prizes? For whom were they making their searches? The Convocation of Canterbury in 1870 resolved after much debate: "That it is desirable that Convocation should nominate a body of its own members to undertake the work of revision, who shall be at liberty to invite the co-operation of any eminent for scholarship, to whatever nation or religious body they may belong." Their stated aim was "to adapt *King James Version* to the present state of the English language without changing the idiom and vocabulary...and to the present standard of Biblical scholarship."

English revisionists would begin the New Testament using the American Bible Union's version for consultation but employ the (work-in-progress) Westcott-Hort New Greek Text (and their putative trove of exotic source papers) as its textual basis. American Philip Schaff, acclaimed Swiss-born, German-educated Protestant theologian, makes notes in his diary in the summer of 1871 concerning his meeting in the Deanery of Westminster with the "Bible Revisers":

> The meeting of the New Testament Revisers was intensely interesting. Lightfoot, Westcott, Hort, Scrivener, Angus, Merivale, Eadie, David Brown, the Bishop of Gloucester...the Bishop of Salisbury and others were all there. No outsider is admitted except the Archbishop of Canterbury (Edward White Benson).

Although pre-occupied with their New Greek Text, Westcott and Hort together with Canon of St Paul's Cathedral, Joseph Lightfoot, find time during 1871 to establish the "Eranus," an elite club for senior Apostles members.

President of Yale University, Timothy Dwight V, a member of the Skull and Bones Society since 1849, was drafted into the American New Testament revision committee in 1873. Officially, the Order of Skull and Bones was founded at Yale University in 1832 by William Huntington Russell and Alphonso Taft. This is challenged in a century-old pamphlet published by an anonymous group that called itself File and Claw after the tools they used to break into the Order's premises. There they found information that indicated that the Order is a chapter of a corps of a German university. Skull and Bones co-founder Russell was in Germany before his senior year and formed a warm friendship with a leading member of a German society. The pamphlet suggests that the number "322" present in all Bones literature is to illustrate that the Order was founded in 1832 as the second chapter of the German society. The File and Claw team go on to describe a German slogan painted "on the arched walls above the vault" of the sacred room, 322. It appears above a painting of skulls surrounded by Masonic symbols, a picture said to be "a gift of the German chapter." The slogan reads:

> "Wer war der Thor, wer Weiser, Bettler oder Kaiser? Ob Arm, Ob Reich, im Tode gleich." (Who was the fool, who the wise man, beggar or king? Whether poor or rich, all's the same in death.)

The slogan is to be found in a 1798 Scottish anti-Illuminist tract reprinted in 1967 by the John Birch Society. The tract (*Proofs of a Conspiracy* by John Robison) reproduces alleged excerpts from Illuminist ritual manuals confiscated by the Bavarian police when they outlawed Johann Adam Weishaupt's Society in 1785. According to the tract, toward the end of the ceremony of initiation into the "Regent degree" of Illuminism a skeleton is pointed out to the initiate, at the feet of which are laid a crown and a sword. The initiate is then asked whether it is the skeleton of a king, nobleman or a beggar.

Based on such revelations, researchers have claimed that the German secret society with which Russell was friendly was established around 1786 when the Bavarian Elector banned the Bavarian Illuminati, whose papers and guiding principles eventually became the foundation of the "Bonesmen." Once more we have a putative link between the nineteenth-century revision work and the global reach and dominion of occult societies in Germany.

Westcott and Hort published the *New Testament in the Original Greek* in two volumes in 1881. Volume 1, containing the Greek text, appeared 12 May, and Volume 2, detailing the scholars' methodology, 4 September. The Westcott and Hort text, as it is alternatively called, appeared as a companion to and the basis of the revised *New Testament of our Lord and Saviour Jesus Christ*, which was published just days later.

This coincidence of near simultaneous publication of the two works initially led critics to confound the two texts, a state of confusion that appeared to bemuse Westcott's son, Arthur. He later stated that the Greek text underlying the *Revised New Testament* differed considerably from that used by Hort and his father. Although copies of the latter had been placed in the hands of the Revisers, he said they did not accept any new reading unless after full discussion a majority of two-thirds was in favour of the change.

Arthur Westcott's position contradicts both the 1870 Convocation of Canterbury resolution that "English revisionists would (use) the Westcott-Hort New Greek Text as its textual basis," and the preface notes[85] accompanying the publication in May 1881 of the *Revised New Testament*. It would appear that Arthur was attempting to put a different

[84] Westcott, A., *Life and Letters of Brooke Foss Westcott,* London: Macmillan & Co., 1903

[85] "The RV is a revision of the *King James Version* made on the basis of Westcott and Hort's 1881 *Greek Language New Testament* and Tregelles' *Gesenius Hebrew Chaldee Lexicon Old Testament Scriptures,* 1857

spin on the nature and origin of the source documents for the revised scripture.

Critical opinion stated that the *New Testament in the Original Greek* was probably the most important contribution to Biblical learning in their generation. *The Times* later wrote a glowing review:

> To the world at large Westcott's tenure of the Regius Professorship will always be associated with the so-called *Cambridge Text* of the New Testament, little as his professorship really had to do with it. Probably the whole history of the New Testament since the time of Origen there has been nothing more remarkable than the quiet persistence with which these two Fellows of Trinity--Westcott, aged twenty-eight, and Hort, some three years younger--started "in the spring of 1853" to systematise New Testament criticism.
>
> They found themselves aware of the unsatisfactoriness of the *Textus Receptus*, and conscious that neither Lachmann nor Tischendorf gave "such an approximation to the Apostolic words as we could accept with reasonable satisfaction." So they agreed to commence at once the formation of a manual text for (their) own use, hoping at the same time that it might be of service to others. It says something at once for their determination and their care that the two famous volumes were not published till 1881, twenty-eight years from their inception...
>
> —*The Times*, 29 July 1901

The *Revised New Testament* appeared 17 May 1881.[86] Seventeen Episcopalians, two of the Scottish Church, two dissenting Presbyterians, one Unitarian, one Independent and one Baptist had carried out the work. A board of American scholars had co-operated but they did not succeed in winning acceptance of their submitted "list of readings and renderings," their "English brethren" choosing not to adopt them. Dean John Burgon recorded that committee members were bound to a pledge of silence. The revisers had been charged with introducing alterations only if they were required in order to be faithful to the original text. In the New Testament alone around 36,000 changes were made, over 5,000 of them on the basis of a better Greek text (Hort and Westcott's). During the ten and a half years consumed in their work the Revision Committee met in the Jerusalem Chamber at Westminster each month for ten months of every year, each meeting lasting four

---

[86] Ellicott, C., et al., *The New Testament of our Lord and Saviour Jesus Christ, Translated out of the Greek: Being the Version Set Forth A.D. 1611, Compared with the Most Ancient Authorities and Revised, A.D. 1881*. Oxford: Oxford University Press, 1881

days between 11:00 a.m. to 6:00 p.m.

Right from the start, all was not plain sailing. The Committee was divided, the majority of two-thirds being in favour of applying German methods of higher criticism to the revision process. The first chairman, Bishop of Winchester Samuel Wilberforce, resigned very soon after commencement of the program, calling the work a "miserable business." Charles Ellicott, Bishop of Gloucester and Bristol, succeeded him.

Wilberforce had vehemently protested the presence on the committee of a Unitarian scholar, Dr. G. Vance Smith, who denied the divinity of Christ. Despite Smith's anti-Christian opinion, he had nonetheless participated in a communion service at Westminster Abbey upon the invitation of Bishop Westcott prior to the first committee meeting. May "doubting Thomas" Smith, the unbeliever, have been following a secret agenda under Westcott's direction?

In 1883 the American and Foreign Bible Society and the American Bible Union resolved their differences and accepted the English revision, based on the *Westcott-Hort New Greek Text*, and agreed to publish the *English Revised Version* of the KJV and the American Bible Union version.

With the publication of the revised Old Testament in four volumes in 1885 it was mission accomplished for the Revision Committee. Their Bible was a great success, the ERV selling three million copies in its first year of publication.

In the context of this present work what is relevant to our understanding is that Westcott and Hort's New Greek Text was not only the textual basis for the ERV but, as described by the Revision Committee, its companion publication. In other words, without the Westcott-Hort text there would have been no ERV. Westcott and Hort's input was mission critical for the ERV's success. The Committee's emphasis on the critical importance of the New Greek Text would present no cause for query were it not for the fact that Westcott and Hort's source papers were not what they seemed

Westcott and Hort's *New Testament in the Original Greek* is a critical text compiled from some of the oldest New Testament fragments and texts discovered by the time they embarked on their project. They took the precaution to praise the integrity of the extant texts, saying: "It is our belief that even among the numerous unquestionably spurious readings of the New Testament there are no signs of deliberate falsification of the text for dogmatic purposes." In making this claim, of course, the pair could also be said to have been avoiding any suspicion that they were seeking hidden knowledge in documents such as Bacon's KJV revision papers.

There are three major Greek language Codices that have been used in Bible revisions: Vaticanus, Sinaiticus and Alexandrinus. Codex Vaticanus is owned by the Vatican; "Tischendorf's" Codex Sinaiticus, a 4th century Alexandrian parchment, has its parts dispersed between St Catherine's Monastery, the British Library, Leipzig University Library and the National Library of Russia; and Alexandrinus, one of the earliest and most complete manuscripts of the Bible, passed from Alexandria to Britain in the 17th century.

The Codex Vaticanus is regarded as the oldest extant manuscript of the Greek Bible (Old and New Testament), and is so named after its place of conservation in the Vatican Library. It is considered by scholars today to be one of the best Greek texts of the New Testament.

An extract from the Codex Vaticanus

In order of preference, Westcott and Hort favoured Codex Vaticanus followed by Codex Sinaiticus. They believed that the two codices, in combination with Codex Bezae Cantabrigensis, a document of the New Testament dating from the 5th century, represent the original form of the New Testament text.

The Codex Vaticanus has a fascinating and chequered history. Regarded as the most ancient of all Greek manuscripts, it was brought in 1448 by Pope Nicholas V to Rome, since which time papal officials have guarded it zealously. Erasmus in 1533 knew of its existence but it is said that he was not permitted to study it, nor was anyone else allowed access for nearly three hundred years. Finally, in 1843 after months of delay, Tischendorf was allowed to see it for just six hours! Another specialist, de Muralt, in 1844 was afforded access for a more generous nine-hour period. In permitting these snapshot readings, the Vatican thought it was being canny. They did not, however, count on the brilliant memorizing abilities of English Biblical scholar, Dr. Samuel Prideaux Tregelles.

In 1845 Tregelles was permitted to study the Codex for an open-ended period. Denied writing paper, pen and ink, Tregelles was allowed into the reading room on a daily basis. As an added precaution his pockets were searched on entering and leaving the room. However, despite the formidable obstacles put before him Tregelles' prodigious memory allowed him to eventually retain and commit to paper in his quarters all of the principle variant readings of this most ancient text. He pulled off this amazing feat even when handicapped by the practice of eagle-eyed officials to snatch away a particular leaf if they considered that the Englishman was paying it too much attention.

Eventually, officials discovered that Tregelles had as good as stolen the text and that the Biblical world knew the essential contents of the historic manuscript. Recognising the *fait accompli,* Pope Pius IX felt he had no choice but to announce that the Catholic Church would bring out its own edition of the Vaticanus, which it released in five volumes in 1857 under the auspices of Cardinal Mai and his assistants who, frankly, were grossly incompetent. Mai had commenced his edition in 1836 but well aware of its embarrassing faults

Dr. Samuel Tregelles

held back its publication for twenty years. It was therefore no surprise that in the opinion of scholars the Vatican should have spared itself the time and effort because of the very poor quality of Pius's edition. The Vatican did not present a more widely acclaimed version until Pius sanctioned the release of 100 limited-edition copies of Joseph Cozza's edition in 1889.

What all of this means is that when Westcott and Hort commenced their *New Testament in the Original Greek,* and for the greater part of its execution, they knew full well that they were not referencing a good quality Codex Vaticanus, their principle source document of choice. Although the project had proceeded on the understanding that Tischendorf would supply textual materials, his six-hour perusal of the Codex Vaticanus and his subsequent issue of its first twenty pages of text were obviously of limited value. As for Tregelles's contribution, although he is regarded as a key influence on the Westcott and Hort work his own knowledge of Vaticanus was restricted to its variants. It therefore follows that both the *Westcott and Hort Greek New Testament* and the ERV were deficient insofar that they were based on an incomplete Codex Vaticanus. It would have been a wholly dispiriting twenty-eight years if during that whole time Westcott and Hort were proceeding in the belief that they had nothing better to guide them in their monumental labours than a less-than-perfect Codex.

What other documents might they have had on their desks? Hort told Ellerton at the commencement of the project that they proposed to use "Oriental versions" unblemished by "Byzantine corruptions." That sounds like an exciting option except that in a search through Westcott and Hort's main items of correspondence from 1853 until 1881,[87] the phrase "Oriental versions," except in Hort's letter to Ellerton in April 1853, does not re-appear.

Perhaps the pair did not need to use "Oriental versions"; maybe they were a red herring. After all, through their peers and various intertwining circles of influence Westcott and Hort and their colleagues in the revision committee had other choices at their disposal. They could, for example, make use of the Cambridge Apostles' intelligence network and, importantly, the alchemic papers of the Society's progenitor, the sixteenth-century Order of the Lovebirds. They would surely also have had knowledge of what the Palestine Exploration Fund was really doing in the Holy Land and of the true nature and import of Warren and Conder's discoveries. Stories handed down through the centuries speak of the Templars having cached beneath Solomon's

---

[87] http://prophets-see-all.tripod.com/46641.htm, accessed 6 August 2018

stables documents whose contents, if revealed, would bring the Church to its knees. Through the presence of Timothy Dwight on the American New Testament Revision Committee, Westcott and Hort also had access to Weishaupt's occult papers, which through ensuing German secret societies eventually came into the possession of the infamous Skull and Bones Society. And, finally, the Codex Vaticanus did, after all, have its own secrets.

Glen Claston, a world expert in cryptography and the *Voynich Manuscript*, replied to my message like one who had been mulling over its topics well before it reached him. He began by describing John Dee as, above all, a master mathematician who consorted with geometer Gerardus Mercator and Sir Henry Billingsley, the first to translate into English *Euclid's Elements* for which Dee wrote its preface. Claston then brought a further dimension, cryptography, into the equation when he referred to Sir Francis Walsingham (Queen Elizabeth's spymaster) and Dee as masters of complex ciphers, and, finally Lewis Carroll, the logician who concealed his ciphers in the Looking Glass world and who, coincidentally, wrote *Euclid and his Modern Rivals* in 1879. Claston then concludes his response by suggesting that one should look to non-standardised spelling in contemporary Biblical translation *"to ferret out the truth behind the 'looking glass.'"* He could not have been any clearer. In Claston's view, an understanding of number, measure, sign and symbol and the application of the reverse logic of the looking glass world will help solve the riddle of the Whitechapel murders.

Officially, the discovery of the mysterious "umlauts" in the Codex Vaticanus were not discovered until 1995 when Philip Payne, specialist in New Testament studies, noticed the double dots peppered throughout the Vaticanus pages in the margin of the columns next to a line. Payne concluded, and all scholars seem to agree, that these umlauts indicate lines where a textual variant was known to the person who inserted the dots. There are 795 of them in the text and around another 40 that are uncertain. Researchers believe that the umlauts may have been added in the 15th century by Renaissance theologian, Juan Ginés de Sepúlveda (1490-1574) On page 1512, next to Hebrews 1:3, the text contains a margin note: *"Fool and knave, can't you leave the old reading alone and not alter it!"*

Considering the depth of scholarship with which the Vaticanus has been investigated over the centuries it would beggar belief if the umlauts had not been seen prior to 1995. In fact, Tregelles is believed to have seen them during his many hours ensconced in the Vatican library, and was intrigued by the margin note on page 1512. The admonishment piqued Tregelles' interest because he believed that Sepúlveda had knowledge of adulterations made to the Vaticanus text by Dr. John Dee, which the Elizabethan magus had referenced in the marginalia.

Contemporaries John Dee and Francis Bacon shared a mutual interest in a vast array of topics, including science, philosophy, esoteric learning and, of course, cryptography. Dee travelled in Europe extensively in the late 1540s to the early 1550s to consult with learned men on a wide range of scientific and philosophic topics. In this period he spent time in Italy and, besides meeting noted mathematician Federico Commandino, Dee had ample opportunity to meet with intellectuals such as Sepúlveda.

It was Sepúlveda that provided Dutch humanist Erasmus (Desiderius Erasmus Roterodamus 1466–1536), described as the greatest scholar of the northern Renaissance, with 365 readings of Codex Vaticanus. With barely ten years having passed since Erasmus' death, Sepúlveda, his memory fresh, would have had plenty to discuss with a fellow giant of sixteenth-century scholarship about his collaboration with the Dutchman on the secrets of the Codex Vaticanus. He could also have arranged for Dee to peruse the Codex during which opportunity the Englishman had the opportunity to make the adulterations discovered subsequently by Sepúlveda and, much later, by Tregelles. It is therefore not beyond the bounds of possibility that Dee revealed to Bacon the substance of what he had learned on his travels and of his adulterations to the Codex, and that Bacon later provided clues to their nature in an encrypted form in the KJV.

Francis Bacon and the equally famous philosopher, wizard and Franciscan friar Roger Bacon (1219/20-1292), known as Doctor Mirabilis, were descended from the Norman Mollei-Bacon family, which hailed from the arrondissement of Bayeux.[88] This would make the two English Bacons direct descendants of Jacques de Molay (also Molai), the last Grand Master of the Knights Templar who took the Order's secrets to his grave after he was roasted alive on a spit on the orders of Philip IV of France.

The *Voynich Manuscript* is also known as the Roger Bacon cipher because of the weight of scholarly opinion that attributes its creation to the Friar. Roger Bacon was reported to use a talking head fashioned from brass that could answer any question. It is said that he learned the secret of the head from the Knights Templar. In turn, a recurring charge laid against the Templars was their reputed worship of a human skull

---

[88] *Escutcheons of Science*, http://www.numericana.com/arms/bacon.htm, accessed 7 August 2018

they called Baphomet which, according to the court of Rome's indictment of heresy, "bestowed on the order all its wealth, made the trees flower and the plants of the earth to sprout forth."

The Templars are said to have inherited the secrets of the Cathars, a unique Christian sect in the South of France that counted among their number a "Living Bible." Some claim that the "Living Bible" was a talking head that was passed to the Templars after the last of the Cathars were put to the stake in the mid-thirteenth century.

In connection with the story that Mary Magdalene came to France after the Crucifixion, there is mention in legend that she brought to Narbonne a crystal skull reputed to contain the living essence of Jesus, a fabulous artefact that was subsequently handed down to trusted custodians (Cathars, Templars et al.) through the ensuing centuries. May clues to this object's existence and its unlimited power have been the source of secrets encoded by initiates during the Christian era in key documents such as the *Voynich Manuscript* and the KJV?

In 1883 Pope Leo XIII authorised the opening up of the Vatican archives. Almost as soon as Leo gave the authorisation, a Greek Bible translation, said to be a copy of the Codex Vaticanus hitherto not seen by scholars, was stolen by agents working on behalf of a secret group within the Oxford University academic team tasked with producing a New English Dictionary. The story goes that two years later, the insider group in the Oxford English Dictionary offices published in secret its own *Revised New Testament Bible*. It was rumoured that the group was working hand-in-hand with the founding members of the Fabian Society. It would appear that when producing their clandestine scripture the OED group had better quality source material at their disposal than had Hort and Westcott during their twenty-eight year program.

More or less concurrent with the appearance of the OED's secret Bible, Leo came out very strongly against Freemasonry in his encyclical *Humanum Genus*. Revealing his knowledge of a Masonic connection to the theft of the Codex and of the OED's ensuing secret Bible work, Leo wrote that as a convenient manner of concealment Freemasons "assume the character of literary men and scholars associated for purposes of learning." "Literary men and scholars" rather neatly sums up the OED group responsible for the theft and the subsequent publication of their own secret Bible.

Sources within the SAGB membership report receiving a communication in the early 1970s that a copy of the OED's secret Bible was buried in a Hampshire location. SAGB sources also report that an unnamed cryptographer working on cracking German ciphers during

WWII discovered a copy of the OED Bible, the implication being that they either learned of its location through his cipher work or was told of it by another source.

Any prizes sought or gained as a result of Bible translation did not accrue from the finished product, albeit welcomed by the Christian faithful, but from the source material. Stories reporting clandestine activities well into the twentieth century indicate that the search for hidden booty was not resolved, at least in part, by 1888.

In the penultimate chapter we consider the vexed questions of commission and participation concerning the Whitechapel murders. Why might at least six women have been slain in varying degrees of brutality, the most heinous of which suggest acts of sacrifice as distinct from "run of the mill" murder?

I declare at once that I do not pretend to have the answers but I do provide food for thought such that, appetite whetted, others might be moved to make investigations of their own.

Joshua passing the River Jordan with the Ark of the Covenant by Benjamin West

Chapter 16

Basle, 1897

Over the years I have been unable to shake off the feeling that there is a "Royal" dimension to the Ripper story. By this, I am not referring directly to a British royal connection but to a wider involvement within the Imperial Houses of Russia, Germany, Prussia and Austria-Hungary. The thought first took hold while I was watching the BBC's *Fall of Eagles*. As I observed the interplay between the royal leaders it occurred to me that somehow, somewhere behind the truth of the Whitechapel murders there may have taken place an associated event involving one or more of these powerful sovereigns at a personal level.

As soon as this idea came to me, for no reason other than an intuitive leap, I quickly thought of Alan Moore's *League of Extraordinary Gentlemen,* a nineteenth-century story about British Intelligence assembling through intermediaries a cadre of extraordinary individuals to protect the interests of the Empire. In *From Hell* Moore was similarly insightful in his treatment of the Ripper murders, and so I treated my synchronous musings with respectful deliberation.

It felt to me that operating at the level of the sovereigns a similar undercurrent might have been at work in 1888 concerning matters of political intrigue and esoteric ambition. On further consideration, I felt that a connection with Whitechapel need not have been something grandiose or mysterious but could just as well have been, for example, a tawdry bit of business such as a fling with a woman from the "lower classes" and its attendant unwelcome consequences.

Others thinking along these lines suggest an incident of scandal within the ruling Habsburg family, pointing, for example, to the remarkable case of Johann Orth. On 16 October 1889, Archduke Johannes von Habsburg (Johann Nepomuk Salvator), cousin of the Emperor of Austro-Hungary, resigned his army commission and renounced his title and the priviliges he enjoyed as a member of the Austrian Imperial Family. He then assumed the name "Johann Orth," the surname deriving from the name of a castle he once owned. No one knows for certain what prompted Orth to renounce his titles and retire from the Imperial scene. However, he did say in an interview that he was looking for a safe haven as he felt that the Habsburgs were about to be ousted from Austria. It appears that that was not all that Orth was looking for.

It is known that between November 1889 and February 1890 Orth visited Rennes-le-Château in the Languedoc region of southwestern France. Stories of extraordinary finds by village curé Abbé Bérenger Saunière in the 1890s have made the area a hot topic for conspiracy theorists and treasure seekers. Orth later claimed that he only reached the village because he got lost while travelling from Italy to Spain.

Orth's account does not entirely square with the fact that he and Saunière had consecutively numbered bank accounts at Perpignan, indicating they had opened them together and that they shared financial arrangements of a repetitive nature. It goes without saying that any major issues faced by the House of Habsburg and the German and Russian Royal Families in this period impacted directly on the British Royals as they were all directly linked by close family ties and bloodlines. Orth and his wife, opera dancer Ludmilla ("Milli") Stubel, were officially declared dead in 1911, twenty-one years after going missing after their ship was lost off Cape Horn *en route* to Argentina.

The Orth story as a backcloth to the Whitechapel murders may not be a long shot. Sir Arthur Conan Doyle seemed to believe there might be a connection. The writer is said to have based the character of Irene Adler on Stubel. Adler was both Holmes' only true love and, in "A Scandal in Bohemia" published in June 1891, the only woman ever to have defeated his powers of investigation. Written around the time of the couple's disappearance at sea, it is Conan Doyle's first short story to feature Holmes. It tells the story of one Wilhelm Gottsreich Sigismond von Ormstein, Grand Duke of Cassel-Felstein and the hereditary King of Bohemia (in 1891, a part of the Austro-Hungarian Empire), who begs Holmes to find incriminating love letters. The Grand Duke is to become engaged to Clotilde Lothman von Saxe-Meiningen, a young Scandinavian princess. However, five years earlier he had had a fling with a "well-known adventuress," the American opera singer Irene Adler whilst she was prima donna of the Imperial Opera of Warsaw. She had since retired and now lives in London. Love letters and photographs had to be recovered in order to save the King's forthcoming marriage. Holmes does his best to fulfill the commission but is thwarted by Adler who nevertheless promises in a note found after her flight from London not to compromise the King.

In "A Scandal in Bohemia" Conan Doyle writes an engaging story that centres upon scurrilous affairs in London that involve a royal personage from the Habsburg region who is seeking the return from a former lover of compromising material. If one were looking for a motive behind murderous attacks in London the events described in "A Scandal in Bohemia" would not be out of place in a basket of credible scenarios. But perhaps there is more to the story than meets the eye.

As we have noted, Conan Doyle was an inveterate spiritualist and a fervent devotee of all things of an esoteric nature. In January 1931, six months after Conan Doyle's death, a man calling himself Zam Bhotiva contacted acclaimed London medium, Grace Cooke. Through Cooke's mediumship, Bhotiva heard Conan Doyle affirm that a group called La Fraternité des Polaires was "destined to help in the molding of the future of the world...for the times are near." Mrs. Cooke's spirit guide, a Tibetan Sage named White Eagle, stated that Bhotiva had come on instructions from Tibetan masters. A Rosicrucian initiate known as the Chevalier Rose-Croix confirmed via Cooke that Conan Doyle was to help the Brotherhood: "See the star rises in the East; it is the sign of the Polaires, the sign of the two interlaced triangles."

The Polaires, mentioned in passing in chapter 6, nailed its colours to Theosophy and to 19th century supporters of the mythical subterranean realms of Agartha and Shamballah. One can trace its origins to a day in 1908 when twelve-year old Franco-Italian Mario Fille met a hermit named Father Julian in the hills near Rome. The hermit gave to Mario a number of old parchments containing L'Oracle de Force Astrale, which, once decoded, purports to be an actual channel of communication with the Rosicrucian initiate centre of Asia Mysteriosa in the Himalayas. This channel was directed by the "Three Supreme Sages" or the "Little Lights of the Orient" who live in the invisible world of Agartha. Father Julian was a member of this mystical body. After his death in 1930 the baton passed to "Chevalier Rose-Croix," rumoured to be the legendary and immortal Comte de Saint-Germain. Many years later, Mario

Bulletin of the Polaires

Fille, together with Cesare Accomani whom Fille is said to have met in Egypt in 1920, moved to Montmartre in Paris where the Oracle was shown to a group of journalists and writers. Some were sufficiently moved to publicise it and to contribute to Accomani's 1929 book *Asia Mysteriosa*, published under the pseudonym "Zam Bhotiva."

Author Leo Lyon Zagami claims that La Fraternité des Polaires was established as an Illuminati Order and that, subsequently, Fille and Accomani were inducted into the Order as intelligence operatives. Zagami's research unearthed German sources which state that Fille, responding to instructions from the Himalayan Masters, demonstrated the Oracle to a "small number of experts" as a first step toward finding suitable candidates to form an occult working group that included René Guénon. This group became La Fraternité des Polaires.

During 1929 and 1930 the Polaires made excavations in the Montségur area of the French Pyrenees. German Grail historian and explorer Otto Rahn, named incorrectly as Rams and Rahu in the local press, was said to be the group's expedition leader. The stories claimed that Rahn's group had found traces of Christian Rosenkreutz's travels in the ruins of Lordat castle.

By 1936 there were separate Polaires groups for men and women in capital cities in Europe and America, each dedicated to working for the good of mankind under Mario Fille's direction. Information on the Polaires is hard to come by. The Fraternity's papers were seized from the Paris headquarters of the Theosophical Society by German forces during the Occupation, an action ordered by Alfred Rosenberg who sought the documents for his academy at Frankfurt, a cultural and learning centre established to provide a historical foundation for the justification of Nazism.

"A Scandal in Bohemia" is a London-based story about a powerful man's desire to retrieve documents. Its protagonists include former lovers whose fictional identities, it appears, Conan Doyle conflates with those of Orth and his lover, Milla. Orth collaborated with Saunière in a search for Rennes-le-Château's riches, whose nature has never been verified but is said variously to be Blanche of Castile's gold, the Treasures of the Temple of Solomon (including the Ark of the Covenant), Cathar documents, even a gateway to Agartha.

Jules Verne is said to have inserted clues in his novels as to the nature of the treasure. Grace Cooke communicated that Conan Doyle in the world of spirit was affirming that the Polaries should be

---

[89] Zagami, L. *Invisible Masters The Puppeteers Hidden Power*, CCC publishing, 2018
[90] Lamy, M., *Jules Verne, Initié et Initiateur*, Payot + Rivages, 1984

supported because its work was vital for the world's future. As lofty as may have been this noble objective, the Polaires were also not above digging around caves in the South of France with Rahn in a search for the secrets of the Rosicrucians, including their passageways to the higher worlds of Asia Mysteriosa.

London in 1888 was full of influential men who, in collaboration with powerful occultists in Europe and in America, lusted for such fabulous prizes, prizes worth killing for if circumstances demanded. Wars have been started over less. Perhaps Conan Doyle possessed more knowledge of the Whitechapel murders than he dared voice in public and, like Verne, inserted clues in his work. It is food for thought.

The Orth scenario is a rich tableau that incorporates a wealth of material connected with many of the occult themes explored in these pages. Let us now explore an alternative setting closer to home from which one might reasonably infer a credible connection with the events in Whitechapel.

On 20 June 1887 the Golden Jubilee of Queen Victoria was celebrated with a banquet to which fifty royal figures were invited. Of the fifty, the principle guests representing European royalty were:

➤ Crown Prince of Germany and Prussia (Friedrich, 1831-1888) became German Emperor Frederick III and King of Prussia for ninety-nine days in 1888, the "Year of the Three Emperors." He died from cancer of the larynx 15 June 1888;

➤ Prince William of Prussia (Friedrich Wilhelm Viktor Albrecht, 1859-1941) who on the death of his father, Freidrich, became the last German Emperor and King of Prussia. He was accompanied to the Jubilee celebrations by his wife, Augusta Victoria of Schleswig-Holstein, known as "Dona."

➤ Crown Prince of Austria (Rudolf Franz Karl Joseph, 1858-1889), the only son of Emperor Franz Joseph I and Elisabeth of Bavaria. He was heir apparent to the throne of Austria-Hungary from birth. On 30 January 1889 he died in a suicide pact with his mistress, Baroness Mary Vetsera, at the Mayerling hunting lodge. The ensuing scandal made international headlines, fuelled international conspiracy rumours and ultimately contributed to the demise of the Habsburg monarchy.

In spite of attempts by Princess Royal Victoria (Vicky), Wilhelm's mother and eldest daughter of the British queen, to cover up the extent of her husband's illness, Wilhelm rightly concluded the worst and persuaded his grandfather, the 90-year old Kaiser (Wilhelm I), to appoint him his father's appointed representative for the Jubilee celebrations. Friedrich, Vicky and her mother were outraged by the decision. Not that Wilhelm cared a hoot: he loathed his mother and grandmother with equal passion. Queen Victoria received Wilhelm and his wife coldly, seating Dona for the entire occasion behind the queen of Hawaii. Nevertheless, let one keep in mind that Wilhelm and Dona stayed in Britain for two months after the celebrations.

When his father died in June 1888 Wilhelm ordered a military cordon drawn around the Royal Palace to prevent "state or secret documents being conveyed to England by my mother." He acted thirteen months too late. In the early stages of her husband's illness and acutely aware of its severity, Vicky had gathered papers together and asked her mother if she could secrete them in Buckingham Palace.

Wilhelm remained in England for several weeks after the Jubilee celebrations. He was emotionally unstable and intoxicated by the imperial power that lay before him. His grandfather was ninety years old and surely could not last much longer. His father, next in line to the throne, was gravely ill; Wilhelm was confident that his time to rule was not far off. This was a dangerous and intoxicating combination of circumstance and sentiment.

With very little mental effort, one can visualise an evening scenario in which one or more of the the young Turks of European royalty— Wilhelm (28), Rudolf (28) and Prince Albert Victor ("Eddy"), eldest child of the Prince and Princess of Wales and Victoria's grandson (23)—go out on the town, have a few too many drinks and get into a fumble with a woman (or man) in a mean part of town that goes very badly wrong. Maybe there is a pregnancy, maybe blood is spilt or maybe even someone is killed. There is no proof that any of these things happened but they are easily imagined and entirely plausible. The law of unintended consequences is an unyielding and adversary and no respecter of rank, class or position.

Any such transgressions committed in Britain would also have been observed outside the royal bubble. SAGB sources claim that within the early Fabian Society was an inner group whose remit was to observe and record the monarchy's secret undertakings. If something along these lines did take place it had, of course, to be covered up. Those involved had to be silenced through payments or other inducements, even by acts of murder.

---

[91] Kohut, T., *Wilhelm II and the Germans: A Study in Leadership*, Oxford University Press, 1991

Memorial plaque for Prince Albert Victor ("Eddy"),
St. Mary Magdalene Church, Sandringham

Queen Victoria's Golden Jubilee Service, William Ewart Lockhart

Why do these musings matter? Because of a communication conveyed to American author Jim Keith (1949-1999) while he was preparing a new work for publication, from a person purporting to be a Vatican insider. Keith's anonymous correspondent, a member of the Franciscan Order, set out a secret occult history of Western civilisation based on documents in the Vatican library. To provide a measure of provenance for the information, the document copy sent to Keith bore the inked imprint of a Vatican library entrance stamp, which appears to indicate that the Franciscan had formal access to the archives. The stamp is repeated at the end of the document together with a thumbprint. This is the not the place to go into detail on what is a highly sensational document but it elaborates on both the theme of German occult domination of esoteric developments in Europe and America and on the nature of forces at work in Whitechapel in 1888.

In summary, the priest describes how during the Dark Ages tribes in Europe that still worshipped the pagan gods split into several factions, some recognising, at least in part, the Church as their titular head, while others continued to oppose Christian domination. Simply put, tribes in southern Europe formed a generally pro-Church clique while those in the north—the Teutons, Norse, Saxons, et al.—were characterised by a cold indifference to humanity and a delight in atrocity and cruelty.

In 826 AD, the northern clique aligned with Muslims expelled from Spain. Around twenty-five years later, Jews began settling in Germany under the direction of a secretive Israeli group of sorcerers, which forged ties with the most powerful of the Germanic tribes, especially the Prussians and the Bavarians. Although racially different, they worshipped the same dark gods and, the priest claimed, shared a predilection for ritual human sacrifice. Over the following centuries, the two cliques played a game of cat and mouse, each trying to outdo the other in fighting for religious, political and military control in Europe and, later, in America. At times these efforts brought the cliques into open hostility but on the whole a balance of power between them was maintained. The priest claimed that in the 1880s the northern European clique siezed control

Keith's informant's Vatican credentials

[92] Keith, J., *Secret and Suppressed: Banned Ideas & Hidden History*, Feral House, 1993

of the Italian government to put a stranglehold around the Vatican power structure, but not before "solving a sticky problem for the Royal Family" through "ritual sacrifice of several prostitutes in Whitechapel." The priest then goes on to claim that the northern clique held a full meeting in Basle in 1897 to:

> …lay the groundwork for their plans for domination of those territories not yet directly under their control. Included in these discussions were plans for an Holocaust, a massive extermination-sacrifice of European Jewry and others.

It is a truly shocking narrative, not least because while introducing the subject of the Holocaust the Franciscan casually mentions that those behind it took time out from their long term planning to "solve a sticky problem for the Royal Family." And in so doing, the enforcers did not just carry out simple murders but arrogated occult power to themselves by killing women in ritual fashion on London's streets. But is the priest's tale an historical account, a gruesome story or a sensationalist blend of fact and fiction?

The account remained largely uncorroborated until investigator Joseph Farrell[93] discovered an extract from a novel by Gloria Vitanze Basile[94] where she reproduces a quote from Zionist leader Max Nordau in which he speaks in 1911 of: "righteous governments…preparing the complete annihilation of six million Jews." Stunned that Basile had referenced a quote that seemingly foresaw the Holocaust by thirty-one years, Farrell sought verification of Nordau's powers of prophecy. Ten years later he found in *Max Nordau to his People*[95] the proof he had been looking for.

In 1897, Max Nordau (Simon Maximilian Suedfeld, 1849–1923), physician, writer, orator, and co-founder of the World Zionist Organization, attended the First

Max Nordau

[93] Farrell, J., *Hess and the Penguins*, Adventures Unlimited Press, Illinois, 2017

[94] Basile, G., *The Eye of the Eagle*, Pinnacle Books, 1983

[95] Nordau, M., *Max Nordau to his People,: A Summons and a Challenge*, Published for Nordau Zionist Society by Scopus Pub. Co., Inc. c1941

Zionist Congress. The Congress, held in the concert hall of the Stadtcasino Basel, was a 3–day event which ended on 31 August, incidentally the ninth anniversary of Mary Ann "Polly" Nichols' murder.

Born in Pest, the son of Rabbi Gabriel Suedfeld, Nordau received a traditional Jewish education and remained an observant Jew until his eighteenth year when he became a militant naturalist and evolutionist. In 1875 he earned an M.D. degree at the University of Pest and settled in Paris in 1880 as a practising physician.

The Basle Congress was the first interterritorial gathering of Jews on a national and secular basis. Here the delegates adopted the Basle Program (drafted by Nordau) and the program of the Zionist movement. Congress declared, "Zionism seeks to establish a home for the Jewish people in Palestine secured under public law." At the Congress the World Zionist Organization was established as the political arm of the Jewish people.

Nordau's friend, Theodor (Binyamin Ze'ev) Herzl (1860-1904), was elected its first president. Herzl was the visionary behind modern Zionism and the reinstitution of a Jewish homeland. His ideas were met with enthusiasm by the Jewish masses in Eastern Europe but when he tried to muster support among Jewish leaders he was far less successful. Herzl appealed to wealthy Jews such as Baron Hirsch and Baron Rothschild to join the national Zionist movement but they were unmoved.

In his capacity as vice-president of the First to the Sixth Zionist Congresses and as president of the Seventh to the Tenth Congresses, Nordau's addresses to Conference surveyed the Jewish situation in the world. He described and analysed the physical and material plight of the Jews in Eastern Europe as well as the moral plight of the Western Jew, who had lost contact with fellow-Jews and endured antisemitism, which excluded him from non-Jewish society. In his speech to the Tenth Congress in Basle in 1911, reproduced in *Max Nordau to his People*, Nordau said:

> The virtuous Governments, which work with such noble zeal for the spread of eternal peace acquiesce in the downfall of six million creatures [in the Russian Empire and other East-European countries] -acquiesce, and no one, except the victims raises a voice against it....
>
> The administration of hero funds and the distribution of the interest is [sic] laid in the hands of authorities who favor the massacres of Jews even if they themselves do not directly instigate them.

Nordau's words were re-quoted in 1949.[96] The journal's article claims:

> Had Nordau's councels been listened to, the six million lives in Hitler's furnaces might now be living and working in Israel...In the State of Israel and in the future of the Jewish people, Max Nordau has an immortal monument.

The Basle Congress of 1897 is a historical reality. It was convened to inaugurate the Zionist movement and to make an agreement "to establish a home for the Jewish people in Palestine secured under public law." Nordau was in attendance. The Vatican informant described a meeting in Basle in 1897 that lay "the groundwork for...an Holocaust, a massive extermination-sacrifice of European Jewry and others." This appears to be a direct reference to the First Congress. In 1911 at the Tenth Congress, Nordau is on record as prophesying the massacre of "six million" European Jews, a description and number that parallels the actions of Hitler's forthcoming Nazi regime.

Did Nordau hear something during or, later, in connection with the First Congress which was so shockingly credible that he felt confident about publicly making his sensational remarks? Any time-gap between Nordau hearing about such plans and referring to them in a public forum may be attributed to his seeking some form of corroborating evidence before speaking about imminent mass murder on an unprecedented scale.

The Franciscan makes it clear that one of the two parties that had been behind the northern clique's occult ambitions since the ninth-century was a powerful elite group of Israeli sorcerers. Elsewhere in his account to Keith, the priest remarks about how the elite care nothing for the common mass of Jewry, considering it to be nothing more than fodder for sacrifice.

Anyone who has attended a conference knows that the main action often does not take place in plenary but within meetings of fringe groups where gather people of influence and authority in side rooms or other areas where conversations can be held in comparative quiet. One can visualise a situation where a small group representing this elite meets away from the hubbub in the auditorium. Under a shroud of delegate legitimacy, men gather to consider ostensibly the finer points of conference proceedings but quietly discuss and plan future actions of

---

[96] *Nordau, the Man Who Foresaw*, The Jewish Advocate, The Organ of Indian Jewry, Bombay, XVIII, No.5, [August, 1949]. 10-11

a diabolical nature.

Further corroboration of Keith's informant's account may be found in connection with a story that was circulating among a small circle more than forty years ago in Tuscany. A man known to me heard it while visiting friends in the region in the late 1970s. One night over dinner, a retired priest in his late eighties disclosed a remarkable tale.

His account concerned secret activities that he undertook at the request of Pius X in the weeks prior to the outbreak of war in 1914. At the time, the priest would have been around twenty-four years of age. Pius employed a small network of operatives in Italy and France. Its task was to gather intelligence that would help Pius, openly a Conservative, to secretly steer the Church into a more Modernist direction. Ultra-conservatives within the Vatican were extremely hostile to any such moves and they needed careful watching, especially at a time when it was clear that war in Europe was rapidly approaching. The Tuscan priest was chosen to head Pius's small group because of his even temperament and his impressive gift for languages.

One branch of Pius's network was a brothel in the Rue d'Amboise in Paris. Pillow talk and things blurted out during lovemaking were a very useful source of intelligence. When the priest visited the brothel for the first time to meet his contacts he was told of an event that took place there in 1906. Two men that appeared to be friends came one day and requested the establishment's female services. In the heat of passion, one of them whispered words along the lines of "Oh, my God, my God, by my mort…oath may you be praised and protected." The other man, a bisexual, said, "Shhh, Abby, the walls have ears!"

After the men's departure a calling card was found bearing the engraved name of Dr. Ernest Engels and five handwritten names—Maitland, Verne, Curie, HRC Richard and Sarto. The first three names had been crossed out with the notation "mort." Engels returned to the brothel later that day, demanding to know if his calling card had been found. The prostitute, who had recorded details of the incident in the brothel Madam's diary, feigned innocence

GeorgeTyrell alias Ernest Engels

and received a fierce beating (sustaining broken ribs and cuts) until the brothel bouncer appeared and threw Engels out of the front door into the arms of a passing policeman.

Engels was one of two pseudonyms used by Jesuit writer George Tyrrell (1861-1909). He also wrote as Hilaire Bourdon. Briefly, Tyrrell was born in Dublin and baptized as an Anglican. His subsequent search for religious meaning brought him in 1879 to London where he was involved with a social project at St. Albans Anglo-Catholic Church. Soon afterwards he converted to the Catholic faith and in 1880 became a Jesuit. Until 1885 Tyrrell was a student at the Jesuit College at Stoneyhill in Lancashire where he studied scholastic philosophy.

He then moved on to a college in Malta, which Tyrrell described in a letter to a friend as the "the hardening school for religious life." He returned to Britain in 1888 to undertake a four-year theological study course at St Buenon's College in St. Asaph in Denbighshire. The precise date and month of Tyrell's return in 1888 is not recorded but one may assume that he arrived prior to the commencement of the new academic year's first semester. Bishop Knight of Shrewsbury ordained him priest in September 1891. Tyrell's position as a Modernist upset the established Church and Pius X dismissed him from the Society of Jesus in 1906 and excommunicated him in 1908.

A likely candidate for "Abby" is Tyrrell's close friend, French literary scholar, sometime Jesuit, philosopher and Catholic modernist, Abbé Henri Brémond (1865-1933). Born and educated in Aix-en-Provence, Henri Brémond entered the Society of Jesus in 1882. For the next ten years he studied for his novitiate in the Church of the Most Blessed Blood, established in 1880 at Peak House in Sidmouth in Devon by exiled French Jesuits. Brémond left the Society of Jesus in 1904 but remained a priest. For making an address at Tyrrell's funeral and, in particular, for making the sign of the cross over the grave, Brémond was briefly suspended *a divinis* by Bishop Amigo but later reintegrated into the Church.

Abbé Henri Brémond

Edward Maitland died in 1897 after rapid physical and mental decline; Verne died at his home in Amiens in 1905, the cause attributed to diabetes; Pierre Curie, husband of Marie Skłodowska Curie, died in 1906 from a fall under a horse-drawn cart (coincidentally, as did carman John Netley, accused by Stephen Knight of complicity in the Ripper murders, who in 1903 died from a crushed head after his van struck an obelisk and he was thrown under the hooves of his horses).

It later became obvious that Richards and Sarto were references to Archbishop of Paris, Cardinal François-Marie-Benjamin Richard de la Vergne (1819-1908), and Pius X (Giuseppe Melchiorre Sarto, 1835-1914). Richards' cause of death was attributed to lung congestion. Pius fell ill on the Feast of the Assumption of Mary, 1914, and did not recover. He confided to the young priest that he believed he was being poisoned.

The priest made discreet enquiries and learned of the existence of an order whose remit was to protect the Church at any cost. When necessary, its activities extended to assassinations. One member of Pius's network told the priest that he had once seen a silver menorah candelabrum in a small chapel in the Vatican.

He learned that at the behest of Louis XII, Cesare Borgia in collaboration with his father, Pope Alexander VI, and Cardinal Giuliano della Rovere (the future Pope Julius II), revived a Vatican-based group that was formed around the ninth-century to fight the scourge of heresy. The King and the Vatican authorities in the fifteenth century did not want another Albigensian crusade or Pope Joan, a reference to the scandalous elevation of an Englishwoman to the papacy in 1099. The order of assassins was therefore resurrected in 1498, the year Louis XII acceded to the throne, when Cesare visited the French court to present the King with an annulment signed by his father to dissolve Louis' marriage to Louis XI's daughter, Joan of France. Under the terms of a contract drawn up by Louis XI, Louis of Orléans was obliged to

Cesare Borgia by Altobello Melone

---

[97] Knight, S., *Jack the Ripper: the Final Solution*, Bounty Book, London, 1976

marry the King's daughter. When the wedding took place in 1476, Louis was 14 and Joan was 12.

For political reasons, Pope Alexander agreed the annulment on the grounds that Joan's father had forced Louis XII into the marriage. In fact, Louis was anxious to marry Charles VIII's widow, Anne of Brittany. So desperate was he to be rid of his wife that Louis even claimed that Joan had a physical deformity that made it impossible to consummate the marriage, although no evidence was offered to support this charge.

After the annulment Joan, as Duchess of Berry, founded the monastic Order of the Sisters of the Annunciation of Mary, where she served as Abbess. From this Order sprang the religious congregation of the Apostolic Sisters of the Annunciation.

The objectives of the revived assassins group were of a similar nature to the Chivalrous Order of the Holy Vehm mentioned in Chapter 6. The Holy Vehm began life as a secret vigilante society formed in Westphalia in the mid-thirteenth-century to protect free men and commoners from bandits that roamed the lawless territory between the Rhine and the Weser rivers. In the beginning, the resistance group had the approval of both the church and the Holy Roman emperor but as time passed the Holy Vehm became a law unto itself, passing judgement and pronouncing a death sentence.

Similarly, down through the years the Borgia group was used by ambitious Vatican Princes to make sure that the wealth, dogma and male dominance of the Holy Church was never questioned or threatened. The group's maxim was, "Dead men carry no tales." Members were required to swear an oath to this effect. "Abby's" intemperate outburst in the brothel imprudently revealed the pair's allegiance to the order.

The Tuscan understood that the order was one component of a worldwide occult patriarchy consisting of members drawn from the Freemasons, Sufis, Templars and other exclusively male groupings dedicated to attainment of unlimited power and influence. It is a set-up that matches the occult fraternity described by Jim Keith's Vatican informant. The informant told Keith that the Whitechapel murders were committed by members of Europe's occult elite who took time out from their objective of accumulating ever-increasing global power to do a favour in 1888 for the British Royal Family. Twenty-six years later the Tuscan priest learned of the occult allegiances of George Tyrell and Henri Brémond and their attachment to an order of assassins controlled by senior Vatican clerics.

I was not being flippant when I said at the start that this book is not about proposing a new name for the Ripper. Nonetheless, I would consider these pages incomplete if I did not offer these observations, which are doubtless little more than coincidental connections.

Tyrell returned to England from Malta in 1888. In this year Brémond was in Devon studying for his novitiate. John Best described the man he saw with Elizabeth Stride as having "rather weak eyes...sore eyes without any eyelashes." Mathew Packer reported selling grapes from his shop in Berner Street to a man aged 25-30. Police Constable William Smith saw Stride with a man aged around 28-years on the same street. Israel Schwartz described the two men he saw later in Berner Street as aged about 35 and 30. Joseph Lawende described seeing Eddowes by Church Passage leading to Mitre Square in the company of a man aged 30. The not entirely reliable Hutchinson described seeing Mary Kelly in the company of a man aged about 34 or 35. Rent-collector Thomas Bowyer reported seeing Kelly talking to a man aged 27-28 with "very peculiar eyes" in Miller's Court. In 1888, Tyrell, a man who paid for sex, who would later beat up a Paris prostitute and whose photograph shows a man with distinctive dark-rimmed, sunken eyes was 27-years old. Brémond was 23. These ages and descriptions are not that far removed from witness accounts; and not too wide of the mark such as to rule out the involvement of slightly younger men who out of necessity were disguising their features and appearance. I cannot put hand on heart and say unequivocally that Tyrell and Brémond carried out the Whitechapel murders. Nevertheless, who knows what might be discovered if the necessary diaries and records could be found?

Evidently, Tyrell was a man weighed down by conscience. The essay that elicited the greatest outcry from the Vatican, "A Perverted Devotion" written in 1899, was one in which Tyrell lampooned the concept of hell as a place of eternal punishment. Not for him eternal torture in a fiery pit, Tyrell argued that the conventional image of a vengeful Underworld sat uneasily with the idea of a God who took the suffering and sins of humanity upon Himself so that all mankind might be saved. Tyrell, knowing that he would pass over with bloodied baggage, sought to safeguard his transition by substituting the traditional idea of hell with an afterlife in which all souls, sinners and saints alike, are welcomed with open arms by a forgiving God. Another ten years would pass until Tyrell, yet another victim of the Whitechapel curse of Bright's disease, got the opportunity to prove his theorem.

Chapter 17

Through the Looking Glass

The Whitechapel murders were committed at the height of nineteenth-century occultism. Seen from the standpoint of logic, their enactment was not predicated on the rapid growth of occultism. However, pure reason was in scant supply at the height of the Age of the Irrational.

James Webb[98] observed that the obsessive nature of occult beliefs almost always results in their domination of the possessor's mind. Unorthodox ideas exert a very powerful pull and often move men in directions that in hindsight they would have preferred not to travel. Indeed, the more unorthodox the idea or belief, the more powerful is the obsession because of the increased effort required to "sell" the concept favourably to others.

We have seen that a notable component of the Whitechapel era was man's search for spiritual meaning. He pursued this quest in many ways. He sought answers by joining or promoting societies that promised the prize of revelation concerning life's eternal mysteries. Others grasped for enlightenment through Bible study and theological scholarship. Some thought they could discern in the KJV and in ancient Codices a glimpse or pathway to arcane knowledge that would signpost them to unimaginable treasures both secular and spiritual.

This final chapter is not so much concerned with these largely innocent souls that just wanted to make a little more sense of their place in what can be a challenging and baffling world. It is about those who had it in them to kill the women in Whitechapel in the way that they did.

To observers in 1888, the horrific manner of the Ripper murders must have exceeded their capacity to imagine that such bestial cruelty could be inflicted by one member of humankind upon another. However, I do not believe that what we are dealing with here can be interpreted in terms of Hannah Arendt's famous principle of the

---

[98] Webb, J. *The Occult Establishment*, Open Court Publishing, 1976

"banality of evil," her phrase about Adolf Eichman who at his trial displayed neither guilt for his actions during the Holocaust nor hatred for those trying him. His defence was that he bore no responsibility for the extermination of millions of human beings because he was simply "doing his job" under the ultimate command of his leader, Adolf Hitler (Eichman emphasized that he did his *duty,* he obeyed *orders* and obeyed the *law*). Similarly, Deputy Führer Rudolf Hess tried to blame the Nazis' excesses on mass hypnotism as if the wizard Hitler held his enthralled army in the palm of his hand by a supreme effort of will.

Arendt made her remark about Eichman after having observed the man in the dock only during the trial's initial proceedings. It has been pointed out that had she stayed longer she would have seen a very different Eichman, one who identified strongly with anti-semitism and Nazi ideology, did not simply follow orders and was a pioneer of creative new extermination policies: overall, a man who was well aware of what he was doing and was proud of his murderous "achievements."

In the past, psychologists and historians have tended to agree that when ordinary people under the influence of leaders and groups commit evil they become blind to the consequences of their actions. More recently, a new view among professionals has emerged which radically contradicts this earlier mindset. Critical scrutiny of both historical and psychological evidence indicates that people do great wrong, not because they are unaware of what they are doing but because they consider it to be *right*.

This is possible because they actively identify with groups whose ideology justifies and condones the oppression and destruction of others. This new thinking raises important questions about human malevolence and about the eternal cyclical nature of "good" and "evil." John Steinbeck put his finger on it in his letter to Arendt: "All the goodness and the heroisms will rise up again, then be cut down again and rise up. It isn't that the evil thing wins—it never will—but that it doesn't die."

Recent studies, notably that of Haslam & Reicher, prove that with few exceptions Nazi did not "simply follow orders," not least because orders issued by the Nazi hierarchy were typically very vague. Consequently, individuals needed to display imagination and initiative to interpret the commands they were given and to act upon them. As Ian Kershaw notes, Nazis did not obey Hitler; they worked *towards* him, seeking to surpass each other in their efforts.

---

[99] Haslam, S.A. & Reicher, S.D. (2007a). *Beyond the banality of evil. Personality and Social Psychology Bulletin,* 33, 615–622

[100] Kershaw. I., *Hitler: A Biography,* W. W. Norton & Company; Reprint edition, 2010

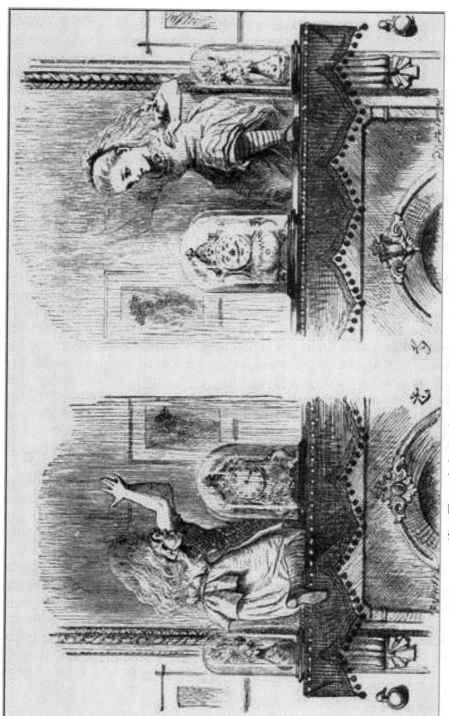

Alice Through the Looking Glass illustrated by John Tenniel

Moreover, in carrying out these excessive actions the camp guards and administrators possessed a large degree of discretion. Indeed, Laurence Rees remarks that it was this latitude that made the Nazi system so dynamic. Even in the most brutal of circumstances, people did not *have* to kill but some actively *chose* to do so. These participants did not act from the perspective of one simply finding themselves trapped in inhumane situations or inhumane groups but, enthusiastically committed to the work of such groups, placed themselves at their epicentre and carried out mass murder routinely. They actively created inhumane situations and demonstrated commitment to inhuman deeds by working on their own initiative with greater brutality than their orders called for. This routine excess of inhumane action reflected a group structure where it was expected that members surpassed the limits of normal violence. They saw clearly what they did and believed it to be the right thing to do.

I make this analogy because of its similarity with the actions in Whitechapel, not the least being that the Franciscan said that the murderers reappeared in Basle; and that Nordau, in turn, described them as the architects of a rapidly approaching mass extermination program.

Our study of the rapidly evolving occult dynamic in nineteenth-century European society and its religious and political affairs has revealed at its core the insidious presence of a long established Germanic negative mystical tradition and structure. For every new esoteric group that sprang forth during the Age of the Irrational, whether under the flag of spiritualism, Theosophy, Hermeticism, Rosicrucianism, neo-Templarism, ceremonial magic or other sundry "isms," one can trace its occult genesis to the corrupting influence of ancient Teutonic tribal ambition.

From the ninth century onwards, Central Europe's tribal overlords made alliances with similar groups in other parts of the world that worshipped the same idols and were characterised by extreme occult-focused ambition. Always these unholy confederacies were wholly male-oriented and dedicated to the protection of global patriarchy.

Tens of millennia in the past, matriarchy had reigned supreme in communities dedicated to worship of the Mother Goddess. The power and positivity gifted to humanity in an era of matriarchal hegemony was recognised in the early days of the developing Christian Church, especially in Western Europe in the first centuries after the Crucifixion. The word "church" comes from the Greek, *kyriakon*, meaning roughly "to be within," a perfect description of the purpose of a holy place in

---

[101] Rees, L., *Auschwitz : the Nazis and the Final Solution*, BBC for the Book People, 2005

which worshippers through prayer may experience spiritual unfoldment.

The first Christians believed that spiritual unfoldment is a process of constant rebirth of personal revelation achieved through conception and incubation of high ideals, precisely the innate process together with nurturing that they regarded as the defining experience of womanhood. Enlightened with this understanding, the early Fathers believed that in a profoundly symbolic sense woman *is* the Church, a position of power and grace that places her higher than the male priesthood whose duty is to incorporate the physical experience of woman into the spirit of humanity. This enlightened thinking held true for the first three centuries but subsequent Councils such as those held at Nicaea and Ephesus developed a new doxology founded upon the principles of Mary Mother of God and the Virgin Birth, which introduced an underlying theme of sexuality into the Church. This new theology adulterated the earlier thinking about the feminine essence of spiritual growth.

Ultimately, it contributed to the Church's policy of misogyny, which evolved rapidly in Europe especially as new pacts were made between ultra-traditionalist clerics in the south and the Teuton-Hebraic tribal alliance in the north. The "fruits" of these federated occult efforts culminated in the slaughter of millions of women as heretics and witches in the Middle Ages.

In 1888 these forces were still very much in existence and wielded immense authority over global affairs. In these pages we have glimpsed an insight into the kind of people that aligned themselves with the occult elite. Moreover, just as in the death camps, the enforcers on the ground doing the elite's dirty work proved their commitment to their masters and to inhuman deeds by using creative self-initiative and exercising far greater brutality than necessary to get the job done. For them, an ad hoc assignment to do away with a handful of women in London was just another opportunity to conform to a "group structure where it was expected that members surpassed the limits of normal violence."

A truly shocking aspect of the Nazis' extermination policies was the level of support for them in Britain. I learned this first hand when I interviewed in 1999 Cecil Williamson, founder of the Witchcraft Research Centre and former member of MI6's occult bureau during WWII. Williamson's lifelong passion for the occult began in his school years when an elderly woman showed him how to cast a spell to harm a boy who was bullying him at school. The spell took the form of sitting on a garden swing and swinging to and fro over a lighted and smoky bonfire. A short while later, Williamson claimed, the bully had a skiing accident that made the boy a cripple. Williamson was delighted. As far as he had been concerned the spell had worked a treat. This had a dramatic effect on him, sewing the seeds for a lifelong quest for knowledge and research into witchcraft and occultism.

He enjoyed spending time with his grandmother and her friend, medium and astrologer Mona Mackenzie. Mona's great friend was palmist, Tarot reader and necromancer Madame de la Hey. Williamson assisted Mona's séance sessions by playing the part of the "boy in white."

As the years went by Williamson nurtured his occult contacts, meeting Aleister Crowley at the Folklore Society. He joined the Golden Dawn, which he described as all sets and theatre: calling up spirits, charging them to do this and that, and then banishing them. He said that Crowley's ritual magic was "codswallop" although Crowley, he maintained, was "brilliant and a great writer." Evidently, Williamson sought a harder sort of occultism.

In January 1938, a family friend, Colonel Maltby of the Foreign Office Section MI6, met with the nineteen year old. He asked if Williamson would be interested in helping the Section on occult matters in Britain and Europe from time to time because war with Germany was inevitable and because Hitler and his cronies were obsessed with the occult. When war started, Williamson was promptly summoned by Colonel Maltby and then reported for duty to Brigadier Gambier-Parry at Whaddon Hall, the requisitioned home of the Selby-Lowndes family adjacent to Bletchley.

During two interviews with me Williamson was remarkably frank on the subject of the Jewish race. He told me that he had little time for the Jews whereas he had a great deal of respect for Hitler. It was clear that he was an unapologetic supporter of the Nazis. Disarmingly, he emphasised that this view was commonly shared by the British upper classes and had been prevalent in the wartime security services. He said Himmler was a decent chap and that an awful lot of bad press had unfairly been thrown at Hitler. Williamson sympathised with the Vatican with regard to heavy criticism directed towards it for providing Nazi escape routes.

Williamson expressed strong support for eugenics. He prefaced his supportive remarks about Nazi extermination policies by first referring to the role of the village midwife in Europe up to the 18th century, an aspect of which was to kill "runts and imbecile babies." He then expanded on this, expressing support for the cleansing of "riff-raff," which were the dullards of society (he referred to them as "semen") and even more of a problem for developed countries.

In the face of shocking sentiments such as these one wonders if it was not just the Nazis that enjoyed making occult capital out of the slaughter of millions. Certainly, Williamson, a serious occultist who regarded the notorious Aleister Crowley (the so-called "wickedest man in the world") as a lightweight, spoke as one who believed that acts of ritual euthanasia could be used to invoke enhanced magical powers.

It begs the question as to just how many others in British occult circles believed similarly, not only turning a blind eye to mass murder but also actively welcoming it so that they might "tune in" to diabolic practices and thereby grow their magical abilities.

Fifty years earlier, the Whitechapel murderers following age-old traditions committed their ritual slayings in obeisance to the sacrificial demands of Europe's dark gods. In so doing, they "solved a sticky problem for the Royal Family," gave succour and delight to fellow hardcore blood-and-guts occultists everywhere and, at the same time, imbued their sorcerers' wands with a little more power than they possessed before.

I have no insights into the precise nature of the events that precipitated the Whitechapel murders. Nonetheless, I do believe in the feasibility of something having occurred that set events in motion, perhaps along the lines of the Jubilee celebrations scenario.

I also believe that those who held the reins of power in Britain must share culpability for the outrages in Whitechapel. Between them they must have known, surely *must* have known who carried them out. That knowledge, that acquiescence and that abject failure to prevent the slaughter made those that sat on their hands synarchic apologists for men of no conscience who, in occult federation, conducted ritual murder in London's East End in 1888.

"One, two! One, two! And through and through
The vorpal blade went snicker-snack!
He left it dead, and with its head
He went galumphing back."

— Lewis Carroll, *Jabberwocky*

Bibliography

Andrews, Keith and Slemen, Tom. *Jack the Ripper: British Intelligence Agent*, The Bluecoat Press, Liverpool, 2010.

Basile, Gloria. *The Eye of the Eagle*, Pinnacle Books, 1983.

Begg, Paul. *Jack the Ripper: the Definitive History*, Routledge, 2004.

—, *Jack the Ripper: the Facts*, Pavilion Books, London, 2008.

Besant, Walter and Rice, James. *Monks of Thelema*, Chatto & Windus, London, 1878.

Bharati, Agehananda. *Fictitious Tibet: the Origins and Persistence of Rampaism,* Volume 7, Tibet Society, 1974.

Blavatsky, Helena. *Isis Unveiled*, 2 vols, New York, Bouton, 1877.

Britten, William. *Ghost Land*, Ed. Hardinge Britten, E. published for the editor, Boston, 1876.

Bulwer-Lytton, Sir Edward. *Vril: the Power of the Coming Race*, Whitefish, Montana. Kessinger Publishing LLC, 2005. (First published 1871).

Bushby, Tony. *The Bible Fraud: An Untold Story of Jesus Christ*, Pacific Blue Group, 2001.

Chanel, Christian, John Patrick Deveney, Joscelyn Godwin. *The Hermetic Brotherhood of Luxor. Initiatic and Historical Documents of an Order of Practical Occultism.* York Beach: Weister, 1995.

Cohen, Morton. *Lewis Carroll: A Biography*, Alfred A. Knopf, 1995.

Conan-Doyle, Sir Arthur. *The History of Spiritualism*, Cassell and Company, London, 1926.

Davis, Andrew. *The Great Harmonium being a Philosophical Revelation*, Bela Marsh, Boston, 1862.

Ellicott, Charles et al., *The New Testament of our Lord and Saviour Jesus Christ, Translated out of the Greek: Being the Version Set Forth A.D. 1611, Compared with the Most Ancient Authorities and Revised, A.D. 1881*. Oxford: Oxford University Press, 1881.

Evans, Stewart and Rumbelow, Donald. *Scotland Yard Investigates*, Stroud, The History Press, 2006.

Evans, Stewart and Skinner, Keith. *The Ultimate Jack the Ripper Sourcebook: An Illustrated Encyclopedia*, London: Constable and Robinson, 2000.

Fairclough, Melvyn. *The Ripper and the Royals*, Duckworth, 1991.

Faivre, Antoine. *Theosophy, Imagination, Tradition: Studies in Western Esotericism*, State University of New York Press, 2000.

—, *The Golden Fleece and Alchemy*, State University of New York Press, 2000.

Farrell, Joseph. *Hess and the Penguins*, Adventures Unlimited Press, Illinois, 2017.

Finnan, Mark. *Oak Island Secrets*, Formac Publishing Company, 2002.

French, Peter. *John Dee*, Routledge and Kegan Paul, London and Boston, 1972.

Gauld, Alan. *The Founders of Psychical Research*, New York, Schocken Books, 1968.

Godwin, Joscelyn. *The Golden Thread*, Quest Books, Illinois, 2007.

—, *Theosophical Enlightenment*, State University of New York Press, 1994.

Godwin, Joscelyn and McLean, Adam. *The Chemical Wedding of Christian Rosenkreutz*, Phanes Press, 1991.

Goodrick-Clarke, Nicholas. *Helena Blavatsky*, Berkeley, CA: North Atlantic Books, 2004.

—, *The Occult Roots of Nazism*, N.Y. University Press, 1985.

Graddon, Nigel. *Otto Rahn and the Quest for the Grail,* Kempton, Illinois, Adventures Unlimited Press, 2008.

Guénon, René. *Le theosophisme: Histoire d'une pseudo-religion* Enlarged ed. Paris Editions Traditionelles, 1982. (First ed., 1921).

Hall, Manley. *The Secret Teachings of All Ages*, Los Angeles. The Philosophical Research Society, Inc., 1928.

Hamill, John, ed. *The Rosicrucian Seer. Magical Writings of Frederick Hockley*, Wellingborough: Aquarian, 1986.

Hancox, Joy. *The Hidden Chapter: An Investigation into the Custody of Lost Knowledge*, Byrom Projects, 2011.

Hardinge Britten, Emma. *Autobiography of Emma Hardinge Britten*. Ed. Margaret Wilkinson. Manchester: John Heywood, 1900.

—, *Modern American Spiritualism*. New Hyde Park: University Books, 1970. (First ed., 1870).

Harrison, C.G., *The Transcendental Universe. Six Lectures on Occult Science, Theosophy and the Catholic Faith. Delivered before the Berean Society*. Introduction and Notes by Chrsitopher Bamford. Hudson: Lindisfarne Press, 1993. (First ed., 1984).

Hartmann, Franz. *Secret Symbols of the Rosicrucians*, Boston Occult Publishing Co., 1888.

Haslam, Alexander and Reicher, Stephen. *Beyond the banality of evil*, Personality and Social Psychology Bulletin, 33, 615–622, 2007.

Heydon, John. *The Rosie Cross Uncovered*, A. Reader, London, 1891.

Howard, Michael. *Occult Conspiracy*, Destiny Books, Vermont, 1989.

Howe, Ellic. "Fringe Masonry in England, 1870-1885." *Ars Quatuour Coronatorum* 85 (1972), 242-295. [1972a].

Howells, Martin, and Skinner, Keith. *The Ripper Legacy: Life and Death of Jack the Ripper*. London: Sidgwick & Jackson, 1987.

Jennings, Hargreave. *The Rosicrucians, their Rites and Mysteries*, Volumes 1 and 2, 3rd edition, John C. Nimmo, London, 1887.

Johnson, Paul. *In Search of the Masters. Behind the Occult Myth*. South Boston, VA: Author, 1990.

—, *The Masters Revealed: Madame Blavatsky and the Myth of the Great White Lodge,* State University of New York Press, 1994.

Keith, Jim (Ed.). *Secret and Suppressed: Banned Ideas & Hidden History*, Feral House, 1993.

Kershaw. Ian. *Hitler: A Biography*, W. W. Norton & Company, New

York, Reprint edition, 2010.

Knight, Stephen. *Jack the Ripper: the Final Solution*, London: Bounty Book, 1976.

Kohut, Thomas. *Wilhelm II and the Germans: A Study in Leadership*, Oxford University Press, 1991.

Kretzulesco-Quaranta, Emanuela. *Les jardin de songes: Poliphile et la mystique de la Renaissance*. Paris: Les Belles Lettres. 1986. (First ed., 1976).

Laidler, Keith, *The Head of God: the Lost Treasure of the Templars*, Weidenfeld & Nicolson, 1998.

Lamy, Michel. *Jules Verne, Initié et Initiateur*, Paris, Payot & Rivages, 1984.

Lamont, Peter. *The First Psychic: The Extraordinary Mystery of a Notorious Victorian Wizard*, Abacus, 2005.

Leary, Thomas, *The Oak Island Enigma: A History and Inquiry Into the Origin of the Money Pit*, Omaha, 1953.

Lecky, William. *History of the Rise and Influence of the Spirit of Rationalism in Europe*, London, 1870.

Maitland, Edward. *Anna Kingsford. Her Life, Letters, Diary and Work. By her Collaborator.* 2 vols. 3rd ed. Ed. S.H. Hart. London: Watkins, 1913. (First ed., 1896).

McIntosh, Christopher. *The Rosicrucians: The History, Mythology, and Rituals of an Esoteric Order,* Red Wheel Weiser, 1998.

Michell, John. *Who Wrote Shakespeare?*, Thames and Hudson, 1996.

Moore, Alan and Campbell, Eddie. *From Hell*, Top Shelf Productions, 1999.

Olcott, Henry. *Old Diary Letters*, vol.1, New York and London, 1895.

Osman, Ahmed. *Moses and Akhenaten: The Secret History of Egypt at the Time of the Exodus,* Inner Traditions Bear and Company, 2002.

Paley, Bruce. *Jack the Ripper: the Simple Facts*, Headline Book Publishing Ltd. 1996.

Rahn, Otto. *Luzifers Hofgesind: Eine Reise zu den guten Gelstern Europas,* Schwarzhaupter Verlag, Leipzig, 1937.

Rawson, A.L.,"Mme Blavatsky: a Theosophical Occult Apology." *Theosophical History* 2/6 (1988), 209-20. (First ed., 1892).

Rees, Laurence. *Auschwitz: the Nazis and the Final Solution*, BBC for the Book People, 2005.

Röhl, John. *Kaiser Wilhelm II: A Concise Life*, Cambridge University Press, 2014.

Rosenthal, Bernice (Ed.). *The Occult in Russian and Soviet Culture*, Cornell University Press, 1997.

Smedley, William. *The Mystery of Francis Bacon*, Robert Banks & Son, London, 1912.

Solovyoff, Vsevolod. *A Modern Priestess of Isis*, Abridged and tr. Walter Leaf, London, Longmans, 1895.

Sugden, Philip. *The Complete History of Jack the Ripper*, Robinson, 1994.

Underwood, Peter. *Jack the Ripper - One Hundred Years of Mystery*. London: Blandford Press, 1987.

Waite, Arthur. *The Real History of the Rosicrucians*, London, 1887.

Webb, James. *Flight from Reason*, MacDonald & Co., 1971.

—, *The Occult Establishment,* Open Court Publishing, 1976.

Wegener, Franz. *Heinrich Himmler: German Spiritualism, French Occultism and the Reichsführer-SS*, CreateSpace Independent Publishing Platform, 2013.

Westcott, Arthur. *Life and Letters of Brooke Foss Westcott,* London: Macmillan & Co., 1903.

Wilding, John. *Jack the Ripper Revealed,* London: Constable & Co, 1993.

Wilson, Colin, and Odell, Robin. *Jack the Ripper: Summing Up and Verdict.* London: Bantam Press, 1987.

Wood, Simon. *The Enigmas of Miller's Court*, Ripperologist 62, December 2005.

Woolf, Jenny. *The Mystery of Lewis Carroll: Understanding the Author of Alice in Wonderland*, London: Haus Books, 2010.

Yates, Frances. *The Rosicrucian Enlightenment*, Routledge and Kegan Paul, London and Boston, 1972.

Yost, Dave. *Elizabeth Stride and Jack the Ripper: The Life and Death of the Reputed Third Victim*, McFarland & Co. Inc., Jefferson N.C., 2008.

Zagami, Leo. *Invisible Masters: The Puppeteers' Hidden Power*, CCC publishing, 2018.

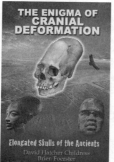

YETIS, SASQUATCH & HAIRY GIANTS
By David Hatcher Childress

Childress takes the reader on a fantastic journey across the Himalayas to Europe and North America in his quest for Yeti, Sasquatch and Hairy Giants. Childress begins with a discussion of giants and then tells of his own decades-long quest for the Yeti in Nepal, Sikkim, Bhutan and other areas of the Himalayas, and then proceeds to his research into Bigfoot, Sasquatch and Skunk Apes in North America. Chapters include: The Giants of Yore; Giants Among Us; Wildmen and Hairy Giants; The Call of the Yeti; Kanchenjunga Demons; The Yeti of Tibet, Mongolia & Russia; Bigfoot & the Grassman; Sasquatch Rules the Forest; Modern Sasquatch Accounts; more. Includes a 16-page color photo insert of astonishing photos!
360 pages. 5x9 Paperback. Illustrated. Bibliography. Index. $18.95. Code: YSHG

SECRETS OF THE HOLY LANCE
The Spear of Destiny in History & Legend
by Jerry E. Smith

Secrets of the Holy Lance traces the Spear from its possession by Constantine, Rome's first Christian Caesar, to Charlemagne's claim that with it he ruled the Holy Roman Empire by Divine Right, and on through two thousand years of kings and emperors, until it came within Hitler's grasp—and beyond! Did it rest for a while in Antarctic ice? Is it now hidden in Europe, awaiting the next person to claim its awesome power? Neither debunking nor worshiping, *Secrets of the Holy Lance* seeks to pierce the veil of myth and mystery around the Spear.
312 PAGES. 6X9 PAPERBACK. ILLUSTRATED. $16.95. CODE: SOHL

THE CRYSTAL SKULLS
Astonishing Portals to Man's Past
by David Hatcher Childress and Stephen S. Mehler

Childress introduces the technology and lore of crystals, and then plunges into the turbulent times of the Mexican Revolution form the backdrop for the rollicking adventures of Ambrose Bierce, the renowned journalist who went missing in the jungles in 1913, and F.A. Mitchell-Hedges, the notorious adventurer who emerged from the jungles with the most famous of the crystal skulls. Mehler shares his extensive knowledge of and experience with crystal skulls. Having been involved in the field since the 1980s, he has personally examined many of the most influential skulls, and has worked with the leaders in crystal skull research. Color section.
294 pages. 6x9 Paperback. Illustrated. $18.95. Code: CRSK

THE LAND OF OSIRIS
An Introduction to Khemitology
by Stephen S. Mehler

Was there an advanced prehistoric civilization in ancient Egypt? Were they the people who built the great pyramids and carved the Great Sphinx? Did the pyramids serve as energy devices and not as tombs for kings? Chapters include: Egyptology and Its Paradigms; Khemitology—New Paradigms; Asgat Nefer—The Harmony of Water; Khemit and the Myth of Atlantis; The Extraterrestrial Question; more. Color section.
272 PAGES. 6X9 PAPERBACK. ILLUSTRATED . $18.95. CODE: LOOS

VIMANA:
Flying Machines of the Ancients
by David Hatcher Childress

According to early Sanskrit texts the ancients had several types of airships called vimanas. Like aircraft of today, vimanas were used to fly through the air from city to city; to conduct aerial surveys of uncharted lands; and as delivery vehicles for awesome weapons. David Hatcher Childress, popular *Lost Cities* author, takes us on an astounding investigation into tales of ancient flying machines. In his new book, packed with photos and diagrams, he consults ancient texts and modern stories and presents astonishing evidence that aircraft, similar to the ones we use today, were used thousands of years ago in India, Sumeria, China and other countries. Includes a 24-page color section.
408 Pages. 6x9 Paperback. Illustrated. $22.95. Code: VMA

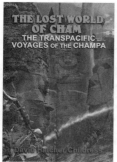

THE LOST WORLD OF CHAM
The Trans-Pacific Voyages of the Champa
By David Hatcher Childress
The mysterious Cham, or Champa, peoples of Southeast Asia formed a megalith-building, seagoing empire that extended into Indonesia, Tonga, and beyond—a transoceanic power that reached Mexico and South America. The Champa maintained many ports in what is today Vietnam, Cambodia, and Indonesia and their ships plied the Indian Ocean and the Pacific, bringing Chinese, African and Indian traders to far off lands, including Olmec ports on the Pacific Coast of Central America. opics include: Cham and Khem: Egyptian Influence on Cham; The Search for Metals; The Basalt City of Nan Madol; Elephants and Buddhists in North America; The Olmecs; The Cham in Colombia; tons more. 24-page color section.
328 Pages. 6x9 Paperback. Illustrated. $22.00 Code: LPWC

OTTO RAHN & THE QUEST FOR THE HOLY GRAIL
The Amazing Life of the Real "Indiana Jones"
By Nigel Graddon
Otto Rahn, a Hessian language scholar, is said to have found runic Grail tablets in the Pyrenean grottoes, unearthed as a result of his work in decoding the hidden messages within the Grail masterwork *Parsifal*. The fabulous artifacts identified by Rahn were believed by Himmler to include the Grail Cup, the Spear of Destiny, the Tablets of Moses, the Ark of the Covenant, the Sword and Harp of David, the Sacred Candelabra and the Golden Urn of Manna. Some believe that Rahn was a Nazi guru who wielded immense influence within the Hitler regime, persuading them that the Grail was the Sacred Book of the Aryans, which, once obtained, would justify their extreme political theories.
450 pages. 6x9 Paperback. Illustrated. Index. $18.95. Code: ORQG

THE LANDING LIGHTS OF MAGONIA
UFOs, Aliens and the Fairy Kingdom
By Nigel Graddon
British UFO researcher Graddon takes us to that magical land of Magonia—the land of the Fairies—a place from which some people return while others go and never come back. Graddon on fairies, the wee folk, elves, fairy pathways, Welsh folklore, the Tuatha de Dannan, UFO occupants, the Little Blue Man of Studham, the implications of Mars, psychic connections with UFOs and fairies. He also recounts many of the strange tales of fairies, UFOs and Magonia. Chapters include: The Little Blue Man of Studham; The Wee Folk; UFOlk; What the Folk; Grimm Tales; The Welsh Triangle; The Implicate Order; Mars—an Atlantean Outpost; Psi-Fi; High Spirits; "Once Upon a Time…"; more.
270 Pages. 6x9 Paperback. Illustrated. $19.95. Code: LLOM

ADVENTURES OF A HASHISH SMUGGLER
by Henri de Monfreid
The son of a French artist who knew Paul Gaugin as a child, de Monfreid sought his fortune by becoming a collector and merchant of the fabled Persian Gulf pearls. He was then drawn into the shadowy world of arms trading, slavery, smuggling and drugs. Infamous as well as famous, his name is inextricably linked to the Red Sea and the raffish ports between Suez and Aden in the early years of the twentieth century. De Monfreid (1879 to 1974) had a long life of many adventures around the Horn of Africa where he dodged pirates as well as the authorities.
284 Pages. 6x9 Paperback. $16.95. Illustrated. Code AHS

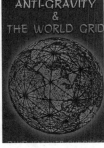

ANCIENT ALIENS ON THE MOON
By Mike Bara
What did NASA find in their explorations of the solar system that they may have kept from the general public? How ancient really are these ruins on the Moon? Using official NASA and Russian photos of the Moon, Bara looks at vast cityscapes and domes in the Sinus Medii region as well as glass domes in the Crisium region. Bara also takes a detailed look at the mission of Apollo 17 and the case that this was a salvage mission, primarily concerned with investigating an opening into a massive hexagonal ruin near the landing site. Chapters include: The History of Lunar Anomalies; The Early 20th Century; Sinus Medii; To the Moon Alice!; Mare Crisium; Yes, Virginia, We Really Went to the Moon; Apollo 17; more. Tons of photos of the Moon examined for possible structures and other anomalies.
248 Pages. 6x9 Paperback. Illustrated.. $19.95. Code: AAOM

ANCIENT ALIENS ON MARS
By Mike Bara
Bara brings us this lavishly illustrated volume on alien structures on Mars. Was there once a vast, technologically advanced civilization on Mars, and did it leave evidence of its existence behind for humans to find eons later? Did these advanced extraterrestrial visitors vanish in a solar system wide cataclysm of their own making, only to make their way to Earth and start anew? Was Mars once as lush and green as the Earth, and teeming with life? Chapters include: War of the Worlds; The Mars Tidal Model; The Death of Mars; Cydonia and the Face on Mars; The Monuments of Mars; The Search for Life on Mars; The True Colors of Mars and The Pathfinder Sphinx; more. Color section.
252 Pages. 6x9 Paperback. Illustrated. $19.95. Code: AMAR

ANCIENT ALIENS ON MARS II
By Mike Bara
Using data acquired from sophisticated new scientific instruments like the Mars Odyssey THEMIS infrared imager, Bara shows that the region of Cydonia overlays a vast underground city full of enormous structures and devices that may still be operating. He peels back the layers of mystery to show images of tunnel systems, temples and ruins, and exposes the sophisticated NASA conspiracy designed to hide them. Bara also tackles the enigma of Mars' hollowed out moon Phobos, and exposes evidence that it is artificial. Long-held myths about Mars, including claims that it is protected by a sophisticated UFO defense system, are examined. Data from the Mars rovers Spirit, Opportunity and Curiosity are examined; everything from fossilized plants to mechanical debris is exposed in images taken directly from NASA's own archives.
294 Pages. 6x9 Paperback. Illustrated. $19.95. Code: AAM2

ANCIENT TECHNOLOGY IN PERU & BOLIVIA
By David Hatcher Childress
Childress speculates on the existence of a sunken city in Lake Titicaca and reveals new evidence that the Sumerians may have arrived in South America 4,000 years ago. He demonstrates that the use of "keystone cuts" with metal clamps poured into them to secure megalithic construction was an advanced technology used all over the world, from the Andes to Egypt, Greece and Southeast Asia. He maintains that only power tools could have made the intricate articulation and drill holes found in extremely hard granite and basalt blocks in Bolivia and Peru, and that the megalith builders had to have had advanced methods for moving and stacking gigantic blocks of stone, some weighing over 100 tons.
340 Pages. 6x9 Paperback. Illustrated.. $19.95 Code: ATP

ANCIENT ALIENS & SECRET SOCIETIES
By Mike Bara
Did ancient "visitors"—of extraterrestrial origin—come to Earth long, long ago and fashion man in their own image? Were the science and secrets that they taught the ancients intended to be a guide for all humanity to the present era? Bara establishes the reality of the catastrophe that jolted the human race, and traces the history of secret societies from the priesthood of Amun in Egypt to the Templars in Jerusalem and the Scottish Rite Freemasons. Bara also reveals the true origins of NASA and exposes the bizarre triad of secret societies in control of that agency since its inception. Chapters include: Out of the Ashes; From the Sky Down; Ancient Aliens?; The Dawn of the Secret Societies; The Fractures of Time; Into the 20th Century; The Wink of an Eye; more.
288 Pages. 6x9 Paperback. Illustrated. $19.95. Code: AASS

AXIS OF THE WORLD
The Search for the Oldest American Civilization
by Igor Witkowski
Polish author Witkowski's research reveals remnants of a high civilization that was able to exert its influence on almost the entire planet, and did so with full consciousness. Sites around South America show that this was not just one of the places influenced by this culture, but a place where they built their crowning achievements. Easter Island, in the southeastern Pacific, constitutes one of them. The Rongo-Rongo language that developed there points westward to the Indus Valley. Taken together, the facts presented by Witkowski provide a fresh, new proof that an antediluvian, great civilization flourished several millennia ago.
220 pages. 6x9 Paperback. Illustrated. References. $18.95. Code: AXOW

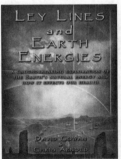

LEY LINE & EARTH ENERGIES
An Extraordinary Journey into the Earth's Natural Energy System
by David Cowan & Chris Arnold
The mysterious standing stones, burial grounds and stone circles that lace Europe, the British Isles and other areas have intrigued scientists, writers, artists and travellers through the centuries. How do ley lines work? How did our ancestors use Earth energy to map their sacred sites and burial grounds? How do ghosts and poltergeists interact with Earth energy? How can Earth spirals and black spots affect our health? This exploration shows how natural forces affect our behavior, how they can be used to enhance our health and well being.
368 PAGES. 6x9 PAPERBACK. ILLUSTRATED. $18.95. CODE: LLEE

THE MYSTERY OF U-33
By Nigel Graddon
The incredible story of the mystery U-Boats of WWII! Graddon first chronicles the story of the mysterious U-33 that landed in Scotland in 1940 and involved the top-secret Enigma device. He then looks at U-Boat special missions during and after WWII, including U-Boat trips to Antarctica; U-Boats with the curious cargos of liquid mercury; the journey of the Spear of Destiny via U-Boat; the "Black Subs" and more. Chapters and topics include: U-33: The Official Story; The First Questions; Survivors and Deceased; August 1985—the Story Breaks; The Carradale U-boat; The Tale of the Bank Event; In the Wake of U-33; Wrecks; The Greenock Lairs; The Mystery Men; "Brass Bounders at the Admiralty"; Captain's Log; Max Schiller through the Lens; Rudolf Hess; Otto Rahn; U-Boat Special Missions; Neu-Schwabenland; more.
351 Pages. 6x9 Paperback. Illustrated. $19.95. Code: MU33

HESS AND THE PENGUINS
The Holocaust, Antarctica and the Strange Case of Rudolf Hess
By Joseph P. Farrell

Farrell looks at Hess' mission to make peace with Britain and get rid of Hitler—even a plot to fly Hitler to Britain for capture! How much did Göring and Hitler know of Rudolf Hess' subversive plot, and what happened to Hess? Why was a doppleganger put in Spandau Prison and then "suicided"? Did the British use an early form of mind control on Hess' double? John Foster Dulles of the OSS and CIA suspected as much. Farrell also uncovers the strange death of Admiral Richard Byrd's son in 1988, about the same time of the death of Hess.

288 Pages. 6x9 Paperback. Illustrated. $19.95. Code: HAPG

HIDDEN FINANCE, ROGUE NETWORKS & SECRET SORCERY
The Fascist International, 9/11, & Penetrated Operations
By Joseph P. Farrell

Farrell investigates the theory that there were not *two* levels to the 9/11 event, but *three*. He says that the twin towers were downed by the force of an exotic energy weapon, one similar to the Tesla energy weapon suggested by Dr. Judy Wood, and ties together the tangled web of missing money, secret technology and involvement of portions of the Saudi royal family. Farrell unravels the many layers behind the 9-11 attack, layers that include the Deutschebank, the Bush family, the German industrialist Carl Duisberg, Saudi Arabian princes and the energy weapons developed by Tesla before WWII.

296 Pages. 6x9 Paperback. Illustrated. $19.95. Code: HFRN

THRICE GREAT HERMETICA & THE JANUS AGE
By Joseph P. Farrell

What do the Fourth Crusade, the exploration of the New World, secret excavations of the Holy Land, and the pontificate of Innocent the Third, all have in common? Answer: Venice and the Templars. What do they have in common with Jesus, Gottfried Leibniz, Sir Isaac Newton, Rene Descartes, and the Earl of Oxford? Answer: Egypt and a body of doctrine known as Hermeticism. The hidden role of Venice and Hermeticism reached far and wide, into the plays of Shakespeare (a.k.a. Edward DeVere, Earl of Oxford), into the quest of the three great mathematicians of the Early Enlightenment for a lost form of analysis, and back into the end of the classical era, to little known Egyptian influences at work during the time of Jesus.

354 Pages. 6x9 Paperback. Illustrated. $19.95. Code: TGHJ

ROBOT ZOMBIES
Transhumanism and the Robot Revolution
By Xaviant Haze and Estrella Eguino,

Technology is growing exponentially and the moment when it merges with the human mind, called "The Singularity," is visible in our imminent future. Science and technology are pushing forward, transforming life as we know it—perhaps even giving humans a shot at immortality. Who will benefit from this? This book examines the history and future of robotics, artificial intelligence, zombies and a Transhumanist utopia/dystopia integrating man with machine. Chapters include: Love, Sex and Compassion—Android Style; Humans Aren't Working Like They Used To; Skynet Rises; Blueprints for Transhumans; Kurzweil's Quest; Nanotech Dreams; Zombies Among Us; Cyborgs (Cylons) in Space; Awakening the Human; more. Color Section.

180 Pages. 6x9 Paperback. Illustrated. $16.95. Code: RBTZ

THE COSMIC WAR
Interplanetary Warfare, Modern Physics, and Ancient Texts
By Joseph P. Farrell

There is ample evidence across our solar system of catastrophic events. The asteroid belt may be the remains of an exploded planet! The known planets are scarred from incredible impacts, and teeter in their orbits due to causes heretofore inadequately explained. Included: The history of the Exploded Planet hypothesis, and what mechanism can actually explode a planet. The role of plasma cosmology, plasma physics and scalar physics. The ancient texts telling of such destructions: from Sumeria (Tiamat's destruction by Marduk), Egypt (Edfu and the Mars connections), Greece (Saturn's role in the War of the Titans) and the ancient Americas.
436 Pages. 6x9 Paperback. Illustrated.. $18.95. Code: COSW

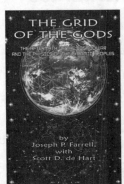

THE GRID OF THE GODS
The Aftermath of the Cosmic War & the Physics of the Pyramid Peoples
By Joseph P. Farrell with Scott D. de Hart

Farrell looks at Ashlars and Engineering; Anomalies at the Temples of Angkor; The Ancient Prime Meridian: Giza; Transmitters, Nazis and Geomancy; the Lithium-7 Mystery; Nazi Transmitters and the Earth Grid; The Master Plan of a Hidden Elite; Moving and Immoveable Stones; Uncountable Stones and Stones of the Giants and Gods; Gateway Traditions; The Grid and the Ancient Elite; Finding the Center of the Land; The Ancient Catastrophe, the Very High Civilization, and the Post-Catastrophe Elite; Tiahuanaco and the Puma Punkhu Paradox: Ancient Machining; The Black Brotherhood and Blood Sacrifices; The Gears of Giza: the Center of the Machine; Alchemical Cosmology and Quantum Mechanics in Stone; tons more.
436 Pages. 6x9 Paperback. Illustrated. $19.95. Code: GOG

THE SS BROTHERHOOD OF THE BELL
The Nazis' Incredible Secret Technology
by Joseph P. Farrell

In 1945, a mysterious Nazi secret weapons project code-named "The Bell" left its underground bunker in lower Silesia, along with all its project documentation, and a four-star SS general named Hans Kammler. Taken aboard a massive six engine Junkers 390 ultra-long range aircraft, "The Bell," Kammler, and all project records disappeared completely, along with the gigantic aircraft. It is thought to have flown to America or Argentina. What was "The Bell"? What new physics might the Nazis have discovered with it? How far did the Nazis go after the war to protect the advanced energy technology that it represented?
456 pages. 6x9 Paperback. Illustrated. $16.95. Code: SSBB

MAPS OF THE ANCIENT SEA KINGS
Evidence of Advanced Civilization in the Ice Age
by Charles H. Hapgood

Charles Hapgood has found the evidence in the Piri Reis Map that shows Antarctica, the Hadji Ahmed map, the Oronteus Finaeus and other amazing maps. Hapgood concluded that these maps were made from more ancient maps from the various ancient archives around the world, now lost. Not only were these unknown people more advanced in mapmaking than any people prior to the 18th century, it appears they mapped all the continents. The Americas were mapped thousands of years before Columbus. Antarctica was mapped when its coasts were free of ice!
316 PAGES. 7x10 PAPERBACK. ILLUSTRATED. $19.95. CODE: MASK

BIGFOOT NATION
A History of Sasquatch in North America
By David Hatcher Childress

Childress takes a deep look at Bigfoot Nation—the real world of bigfoot around us in the United States and Canada. Whether real or imagined, that bigfoot has made his way into the American psyche cannot be denied. He appears in television commercials, movies, and on roadside billboards. Bigfoot is everywhere, with actors portraying him in variously believable performances and it has become the popular notion that bigfoot is both dangerous and horny. Indeed, bigfoot is out there stalking lovers' lanes and is even more lonely than those frightened teenagers that he sometimes interrupts. Bigfoot, tall and strong as he is, makes a poor leading man in the movies with his awkward personality and typically anti-social behavior. Includes 16-pages of color photos that document Bigfoot Nation!

320 Pages. 6x9 Paperback. Illustrated. $22.00. Code: BGN

MEN & GODS IN MONGOLIA
by Henning Haslund

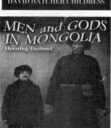

Haslund takes us to the lost city of Karakota in the Gobi desert. We meet the Bodgo Gegen, a god-king in Mongolia similar to the Dalai Lama of Tibet. We meet Dambin Jansang, the dreaded warlord of the "Black Gobi." Haslund and companions journey across the Gobi desert by camel caravan; are kidnapped and held for ransom; witness initiation into Shamanic societies; meet reincarnated warlords; and experience the violent birth of "modern" Mongolia.

358 Pages. 6x9 Paperback. Illustrated. $18.95. Code: MGM

PROJECT MK-ULTRA
AND MIND CONTROL TECHNOLOGY
By Axel Balthazar

This book is a compilation of the government's documentation on MK-Ultra, the CIA's mind control experimentation on unwitting human subjects, as well as over 150 patents pertaining to artificial telepathy (voice-to-skull technology), behavior modification through radio frequencies, directed energy weapons, electronic monitoring, implantable nanotechnology, brain wave manipulation, nervous system manipulation, neuroweapons, psychological warfare, satellite terrorism, subliminal messaging, and more. A must-have reference guide for targeted individuals and anyone interested in the subject of mind control technology.

384 pages. 7x10 Paperback. Illustrated. $19.95. Code: PMK

LIQUID CONSPIRACY 2:
The CIA, MI6 & Big Pharma's War on Psychedelics
By Xaviant Haze

Underground author Xaviant Haze looks into the CIA and its use of LSD as a mind control drug; at one point every CIA officer had to take the drug and endure mind control tests and interrogations to see if the drug worked as a "truth serum." Chapters include: The Pioneers of Psychedelia; The United Kingdom Mellows Out: The MI5, MDMA and LSD; Taking it to the Streets: LSD becomes Acid; Great Works of Art Inspired and Influenced by Acid; Scapolamine: The CIA's Ultimate Truth Serum; Mind Control, the Death of Music and the Meltdown of the Masses; Big Pharma's War on Psychedelics; The Healing Powers of Psychedelic Medicine; tons more.

240 pages. 6x9 Paperback. Illustrated. $19.95. Code: LQC2

ORDER FORM

10% Discount When You Order 3 or More Items!

One Adventure Place
P.O. Box 74
Kempton, Illinois 60946
United States of America
Tel.: 815-253-6390 • Fax: 815-253-6300
Email: auphq@frontiernet.net
http://www.adventuresunlimitedpress.com

Please check: ✓

☐ This is my first order   ☐ I have ordered before

Name

Address

City

State/Province   Postal Code

Country

Phone: Day   Evening

Fax   Email

Item Code	Item Description	Qty	Total

Please check: ✓

	Subtotal ▶	
	Less Discount-10% for 3 or more items ▶	
☐ Postal-Surface	Balance ▶	
☐ Postal-Air Mail (Priority in USA)	Illinois Residents 6.25% Sales Tax ▶	
	Previous Credit ▶	
☐ UPS	Shipping ▶	
(Mainland USA only)	Total (check/MO in USD$ only) ▶	

☐ Visa/MasterCard/Discover/American Express

Card Number:

Expiration Date: Security Code:

✓ SEND A CATALOG TO A FRIEND: